Conflict and Cooperation on South Asia's International Rivers

Law, Justice, and Development

The Law, Justice, and Development Series is offered by the Legal Vice Presidency of the World Bank to provide insights into aspects of law and justice that are relevant to the development process. Works in the series will present new legal and judicial reform activities related to the World Bank's work, as well as analyses of domestic and international law. The series is intended to be accessible to a broad audience as well as to legal practitioners.

Series editor: Rudolf V. Van Puymbroeck

Conflict and Cooperation on South Asia's International Rivers

A Legal Perspective

Salman M. A. Salman
Lead Counsel
*Environmentally and Socially Sustainable Development and
International Law Group
Legal Vice Presidency
The World Bank*

Kishor Uprety
Senior Counsel
*Middle East, North Africa, and South Asia Law Group
Legal Vice Presidency
The World Bank*

THE WORLD BANK
Washington, D.C.

© 2002 The International Bank for Reconstruction and Development / The World Bank
1818 H Street, NW
Washington, DC 20433

All rights reserved.

1 2 3 4 05 04 03 02

The findings, interpretations, and conclusions expressed here are those of the author(s) and do not necessarily reflect the views of the Board of Executive Directors of the World Bank or the governments they represent.

The World Bank cannot guarantee the accuracy of the data included in this work. The boundaries, colors, denominations, and other information shown on any map in this work do not imply on the part of the World Bank any judgment of the legal status of any territory or the endorsement or acceptance of such boundaries.

Conflict and Cooperation on South Asia's International Rivers—A Legal Perspective is also being published in hard cover by Kluwer Law International in its *International and National Water Law and Policy Series* (Patricia Wouters and Sergei Vinogradow, editors), ISBN 90-411-1958-2. Kluwer Law International's edition includes the full text of the treaties discussed in this study. This publication provides complete references to the treaties, both in notes to the text and in summary form in the appendix.

Rights and Permissions

The material in this work is copyrighted. No part of this work may be reproduced or transmitted in any form or by any means, electronic or mechanical, including photocopying, recording, or included in any information storage and retrieval system, without the prior written permission of the World Bank. The World Bank encourages dissemination of its work and will normally grant permission promptly.

For permission to photocopy or reprint, please send a request with complete information to the Copyright Clearance Center, Inc., 222 Rosewood Drive, Danvers, MA 01923, USA, telephone 978-750-8400, fax 978-750-4470, www.copyright.com.

All other queries on rights and licenses, including subsidiary rights, should be addressed to the Office of the Publisher, World Bank, 1818 H Street NW, Washington, DC 10433, USA, fax 202-522-2422, e-mail pubrights@worldbank.org.

Library of Congress Cataloging-in-Publication Data

Salman, Salman M.A., 1948-
  Conflict and cooperation on South Asia's international rivers : a legal perspective / Salman M.S. Salman, Kishor Uprety.
    p. cm. — (Law, justice, and development)
  Includes bibliographical references and index.
  ISBN 0-8213-5352-7
  1. International rivers—South Asia. I. Uprety, Kishor, 1958- II. Title. III. Series.

KZ3700 .S25 2002a
341.4'42'0954—dc21

Library of Congress Cataloging-in-Publication Data has been applied for.

"A river is more than an amenity; it is a treasure. It offers a necessity of life that must be rationed among those who have power over it."

Justice Oliver Wendell Holmes
(*New Jersey v. New York*, **1931**)

Contents

List of Tables ix
List of Maps x
Glossary xi
Foreword xiii
Abstract xv
Preface xvii
Acknowledgments xix

PART ONE   GENERAL INTRODUCTION
Chapter 1   Introduction 3
                   I.   The South Asian Sub-continent 3
                   II.   International Water Law 8
                   III. Scope of the Study 32

PART TWO   INDIA–PAKISTAN RELATIONS
Chapter 2   The Indus River 37
                   I.   Introduction and History 37
                   II.   The Indus Treaty Regime 48
                   III. Conclusion 57

PART THREE   INDIA–NEPAL RELATIONS
Chapter 3   The Kosi River 65
                   I.   Introduction and History 65
                   II.   The Kosi Treaty Regime 70
                   III. Conclusion 80
Chapter 4   The Gandaki River 83
                   I.   Introduction and History 83
                   II.   The Gandak Treaty Regime 84
                   III. Conclusion 93

Chapter 5	The Mahakali River 97	
	I. Introduction and History 97	
	II. The Mahakali Treaty Regime 103	
	III. Conclusion 115	
Chapter 6	The Kosi, Gandaki and Mahakali: An Overview 119	
PART FOUR	INDIA–BANGLADESH RELATIONS	
Chapter 7	The Ganges River 125	
	I. Introduction and History 125	
	II. The Ganges Treaty Regime 170	
	III. Conclusion 189	
PART FIVE	GENERAL CONCLUSION	
Chapter 8	Conflict, Cooperation and Treaties: Retrospect and Prospects 195	

Select Bibliography 203
Appendix 209
Index 211

List of Tables

Table 1.1	Population, Population Growth and GNP Per Capita in the South Asian Sub-continent	6
Table 1.2	Fresh Water Resources and Withdrawals in the South Asian Sub-continent	7
Table 4.1	Water Allocation for Irrigation in Nepal Under the Gandak Agreement	91
Table 5.1	Nepal's Share of the Waters of the Mahakali River Under the Mahakali Treaty	111
Table 7.1	Amounts of the Waters of the Ganges Diverted to the Feeder Canal Under the 1975 Partial Accord	140
Table 7.2	Share of India and Bangladesh of the Waters of the Ganges at Farakka Under the 1975 Partial Accord	141
Table 7.3	Share of India and Bangladesh of the Waters of the Ganges at Farakka Under the 1977 Agreement	153
Table 7.4	Share of India and Bangladesh of the Waters of the Ganges at Farakka Under the 1982 Memorandum of Understanding	161
Table 7.5	Formula for Sharing the Waters of the Ganges Under the 1996 Treaty	172
Table 7.6	Share of India and Bangladesh of the Waters of the Ganges at Farakka Under the 1996 Treaty	173
Table 7.7	Average Flows of the Ganges at Hardinge Bridge in Bangladesh During the Years 1989-1995, and Under the Treaty	178
Table 7.8	Ganges Flow in Bangladesh During the Dry Seasons of the Years 1997-2000, Compared with the Indicative Figures Under the Treaty	186

List of Maps

Map 1	The Indus River Basin	39
Map 2	The Kosi River Basin	67
Map 3	The Gandaki River Basin	85
Map 4	The Mahakali River Basin	99
Map 5	The Ganges River Basin	131

Glossary

The following terms are widely used in the South Asian Sub-continent, and are defined for ease of reference:

Bigha	A unit for the measurement of land in Nepal (one Bigha is equal to 0.6772 hectare)
Crore	A unit of accounting equivalent to 10 million
Cumec	Cubic meters per second
Cusec	Cubic feet per second
Kharif	Monsoon crop
Lakh	A unit of accounting equivalent to one hundred thousand
MAF	Million acre feet
Rabi	Winter crop
Rs.	Rupees, the currency of India, Nepal and Pakistan, with a different value in each country

Foreword

Early civilizations started and were nourished around rivers. The compelling need for water—for domestic purposes and for growing food—prompted people to live close to those rivers; and gradually communities grew into cities, and cities into nations. Soon competing demands for the waters of rivers started to grow, particularly between nations. In recent history, shared rivers have become sources of conflict, as well as catalysts for cooperation. This situation is particularly true about the South Asian Sub-continent. Some 20 major rivers run through it, and the three largest basins, those of the Indus, the Ganges, and the Brahmaputra, affect not only the countries of the Sub-continent (Bangladesh, Bhutan, India, Nepal, and Pakistan), but China as well. Sharp seasonal variations in the volume of water flows due to climatic phenomena, such as monsoons and droughts, occurring in the territory of some countries, add to the difficulty of finding equitable and durable water-sharing arrangements.

The situation is exacerbated by the fact that the Sub-continent is also one of the poorest areas of the world. The overwhelming majority of the 1.3 billion people living there (close to one-fourth of the world's population) suffer excruciating poverty: gross national income ranges from $240 in Nepal (the lowest) to $590 in Bhutan (the highest), translating into average daily incomes of $0.66 in the former and $1.63 in the latter. Moreover, in the last 20 years, the population of the area has increased by 50 percent. Rapid population growth, expanding urbanization, and fast-growing needs for irrigation and power generation are putting ever-increasing strains on the waters of these rivers.

Out of the vicious circle of situations in which both the cause of potential international conflicts and their solution turn on the utilization of shared water resources, the countries of the South Asian Sub-continent have managed to pioneer innovative solutions and craft lasting compromises. This book showcases the treaty regimes between India and Pakistan with respect to the Indus; between India and Nepal for the Kosi, Gandaki, and Mahakali; and between India and Bangladesh for the Ganges. These treaty regimes came about mostly as a result of bilateral efforts; however, with respect to the Indus Treaty, the good offices of the World Bank played an important role.

I commend my two colleagues in the Legal Vice Presidency of the World Bank for taking up this study of conflict and cooperation in South Asia with respect to the use of waters of international rivers. Combining their extensive experience in international water law with their thorough knowledge of the region, the authors have succeeded in clarifying complex legal and technical issues within the difficult context of intricate political and historical legacies. Their contribution is significant, not only in broadening our awareness of specific international water law issues and how they can be resolved, but also, and especially, in reminding us that cooperative solutions to pressing problems between countries can actually be found.

Ko-Yung Tung
Vice President and General Counsel
The World Bank

September 12, 2002

Abstract

This study starts by tracing the development of international water law and by outlining its key current concepts and principles. Against that background, the authors focus on the hydro-politics of four countries of the South Asian Sub-continent: Bangladesh, India, Nepal, and Pakistan. They analyze the problems these countries have encountered as riparians of international rivers and how they have addressed them. In particular, the study reviews the treaty regimes governing the Indus River basin: the Ganges River basin; and the Kosi, Gandaki, and Mahakali river basins. Each of these regimes is described in depth, but special attention is devoted to the main problems each of the treaties sought to address: dispute resolution in the context of the Indus, water-sharing with respect to the Ganges, and an integrated approach to water resources management for India and Nepal with respect to the Kosi, Gandaki, and Mahakali rivers. In the final part, the authors review treaty experience and offer observations on bilateralism and multilateralism, third-party intervention, water rights and benefits, institutional arrangements, and dispute resolution. They conclude by stressing the importance of cooperation throughout the treaty-making process.

Preface

Fresh water is increasingly in short supply in many parts of the world, largely because of population growth and the needs of urbanization and industrialization. The resulting competition for the scarce water gives rise to complex international problems as the states that share the waters of international drainage basins seek to satisfy their pressing needs. These problems are well illustrated by a study of the history of the water resources of the South Asian Sub-continent. The concerned states of that region are Bangladesh, Bhutan, India, Nepal, and Pakistan, the countries of the Himalayan Block; they encompass some 20 major rivers, three of them being of particular international legal importance, namely the Indus, the Ganges, and the Brahmaputra.

After an introductory chapter, in one section of which the present state of international water law is reviewed, the authors examine the history of the dispute between India and Pakistan concerning the waters of the Indus River. This dispute, having brought the parties to the brink of war at the outset, was eventually resolved by the Indus Waters Treaty of 1960, which was reached only through the intervention of the World Bank and the financial aid of other states. The lawyers for the parties disagreed strongly about the applicable principles of international law governing international water resources. The Treaty, however, was not based on any principle of law when it divided the waters of the Indus between the parties; indeed, the Treaty expressly stated that nothing contained in it was to be construed as in any way establishing a general principle of law or any precedent. Nevertheless, the division lent some credence to the principle that co-basin states are under a duty to cooperate and to share the waters of the basin reasonably and equitably among themselves.

The relations of India and Nepal are then discussed. Since about 45 percent of the waters of the Ganges River, the major river in India, have their origins in China and Nepal, this river is of major importance to both of these countries. While India and Nepal have entered into several agreements, the results have not always been happy. Nepal, a small, land-locked, and poor upstream state, finds the development of its abundant water resources, for economic if no other reasons, dependent on agreement with its overwhelmingly larger neighbor downstream. Even when agreement is reached, as in the Mahakali Treaty of 1996, implementation is hampered by differences of interpretation about its terms.

The relations of India and Bangladesh concerning the Ganges River emphasize the difficulties in discerning the general principles of international law applicable to the waters of international drainage basins and applying them to the complex facts of a particular case. While India is the downstream state in relation to Nepal, it is the upstream state in relation to Bangladesh, and is therefore in a position to affect the flow of the Ganges and the Brahmaputra into Bangladesh. In fact, India has diverted water from the Ganges by constructing the barrage at Farakka for the benefit of the port at Calcutta, thus seriously affecting Bangladesh by depriving it of desperately needed water during the dry season. Bangladesh strongly protested this diversion and questioned its legality. After making several temporary agreements providing for allocations of the waters of the river, India and Bangladesh entered into the Ganges Treaty in 1996, allocating the waters for the next 30 years. Another issue, however, remains to be dealt with. Bangladesh urgently needs protection from floods from the Ganges during the monsoon period. Such flood control can only be achieved by storage of the waters upstream, mainly in Nepal, and therefore depends upon the cooperation of the three states, a cooperation that India so far has rejected.

In the final chapter of the book, the authors state the conclusions that they draw from their studies. They take satisfaction in that India and Pakistan, India and Nepal, and India and Bangladesh have reached agreements on some of the major water problems of the region, but they recognize that major problems in the region still need urgent attention. They stress that cooperation among states is essential to the reasonable and equitable utilization of the waters of the international rivers that they share.

The authors of the book, both senior lawyers in the Legal Department of the World Bank, have long been involved in matters relating to international water problems. In that capacity, they have had the opportunity to gain special knowledge of the legal, political, and practical aspects of these problems, and have thus taken a special interest in the utilization of the waters of these rivers. Their detailed historical account of the political and legal relations of India with Pakistan, Nepal, and Bangladesh provides even one who already has a good knowledge of the subject, with a deeper understanding and appreciation of the problems and difficulties that these states have faced and still face. In short, the book makes a worthy contribution to scholarship in the field of international water law.

Charles B. Bourne
Professor Emeritus of Law
University of British Columbia

Acknowledgments

The preparation of this book has been a demanding task, and has benefited from the assistance of a number of colleagues and friends in different parts of the world. We would like to extend our sincere thanks and appreciation to Professor Charles Bourne for his constructive comments and for writing the Preface for this book. We would also like to thank Mr. Jerome Muys, Chairman of the Water Law Committee of the International Bar Association, Mr. W. Paatii Ofosu-Amaah, Deputy General Counsel, and Mr. David Freestone, Chief Counsel, Environmentally and Socially Sustainable Development and International Law Group, both of the Legal Vice Presidency of the World Bank, and Mr. Walter A. Garvey, Lead Water Resources Specialist, South Asia Region of the World Bank for reviewing the manuscript and for providing detailed and helpful comments. Sincere thanks are also due to Ms. Undala Alam, a researcher on the Indus, for reviewing and commenting on the Indus Basin part of the book. We would also like to thank Anup Acharya, J. R. Malhotra, Md. Abdul Ghani, and Thuy Thu Le (Van), Linda Thompson, Laura Lalime-Mowry, Vivien Richardson, Wendy Melis, as well as Dorst MediaWorks for their assistance in various ways with the preparation of the book.

Our thanks go to Dr. Patricia Wouters and Dr. Sergei Vinogradov, editors of the International and National Water Law and Policy Series, for their support with the idea of this book, as well as their intellectual contribution throughout its preparation. Similarly, we are grateful to Mr. Ko-Yung Tung, Vice President and General Counsel of the World Bank, and to Mr. Rudolf V. Van Puymbroeck, editor of the World Bank's Law, Justice, and Development Series, for their encouragement and unwavering support.

We would also like to acknowledge funding from the Bank-Netherlands Water Partnership Program for covering the cost of editing, design, and typesetting the book, and to thank the colleagues who facilitated such funding. However, we should emphasize that the views expressed in this book are our own and do not reflect the views of the World Bank or the Water Partnership Program. Needless to say, any deficiencies in this book are our sole responsibility.

Salman M. A. Salman   **Kishor Uprety**

PART ONE

General Introduction

Chapter 1

Introduction

I. The South Asian Sub-continent

International rivers have, worldwide, been a source of conflict as well as a catalyst for cooperation.[1] The fact that water is a scarce resource, characterized by its spatial and seasonal variations, with no substitute, and over which there is total dependency, has heightened both conflict and cooperation over a large number of international rivers.[2] In some areas of the world, the competing demands of states

---

[1] An international river is one either flowing through the territory of two or more states (also referred to as a successive river), or one separating the territory of two states from one another (also referred to as a boundary river or a contiguous river). *See*, A. H. Garretson, et al., eds., *The Law of International Drainage Basins* (Dobbs Ferry, New York: Oceana Publications, 1967), at 16-17. The use of the terms "international river" and "international waterway" has gradually, over the years, given way to the more appropriate and inclusive term "international watercourse," and the definition has been expanded to include any tributary of such a river. *See, infra,* the "international water law" discussion in the following section.

[2] In 1977 the United Nations reported that there were 214 river basins shared between two or more states. *See* Register of the International Drainage Basins, Report of the Secretary-General of the United Nations (UN DOC. E/C 7/71, 11 March 1977). The same figure of 214 river basins appeared again in another United Nations document published in 1978. *See* United Nations, Register of International Rivers, Prepared by the Centre for Natural Resources, Energy and Transport of the Department of Economic and Social Affairs (1978). The Register refers (on page 1) to an earlier United Nations document, *Integrated River Basin Development,* published in 1958, where the number of international river basins was shown as 166. However, since the publication of the Register in 1978, a number of political boundaries have changed due to the emergence of many new nations. The former Soviet Union split into 15 independent states, the former Republic of Yugoslavia split into five republics, and Czechoslovakia and Ethiopia both split into two states, adding significantly to the number of such international rivers. Peter Gleick estimates that there are now 261 international river basins shared by two or more countries. *See* Peter Gleick, *The World's Water 2000-2001, The Biennial Report on Freshwater Resources,* (Oxford University Press, 2000), at 219, and Table 7, at 220-238. However, one problem with the methodology adopted by this study is that it grouped together major rivers that join above an outlet. This methodology resulted in treating the Ganges, Brahmaputra and Meghna rivers as one basin. These are three separate basins, each with its own riparian and one of them is covered by a Treaty, whereas the other two are not (*see infra* Chapter 7). Similarly, the Juba-Shibeli rivers (Ethiopia, Somalia and Kenya) are presented as one basin, whereas those are two separate basins. The methodology used also fails to include some major rivers like the Mahakali, which is covered by a Treaty between India and Nepal (*see infra* Chapter 5), simply because it joins the Ganges basin at one point, but lists as international rivers some seasonal streams such as the Baraka (Eritrea and Sudan) and Gash (Ethiopia, Eritrea and Sudan), both of which end in the sands of northeastern Sudan. As we shall see in the course of this study, India and Bangladesh have identified 54 rivers as international rivers shared between them. But the above quoted study listed only the Ganges-Brahmaputra-Meghna basin and the Karnafauli river (which is not as important, for example, as the Teesta River that is not included in the study). Moreover, although the title of Table 7 of the study is "International River Basins of the World,"

over the waters of the shared rivers have escalated into tensions and disputes due, in part, to the mistaken notion of absolute national sovereignty over natural resources, including shared water resources. Some of the disputes have led to open conflicts, and defied resolution for a long time. In contrast, international rivers have also provided, in a number of regions, an incentive for riparian states to discuss and agree on modalities for cooperation. Such cooperation modalities have taken various forms covering the quantitative and qualitative aspects of the waters of international rivers, as well as programs for development of the shared resource such as joint hydropower, irrigation and flood control projects. Cooperation has also resulted in the establishment of joint mechanisms for the management of the shared watercourses, and in exchange of data and information on such watercourses. Recognition by the international community of the importance of cooperation is witnessed in the recent conclusion of a number of treaties, protocols and conventions at the bilateral, multilateral, regional and universal levels.[3] A number of those instruments have approached cooperation over international watercourses from the wider angle of sharing benefits, as opposed to the limited approach that deals only with sharing of the waters of such watercourses. South Asia is one region that has had to deal with some of the most difficult disputes over international rivers, while

---

it does include some seven international lakes. Obviously the number of international lakes far exceeds this figure. Table 7 also includes the Aral Sea as an "international river basin" (*id.,* at 220), and does not refer either to the Amu Darya or the Syr Darya rivers that feed the Aral Sea. The study does not include transboundary groundwater because "no assessment of international groundwater has been published" (*id.,* at 219). On the other hand, the World Water Council estimates the number of international river basins as "close to 300." *See* William Cosgrove and Frank Rijsberman, *World Water Vision: Making Water Everybody's Business* (London: Earthscan, 2000), at 43. This discussion clearly underscores the difficulty of even estimating the number of international watercourses.

[3] Such treaties and conventions include the 1992 Helsinki Convention on the Protection and Use of Transboundary Watercourses and International Lakes (*see* 31 I.L.M. 1312, 1992); the 1994 Convention on the Cooperation for the Protection and Sustainable Use of the Danube River (*see* 35 International Environment Reporter 0251, 1998); the 1995 Agreement on the Cooperation for the Sustainable Development of the Mekong River (*see* 34 I.L.M. 864, 1995); the 1995 Protocol on Shared Watercourse Systems in the Southern African Development Community (SADC) Region, 61 FAO Legislative Study, Treaties Concerning the Non-Navigational Uses of International Watercourses – Africa, 146 (1997), which has been revised and reissued as the "Revised Protocol on Shared Watercourses in the Southern African Development Community (SADC)" in August 2000 (40 I.L.M 321, 2001); the 1996 Treaty between India and Nepal on the Integrated Development of the Mahakali River, (*see* 36 I.L.M. 531, 1997); the 1996 Treaty between India and Bangladesh on Sharing the Ganges Waters (*see* 36 I.L.M. 523, 1997); the 1997 United Nations Convention on the Law of the Non-Navigational Uses of International Watercourses (*see* 36 I.L.M. 700, 1997); and the 1999 Convention on the Protection of the Rhine (on file with authors). Along the same cooperative spirit, the ten riparians of the Nile Basin (Burundi, Democratic Republic of Congo, Egypt, Eritrea, Ethiopia, Kenya, Rwanda, Sudan, Tanzania and Uganda) have been engaged, since March 1998, in intensive consultations "on the objectives and approaches for cooperative Nile water resources development and management.... As an outcome of this consultation, the Nile riparian countries are now for the first time cooperating in an inclusive institutional mechanism, the Nile Basin Initiative....Cooperative action is being guided by a Shared Vision which puts socio-economic development and shared benefits from the common Nile waters at its center." *See* Foreword, "The Nile Basin Initiative, Preparatory Phase Working Documents," Report No. 01, Entebbe, June 1999. The Secretariat of the Nile Basin Initiative is located in Entebbe, Uganda.

at the same time, it has been successful in designing some interesting methods of cooperation.

The South Asian Sub-continent includes Bangladesh, Bhutan, India, Nepal and Pakistan (also called "Countries of the Himalayan Block"). It is one of the most densely populated parts of the world, and includes a large number of poor people. Nearly 1.3 billion people live in the countries of the Sub-continent, which represents more than 20 percent of the world population of more than 6 billion. Annual population growth in the countries of the South Asian Sub-continent included in this study (Bangladesh, India, Nepal, and Pakistan) ranges between 1.6 percent to 2.5 percent, and this growth has been translated into an increase of almost 50 percent of the population in each country since 1980. The GNP per capita for the four countries (Bangladesh, India, Nepal, and Pakistan) ranges between $220 to $470, placing them at the bottom of the list of poor countries of the world (Table 1.1). Indeed, the South Asia region has the largest number of poor people in the world, 43.5 percent of the world's poor.[4]

The countries of the Sub-continent are drained by nearly 20 major rivers, of which the Brahmaputra, Ganges and Indus are the largest. Those rivers originate in the Tibetan Plateau of the Himalayas. All parts of the Sub-continent, except peninsular India, depend directly on the water resources supplied by the Himalayan rivers.[5]

The river systems of the Himalayan region can be divided into three sub-regions. The Western Himalayan sub-region includes the Indus system to which the Jhelum, Chenab, Ravi, Beas, and Sutlej Rivers belong. The Indus River system is shared by India and Pakistan, as well as China and Afghanistan. The Central Himalayan sub-region includes the Ganges system of which the Yamuna, Ramganga, Mahakali, Karnali, Gandaki, and Kosi Rivers are part. The Ganges basin is shared by India, Bangladesh, Nepal and China. The Eastern Himalayan sub-region includes the Brahmaputra system to which the Teesta, Raidak and Manas Rivers belong. The Brahmaputra system is shared by India, Bangladesh, Bhutan and China. Several other tributaries of those rivers also flow into more than one country, thus falling into the category of international rivers as well.

River water has always played a critical role in the South Asian Sub-continent, perhaps much more so than most other parts of the world. The major rivers of the

---

[4] See World Bank, *World Development Report 2000/2001, Attacking Poverty* (2000), at 4. The report defines poverty as living on less than $1 a day, and indicates, under this definition, that 1.2 billion people worldwide live in poverty. About 2.8 billion people, almost half the world's population, live on less than $2 a day; *see id.*, at 3. All "$" and "dollars" refer to US$.

[5] There are some major rivers that flow east-west or west-east, and as such do not have their origin in the Himalayas. The Narmada River, which originates in the Indian state of Madhya Pradesh and forms the borders with the state of Maharashtra before entering the state of Gujarat and flowing into the Arabian Sea, represents one of those rivers. Other such rivers in peninsular India include the Mahanadi, the Godavari and the Krishna rivers. For further information *see* generally, B. R. Chauhan, *Settlement of International and Inter-State Water Disputes in India* (New Delhi: Indian Law Institute, 1992).

region played a crucial role in sustaining and nourishing early civilizations, most notably the Indus civilization. Irrigated agriculture provides living for a large number of people and uses a very high percentage of water. Rivers are also a major producer of electric power, a main source for fisheries, and an important conduit for inland transportation, including carriage of goods. During the monsoon season, when the water level is quite high in those rivers, they are an important source for recharging groundwater. Saline intrusion from the Bay of Bengal and the Arabian Sea is counteracted by the upland flows of those rivers.

Table 1.1
Population, Population Growth and GNP Per Capita in the South Asian Sub-continent

Country	Population (in millions; 1980)	Population (in millions; 1999)	Average Annual Population Growth (percent 1990-99)	GNP/per Capita (U.S.$; 1999)
Bangladesh	87	128	1.6	370
India	687	998	1.8	450
Nepal	15	23	2.4	220
Pakistan	88	135	2.5	470

Source: *World Development Report 2000/2001*, (World Bank), 274-275 and 278-279.

Freshwater resources per capita in the Sub-continent, as shown in Table 1.2, indicate a major variation between Bangladesh and Nepal on one hand, and India and Pakistan on the other. However, those figures obscure the sharp seasonal and spatial variations within each country. Indeed, the two basic characteristics of water resources in the South Asian Sub-continent are floods and drought. About 80 percent of the annual precipitation in India takes place during the short monsoon season that usually starts in June and ends in September.[6] Floods could devastate the Sub-continent during this period, as happened in Bangladesh and India in 1988 and 1998, as well as in 2000. During the dry months of March and April when the flow of the Ganges is usually at its lowest levels, Bangladesh could suffer from drought as happened in 1989 and 1997 when the Ganges flow was exceptionally low. In the early months of the year 2000, some parts of Pakistan, and large parts of India, particularly its arid western part in the states of Rajasthan and Gujarat, suffered from severe drought.[7]

---

[6] *See* M. A. Chitale, "Water Resources Management In India: Achievements And Perspectives," in *Country Experience with Water Resources Management – Economic, Institutional, Technological and Environmental Issues*, Guy Le Moigne, et al., eds., World Bank Technical Paper No. 175 (1992), at 157. The author states that, according to the criteria adopted in India, "....drought occurs in an area when annual rainfall is less than 75 percent of the norm. When this situation exists for more than 20 percent of the year, the area is labeled drought prone." *See, id.*, at 157.

[7] *See Frontline*, Vol. 17, No. 10 (May 13–26, 2000), at 23, and 120–133.

Table 1.2
Fresh Water Resources and Withdrawals in the South Asian Sub-continent

Country	Freshwater Resources Cu. meters Per capita (1998)	Annual Freshwater Withdrawal (Billion Cu. meters)	Percent of Withdrawal for Agriculture
Bangladesh	9,636	146	86
India	1,947	500	93
Nepal	9,199	29	99
Pakistan	1,938	155.6	97

Source: World Development Report 2000/2001, (World Bank), 290-291.

By 2015, the population of India is projected to reach 1.2 billion, Pakistan 193 million, Bangladesh 160 million and Nepal 32 million.[8] This is an increase of almost 400 million from the current figures for the region, and of almost 100 percent from the figures of 1980. This steady increase in the population of the Sub-continent, coupled with the increase in urbanization, will continue to put tremendous pressure on the available water resources, and decrease the per capita availability of water. The need to alleviate poverty that afflicts the Sub-continent will increase the pressure on the use of the water resources of the region, particularly in the irrigation sector, which is significantly the largest user of water in the Sub-continent, with figures varying from 86 percent to 99 percent, as indicated in Table 1.2.[9] These factors are leading to an increase in competing demands over the waters of the international rivers of the South Asian Sub-continent, thus heightening the possibilities for conflict. The same factors will also present opportunities for cooperation.

Despite the large number of rivers, and the significant importance of water resources for the basic livelihood of its people, the South Asian Sub-continent has not been successful in designing and establishing treaty regimes for several of its shared rivers. Only a few treaties have been entered into between some of the riparian countries, and not without political and diplomatic difficulties. The Indus Waters Treaty has been entered into between India and Pakistan, and a series of successive treaties on the Ganges River has been entered into between India and Bangladesh. Nepal and India have established treaty relations on three international rivers: the Kosi Agreement (in connection with the Kosi River), the Gandak Agreement (in connection with the Gandaki River) and the Mahakali Treaty (in connection with the Mahakali River). It is worth emphasizing that all these treaties are bilateral, and

---

[8] *See*, World Bank, *1999 World Development Indicators*, at 42-43.

[9] About 73 percent of all water withdrawals, globally, are for irrigation. *See* World Bank, *1992 World Development Report, Development and the Environment*, at 100. Withdrawal for irrigated agriculture is quite high in some states in India, like the predominantly agricultural State of Punjab where irrigation accounts for more than 95 percent of all water used; *see* Salman M. A. Salman, *The Legal Framework for Water Users' Associations – A Comparative Analysis*, World Bank Technical Paper No. 360 (1997), at 2.

none of those countries has entered into an agreement with China on any of the rivers that originate there.

To place those international agreements in context for discussion, and to identify the different principles of international water law included in such agreements, it is essential to outline the evolution of international water law in general.

II. International Water Law

One of the basic characteristics of international water law is that it is still in the formative stage of development with regard to non-navigational uses. Despite the work of a number of scholarly institutions and the United Nations, there is still no universal treaty in force that regulates the non-navigational uses and protection of international watercourses. The United Nations Convention on the Law of the Non-Navigational Uses of International Watercourses (the UN Convention), which was adopted by the United Nations General Assembly on May 21, 1997, after more than 25 years of preparatory work by the International Law Commission and extensive deliberations by the Sixth Committee of the General Assembly,[10] has yet to enter into force and effect. Prior to the adoption of the UN Convention there were no formal rules regulating the use and protection of international watercourses. The Institute of International Law (known commonly by its French name, l'Institut de Droit International) and the International Law Association have attempted to provide guidance in this field through their scholarly work, reports and resolutions. This effort has contributed significantly to the process of codification of the prevailing principles of customary international water law for non-navigational purposes. On the other hand, regulation of the navigational uses of international watercourses predated the efforts of the Institute of International Law and the International Law Association, as described in the next section.

1. The Rise and Decline of the Primacy of Navigational Uses

The process of evolution and codification of the principles of international law with regard to navigational purposes started relatively early. The process commenced with the adoption of the Act of the Congress of Vienna on June 9, 1815.[11] At that

---

[10] On December 8, 1970, the United Nations General Assembly adopted Resolution 2669 (XXV) asking the International Law Commission (ILC) to study the topic of international watercourses. The ILC started working on the draft Convention at its twenty-third session in 1971, and completed its work and adopted the articles of the draft Convention on June 24, 1994, and recommended the draft articles to the General Assembly on that date. *See* 1994 Yearbook of the International Law Commission, Volume II (1997), Part Two, at 88. The Convention was adopted by the General Assembly on May 21, 1997, by a vote of 103 for, and three against (Burundi, China and Turkey) with 27 abstentions; 52 countries did not participate in the voting. For the full text of the Convention, *see* 36 I.L.M. 700 (1997). *See* also Salman M. A. Salman and Laurence Boisson de Chazournes, eds., *International Watercourses: Enhancing Cooperation and Managing Conflict*, World Bank Technical Paper No. 414 (1998), Annex 1, at 173.

[11] For the text of the Act, *see,* Wilhelm G. Grewe (ed.) *Fontes Historiale Iuris Gentium (Sources Relating to the History of the Law of Nations)*, Volume 1 (1992), at 455. *See* generally, Martens

time, navigation was, by and large, the single user of rivers. Non-navigational uses such as irrigation, hydro-power and industry were only in the early stage of development.[12] Other means of transportation for people and their products were also in a similar stage of development. This situation gave considerable importance to navigation.

The Act of the Congress of Vienna included, *inter alia*, 10 articles on navigation on international rivers. Article 108 stated that the Powers whose territories were separated or crossed by the same navigable river undertook to regulate by common agreement all that related to the navigation of such rivers, and for that purpose they would name commissioners who would adopt the principles established in the pertinent articles of the Act. Article 109 established the principle of freedom of navigation on such a river, for all riparians, on a reciprocal basis. The rest of the Articles dealt with issues such as the system for collection of dues and regulation of tariff. As such, the Act of the Congress of Vienna can be considered a landmark in the evolution of international water law.

The trend toward freedom and priority of navigation established by the Act of the Congress of Vienna continued to prevail, and was confirmed in 1885 by the General Act of the Congress of Berlin with regard to the Congo and Niger Rivers,[13] thus extending the freedom of navigation to non-riparian states as well. Although the Madrid Declaration issued by the Institute of International Law in 1911 was intended to deal with non-navigational matters, it did include a reference to freedom of navigation.[14] Article 4 of the Declaration upheld the primacy of navigation by stating that the right of navigation by virtue of a title recognized in international law may not be violated in any way whatsoever.

---

and Cussey, *Recueil Manuel et Pratique de Traités, Conventions et Autres Actes Diplomatiques* (1935).

[12] It should be added that, in addition to the navigational and non-navigational uses, international rivers and lakes may also be used to delimit boundaries between nations. Although boundaries, as a general rule, are established by treaties, the interpretation of treaties as to where the boundaries are actually drawn across the river, often has to take into account the particular characteristics of the international river or lake in question. For a general discussion of international rivers as boundaries, *see*, R. R. Baxter, *The Law of International Waterways* (Cambridge: Harvard University Press, 1964); *see* also, Salman M. A. Salman, "International Rivers As Boundaries: The Dispute Over The Kasikili/Sedudu Island and The Decision of The International Court of Justice," 25 *Water International* (2000), at 580; *see* also International Court of Justice, Case Concerning Kasikili/Sedudu Island (Botswana/Namibia), General List No. 98, (1999). Both the Mahakali and the Ganges rivers are boundary rivers for some stretches between India and Nepal, and India and Bangladesh, respectively (*see infra,* Chapters 5 and 7).

[13] *See* 3 *American J. International Law* (Supp) (1909), at 7. The purpose of the expansion of the concept of freedom of navigation to the Congo and Niger rivers was to facilitate the conquest of Africa by the European colonial powers. *See* for detail, Bela Vitanyi, *The International Regime of River Navigation* (Alphen aan den Rijn, The Netherlands: Sijthoff and Noordhoff, 1979), at 98. *See* also Baxter, *supra* note 12, Chapter III, at 149.

[14] *See* International Regulations Regarding the Use of International Watercourses for Purposes Other than Navigation, adopted by the Institute of International Law at its session at Madrid, April 20, 1911; 24 *Annuaire de l'Institut de Droit International* 365 (1911). *See infra,* the discussion of this Declaration in Section III of this chapter.

The 1919 Peace Treaty of Versailles continued the liberalization trend in navigation by opening all the navigable rivers in Europe to all the European countries.[15] This trend was confirmed 10 years later by the Permanent Court of International Justice in the Oder River Case, where the Court ruled that the jurisdiction of the International Commission for the Oder River extended to certain tributaries of such river.[16]

The changing economic circumstances, however, gradually eroded the primacy of navigation established at the beginning of the nineteenth century. The industrial revolution and the steady increase in population necessitated other uses for the rivers. The industrial revolution brought about new modes of transportation and carriage of goods that reduced the importance of rivers as international *highways*. With the beginning of the twentieth century, economic, non-navigational uses of international rivers started evolving and competing with navigational uses. Although the Madrid Declaration, as we have noted, asserted in 1911 the right of navigation as inviolate, it did provide for other uses of boundary and successive rivers. In 1921 the "Convention and Statute on the Regime of Navigable Waterways of International Concern," which is also known as the Barcelona Convention, was adopted under the auspices of the League of Nations.[17] The Convention confirmed the principle of freedom of navigation. Article 10 (1) of the Statute obliged each riparian state to refrain from all measures likely to prejudice the navigability of the waterway, or to reduce the facilities for navigation, and also to take all the neces-

---

[15] It should be noted, however, that the notion of freedom of navigation did not prevail in the Americas. As Lucius Caflisch noted "The American States have, from the outset, been reluctant to open their waterways even to other riparians and have developed what one may call the regional custom of the "concesion especial." Each riparian State is entitled, on the part of watercourse located on its territory, to prohibit foreign navigation of any kind." See Lucius Caflisch, "Regulation of the Uses of International Watercourses," in *International Watercourses – Enhancing Cooperation and Managing Conflict, supra* note 10, at 7–8.

[16] *See,* Case Relating to the Territorial Jurisdiction of the International Commission of the River Oder, 1929 P.C.I.J. (ser. A) No. 16 (Great Britain, Czechoslovak Republic, Denmark, France, Germany and Sweden v. Poland). The issue before the Permanent Court of International Justice was whether the jurisdiction of the International Commission of the Oder River extended, under the provisions of the Treaty of Versailles, to sections of the tributaries of the Oder, namely the Warthe and Netze, which were situated in Poland. Whereas Poland maintained that the jurisdiction of the Oder Commission excluded sections of those tributaries in Polish territory, the other six countries felt that the navigable portions of those tributaries should not be excluded from the Commission's jurisdiction. The Court ruled that the jurisdiction of the Commission extended to certain tributaries of the Oder River situated within Poland. Along those lines of liberalization, the Permanent Court of International Justice in the *Oscar Chinn* case (Great Britain v. Belgium), (P.C.I.J., ser A/B, No. 63 (1934) stated, five years after its decision in the *River Oder* case, that "...freedom of navigation implies, as far as the business side of maritime or fluvial transport is concerned, freedom of commerce also." *Id.,* at 83.

[17] 7 U.N.T.S., 35. The Convention was signed on April 20, 1921 at Barcelona; *see* also W. E. Burhenne, *International Environmental Law – Multilateral Treaties*, Vol.1 (London: Kluwer Law International, 1997). The Convention included procedural aspects such as signature, accession and ratification, while the Statute laid down the detailed rules regarding the navigable uses of international waterways.

sary steps for removing any obstacles and dangers which may occur to navigation.[18] Although the Convention reconfirmed the principle of freedom of navigation, supremacy of navigation was no longer absolute. Article 10 (6) recognized the right of a riparian state, in exceptional circumstances, to close the waterway, wholly or in part, to navigation if navigation was of little importance to it, and if the state could justify its action on the ground of economic interest clearly greater than that of navigation. Although the Barcelona Convention was intended to address navigational uses of international rivers, it certainly recognized non-navigational uses as well.

Two years later, in 1923, another convention was adopted under the auspices of the League of Nations that also dealt with non-navigational uses of international rivers. This one was the "General Convention Relating to the Development of Hydraulic Power Affecting More Than One State," also known as the Geneva Convention.[19] The Convention dealt with the right of any riparian state to carry out on its territory any operations for development of hydraulic power that it may consider desirable, subject to "the limits of international law." The adoption of this Convention marked another step in the decline of the inherent supremacy of navigation that prevailed throughout the nineteenth century. Freedom of navigation was also affected. After the Second World War and the division of Europe into east and west camps, freedom of navigation was gradually restricted only to the riparian countries of the particular shared river. This situation has continued to prevail, and seems to represent contemporary customary international law in this field.[20]

2. Evolution of Principles for Non-Navigational Uses

It should be noted, however, that the decline of the primacy and freedom of navigation was not accompanied by the evolution and the establishment of any official rules for regulating the non-navigational uses of international rivers. Toward the end of the nineteenth century and the beginning of the twentieth, four varying, and to some extent conflicting, principles were in existence for addressing the rights and obligations of riparian states over international rivers. Those principles were based, to a large extent, on state practice and the work of scholars and experts in the field.

The first of those principles, absolute territorial sovereignty, has been the most controversial. According to this principle, also known as the Harmon Doctrine, a state is free to dispose, within its territory, of the waters of an international river in any manner it deems fit, without concern for the harm or adverse impact that such

---

[18] It should be noted that some jurists like Berber do not regard the Barcelona Convention "...as the expression of prevailing state practice, as in the first 15 years after its conclusion it was ratified by only 20 states. These states, moreover, consisted almost entirely of states in whose territory there were no rivers to which the Convention was applicable." See F. J. Berber, *Rivers in International Law*, (London: Stevens & Sons Limited, 1959), at 123.

[19] 36 U.N.T. S., 75. The Convention was signed in Geneva on December 9, 1923.

[20] See Caflisch, *supra* note 15, at 7. The decline of the inherent supremacy of navigation is reflected in a number of recent instruments. The Helsinki Rules equate all kind of uses (*see infra* note 63). Similarly, the UN Convention states that in the absence of agreement, no use of an international watercourse enjoys inherent priority over other uses (*see infra* note 79).

use may cause to other riparian states.[21] The corollary of this principle, however, is that such a state has no right to demand the continued flow of the waters of an international river from the other riparians. In essence, the principle of absolute territorial sovereignty attests that there is no specific international law on the subject. This principle has been criticized by a number of scholars and was described in 1931 by one jurist as "radically unsound."[22] The United States itself did not adhere to this principle in any of the treaties on shared lakes and rivers signed with its two neighbors, Canada in 1909, and Mexico in 1944.[23] Moreover, a number of arbitral and

---

[21] The opinion given by the Attorney General of the United States, Mr. Judson Harmon, in 1895 regarding a dispute with Mexico over the utilization of the waters of the Rio Grande concluded that there was no settled and recognized right "by which it could be held that the diversion of the waters of an international boundary stream for the purpose of irrigating lands on one side of the boundary and which would have the effect to deprive lands on the other side of the boundary of water for irrigation purposes would be a violation of any established principle of international law." *See,* 21 Op. Att'y Gen. 274, at 283 (1895).

[22] After stating that the principle of absolute territorial sovereignty would give the upper riparian the right to exhaust the whole water of the river irrespective of the injury it would cause to the lower riparian, and that it would equally entitle the lower riparian to flood the lands of the upper riparian, Herbert Smith concluded "It seems obvious that a principle which leads to those consequences must be radically unsound." *See* Herbert Arthur Smith, *The Economic Uses of International Rivers* (London: P. S. King & Sons, 1931), at 8.

[23] The 1909 Treaty between the United States and Great Britain Relating to the Boundary Waters between the United States and Canada, states in Article II that "....Any interference with or diversion from their natural channel of such waters on either side of the boundary, resulting in any injury on the other side of the boundary, shall give rise to the same rights and entitle the injured parties to the same legal remedies as if such injury took place in the country where such diversion or interference occurs..." *See Treaties and Other International Agreements of the United States of America 1776-1949* (compiled by Charles Bevans, [1972], at 319). Furthermore, Article IV states that "...boundary waters and waters flowing across the boundary shall not be polluted on either side to the injury of health or property on the other." It is worth adding that the first part of Article II of this Treaty confirms the exclusive jurisdiction and control of each country "...over the use and diversion, whether temporary or permanent, of all waters on its own side of the line in their natural channels." Some scholars have read this part of Article II as embodiment of the principle of absolute territorial sovereignty; *see* Bonaya Adhi Godana, *Africa's Shared Water Resources: Legal and Institutional Aspects of the Nile, Niger and Senegal River Systems* (London: Frances Printer Publishers, 1985), at 34-35. However this part of the Article that enunciates exclusive jurisdiction has been subjected to the limits discussed above. A similar approach has been included in the Charter of Economic Rights and Duties of States (United Nations General Assembly Resolution No. 3281 (XXIX) adopted on December 12, 1974 (24 I.L.M. 251 (1975). Whereas Article 2 of the Charter endows each state with full permanent sovereignty including possession, use and disposal over all its natural resources, Article 3 subjects the right of the state to exploit natural resources shared by two or more countries to the obligation to cooperate "on the basis of a system of information and prior consultation." The 1944 Treaty between the United States of America and Mexico Relating to the Utilization of the Waters of the Colorado and Tijuana Rivers and of Rio Grande (Rio Bravo) from Fort Quitman, Texas, to the Gulf of Mexico (*see, Treaties and Other International Agreements, supra,* at 1166), follows primarily the principle of equitable and reasonable utilization by allotting to each of the two countries certain specified amounts of the waters of those rivers. It should also be pointed out that in 1903 the United States approved the construction of the Gut Dam by Canada in the St. Lawrence River subject, *inter alia*, to the following two conditions:

    1. That if, after said dam has been constructed, it is found that it materially affects the water levels of Lake Ontario or the St. Lawrence River or causes any injury to the interests of the United States, the government of Canada shall make such changes therein, and provide such

judicial decisions have rejected the principle of absolute territorial sovereignty. In 1941, the Arbitration Tribunal in the Trail Smelter case concluded that "...no state has the right to use or permit the use of its territory in such a manner as to cause injury by fumes in or to the territory of another or the properties or persons therein, when the case is of serious consequence and the injury is established by clear and convincing evidence."[24] In 1949, the International Court of Justice in the Corfu Channel case confirmed the principle of state responsibility for acts contrary to international law that occur within the territory of a state and result in injury to another party.[25] Along those lines, the Arbitration Tribunal in the 1957 Lake Lanoux case concluded that "...according to the rules of good faith, the upstream State is under the obligation to take into consideration the various interests involved, to seek to give them every satisfaction compatible with the pursuit of its own interests, and to show that in this regard it is genuinely concerned to reconcile the interests of the other riparian State with its own."[26] As such, it is widely believed that the principle

---

additional regulation works in connection therewith, as the Secretary of War (of the United States) may order.

2. That if the construction and operation of said dam shall cause damage or detriment to the property owners of Les Galops Island or to the property of any other citizen of the United States, the government of Canada shall pay such amount of compensation as may be agreed upon between the said government and the parties damaged, or as may be awarded the said parties in the proper court of the United States before which claims for damage may be brought.

See Canada-United States Settlement of the Gut Dam Claims, Report of the Agent of the United States Before the Lake Ontario Claims Tribunal, 8 I.L.M. 118 (1969). The imposition of those two conditions by the United States on Canada was a clear indication that the United States believed, less than 20 years after Mr. Harmon issued his famous opinion, that a state was not free to dispose within its territory of the waters of an international river as it pleases, and that such a state is responsible for the damage resulting from the disposition of such waters.

[24] *See Trail Smelter Arbitration* (United States v. Canada), 3 R.I.A.A. 1911 (1941) at 1965. In this case smelting operations in British Columbia in Canada resulted in sulphur dioxide fumes being emitted into the air, causing damage to United States citizens across the border in Washington State. The matter was referred to the International Joint Commission established under the 1909 Boundary Waters Treaty (*supra* note 23). The recommendations of the Commission that included, *inter alia*, assessment of the damage up to 1931 at $350,000, were rejected by the United States. As a result, the parties concluded the Convention for the Settlement of Difficulties Arising From Operation of the Smelter Trail between Great Britain and the United States on April 15, 1935. The Convention provided for the establishment of a three-member tribunal which dealt with the matter and issued its decision in 1941.

[25] *See Corfu Channel* case (U.K. v. Albania), International Court of Justice Reports, 1949, at 3. In this case, a number of British officers lost their lives in 1946 when their warship struck mines in the Corfu Channel in the territorial waters of Albania. The International Court of Justice, confirming the principle of harmless use of territory, concluded that under international law, every state is under obligation not to allow knowingly its territory to be used for acts contrary to the rights of other states. As such, Albania was responsible for the explosion of such mines and for the resulting damage and loss of lives.

[26] *See Lake Lanoux Arbitration* (France v. Spain), 24 I.L.R. 101 (1957). The arbitration dealt with the proposed use by the French government of the waters of Lake Lanoux for carrying out certain hydro-electric works. The lake is fed by some streams originating and flowing through French territory. Its waters emerge by the Font-Vive stream that forms one of the headwaters of the River

of absolute territorial sovereignty does not form part of the law of international watercourses.[27]

The second principle pertains to absolute territorial integrity. It establishes the right of a riparian state to demand continuation of the natural flow of an international river into its territory from the upper riparian or riparians, but imposes a duty on such state not to restrict such natural flow of waters to other lower riparians. At most, this principle tolerates only minimal uses by an upstream state, and in that respect it has similarities with the common law doctrine of riparian rights.[28] In essence, this principle is the exact opposite of the principle of absolute territorial sovereignty as it is intended to favor down-stream riparians, often by protecting existing uses or prior appropriations. The principle is supposed to protect lower riparians from any harm or injury that may be caused by the uses of the waters of the international river by the upper riparian. This contrasts with the principle of absolute territorial sovereignty where the state, often the upper riparian, is free to dispose of the water of the international river the way it deems fit. For the same reasons that the principle of absolute territorial sovereignty was rejected—failure to take into account the rights and interests of other riparian states—the principle of absolute territorial integrity could not be accepted as a part of international water law.

The third principle combines the principles of limited territorial sovereignty and limited territorial integrity. It restricts both principles by asserting that every riparian state has a right to use the waters of the international river, but is under a corresponding duty to ensure that such use does not significantly harm other riparians. In essence, this principle establishes the right of every riparian state over the shared river. One of the earliest cases to which this principle can be traced is the Meuse River dispute between Holland and Belgium. In a letter issued by the Dutch Government in 1862, it was stated that: "The Meuse being a river common both to Holland and to Belgium, it goes without saying that both parties are entitled to make

---

Carol, which flows into Spain, where it joins the River Segre. Spain opposed the use of the waters of Lake Lanoux by France, claiming adverse effects as a result. While the Tribunal decided that the works did not constitute infringement of Spain's rights, it also ruled that France was entitled to use the waters of Lake Lanoux but could not ignore Spain's interests, and that Spain was entitled to demand that Spanish rights be respected and interests be taken into account.

[27] Jerome Lipper concluded, after an analysis of the principle of absolute territorial sovereignty, that "...the Harmon Doctrine was not an expression of international river law. Rather, it was an assertion that there being no rules of international law which governed, states were free to do as they wished." *See* Jerome Lipper, "Equitable Utilization," in *The Law of International Drainage Basins,* Garretson et al., eds. (1967), at 22-23. *See* also, Stephen McCaffrey, "The Harmon Doctrine One Hundred Years Later: Buried, Not Praised," *Natural Resources Journal* 36 (1996), at 549.

[28] Under the common law doctrine of riparian rights, as originally conceived, the upper riparian land owner should allow the water to flow down its natural course without interfering with its quantity or quality. However, the principle of riparian rights gradually developed to allow each riparian a reasonable use of the available amount of water. For a discussion of the doctrine of riparian rights, *see* Ludwik A. Teclaff, *Water Law in Historical Perspective* (Buffalo, New York: W. S. Hein, 1985), at 6-20. *See* also David H. Getches, *Water Law in a Nutshell* (1997), at 15–55.

the natural uses of the stream, but at the same time, following general principles of law, each is bound to abstain from any action which might cause damage to the other. In other words, they can not be allowed to make themselves masters of the water by diverting it to serve their own needs, whether for purposes of navigation or for irrigation."[29]

In the River Oder case, the Permanent Court of International Justice referred to "the principles governing international fluvial law in general." After discussing the principle of community of interest of riparian states, the Court concluded that "This community of interest in a navigable river becomes the basis of a common legal right, the essential features of which are the perfect equality of all riparian States in the use of the whole of the course of the river and the exclusion of any preferential privileges of any one riparian State in relation to the others."[30] The concept of the right of each riparian state to a share in the international river, and the corresponding duty not to ignore the rights of other riparian states, have been the basis of the decision of the arbitral tribunal in the Lake Lanoux case.[31] The principle of "equitable and reasonable utilization" is the guiding principle in contemporary international water law and stems from the concept of equality of rights for all the riparian states, which has its roots in the principles of limited territorial sovereignty and limited territorial integrity.

The fourth principle is the community of co-riparian states in the waters of an international river. According to this principle, the entire river basin is an economic unit, and the rights over the waters of the entire river are vested in the collective body of the riparian states, or divided among them either by agreement or accord-

---

[29] For the full text of the letter, *see* Smith, *supra* note 22, Appendix II, at 217. Smith considered the letter to be "the first formal statement of a general principle of law" for the economic uses of international rivers (*id.*, at 217). In this regard, the letter would have a similar place in the history of international water law as that of the Act of the Congress of Vienna of 1815 (*supra* note 11) which is also considered a watershed in the history of the navigational uses of international rivers. The Meuse River originates in France before entering Belgium, becomes a border river between Belgium and Holland and then flows into Holland before joining the Rhine. During the nineteenth century and the beginning of the twentieth century, a bitter dispute arose between Belgium and Holland over the uses of the waters of the River. In the mid-nineteenth century, Belgium started digging a canal for diverting the waters of the Meuse for navigation and irrigation, and Holland complained about the adverse impact of such works in 1851. Two treaties were entered into to address this issue in 1863 and 1865. However, the dispute between the two countries persisted and was finally taken to the Permanent Court of International Justice, which issued its judgment in 1937. For the history of the dispute, *see id.*, at 24-39. Because the questions at issue between the two countries were governed by the 1863 Treaty, the Court concentrated on interpretation of the Treaty, and did not address the general rules of international water law. As such, the decision of the Court has not contributed much to the evolution of the principles of international water law. For the judgment of the Court, *see Diversion of Water from the Meuse* (Neth v. Belg), 1937 P.C.I.J. (ser. A/B) No. 70, at 6 (June 28).

[30] *See supra* note 16, at 27. The reference by the Permanent Court of International Justice to "international fluvial law in general" led many scholars to conclude that the notion of "the equality of all riparians" enunciated by the Court goes beyond navigation and applies equally to non-navigation. *See* Jerome Lipper, *supra* note 27, at 29.

[31] *Supra* note 26.

ing to proportionality.[32] This principle tends to overlook the political boundaries in favor of the optimal and integrated development of the entire river basin.[33] However, nationalism, absence of political will, lack of trust between and among the riparian states, and the varying degrees of development of the different basin states, are all factors that could undermine this idealistic principle.[34]

Codification of the principles of international water law can be attributed mainly to the work of the Institute of International Law, the International Law Association, and most notably the International Law Commission. The work of these institutions is based largely on the principle of limited territorial sovereignty, and its counterpart, limited territorial integrity. As such, the rules and resolutions adopted by these institutions reflect those principles.

3. Contribution of the Institute of International Law

The first attempt toward codification of principles and regulations for non-navigational uses of international waters was enunciated by the Madrid Declaration, adopted by the Institute of International Law in 1911.[35] The Declaration makes a distinction between streams that form boundaries between two states, and streams that traverse successively through two or more states.[36] For frontier streams, the first article of the Declaration states "…neither of these (riparian) States may, without the consent of the other, and without special and valid legal title, make or allow individuals, corporations, etc. to make alterations therein detrimental to the bank of the other State. On the other hand, neither State may, on its own territory, utilize or allow the utilization of the water in such a way as seriously to interfere with its utilization by the other State, or by individuals, corporations, etc. thereof."[37] The sec-

---

[32] For discussion of those principles *see* Jerome Lipper, *supra* note 27, at 13; *see* also Berber, *supra* note 18, at 11.

[33] As we have seen, the Permanent Court of International Justice addressed the issue of community of interests of riparian states in the *Oder River* case, *supra* note 16.

[34] The World Bank, in its mediation efforts between India and Pakistan, attempted an integrated approach to the Indus Basin, based on the principle of "Community of Co-riparian States" (*infra*, Chapter 2). However, the political realities forced the World Bank to abandon that approach and agree instead to the proposal to divide the Indus Basin between India and Pakistan.

[35] *See* "International Regulations Regarding the Use of International Watercourses for Purposes Other than Navigation" (the Madrid Declaration); *supra* note 14; also International Law Association, Principles of Law and Recommendations on the Uses of International Rivers, Statement of Principles of Law and Recommendations with a Commentary and Supporting Authorities Submitted to the International Committee of the International Law Association by the Committee on the Uses of Waters of International Rivers of the American Branch, New York University Conference (1958), at 54-55.

[36] Although often stressed to an extreme, international law, in terms of rights and duties, does not draw any legal distinction between boundary rivers and successive rivers. The same rules of international law apply to both types of rivers. This has been concluded by the Permanent Court of International Justice in the *River Oder* case. *See* The International Commission of the River Oder, *supra* note 16, at 27.

[37] *See* the Madrid Declaration, *supra* note 35, Article 1. The same Article extends the application

ond article deals with successive streams and obligates the riparian states not to change the point where such a stream crosses the frontiers of such states, by establishments of one of the states without the consent of the other. It also forbids all alterations injurious to water, and the emptying therein of injurious matter such as from factories. The Declaration also prohibits establishments such as factories from taking so much water as to seriously modify such stream. It also prohibits construction that would subject other states to inundation. The Declaration clearly rejects the principle of absolute territorial sovereignty by imposing certain restrictions on each riparian state, including the requirement of obtaining the consent of the other riparians. As such, the Declaration codifies the principle against causing appreciable harm to other riparians. Under this principle, it may be noted, a state is entitled to use the flow of an international watercourse in its territory but only in such manner as not to cause appreciable harm to another riparian.[38] Hence, the Madrid Declaration embodies the principle of limited territorial sovereignty, but establishes absolute prohibition against activities that would result in injury to other riparians.

The Geneva Convention, which was adopted under the auspices of the League of Nations 12 years later, in 1923,[39] subjected the rights of any state to carry out on its territory any operations for development to "the limits of international law."[40] The Geneva Convention calls for joint investigation by the Contracting States for the reasonable development of hydraulic power involving international investigation, and obliges the parties to pay due regard to any works already existing, under construction or projected. If such development involves the use of the territory of another state, or may cause prejudice to another state, those states shall enter into negotiations with a view to conclude an agreement. As such, "the seemingly absolute prohibition of the Madrid Declaration against upper riparians undertaking construction that might alter the regime of the waters was superseded at Geneva by the principle of reasonableness, and the necessity of negotiations."[41]

The Institute of International Law continued its work on the uses of international watercourses and in 1961 adopted the Salzburg Resolution.[42] The provisions of the

---

of this rule to "a lake lying between the territories of more than two States." Perhaps the intention was "two or more states," rather than "more than two states."

[38] The no harm rule, *sic utere tuo ut alienum non laedas* (so use your own property as not to injure your neighbor), covers, under international law, a whole range of neighborly relations, including issues pertaining to the protection of the environment, as we noted in the *Trail Smelter Arbitration*, supra note 24.

[39] *Supra* note 19.

[40] *See* Article 1 of the Geneva Convention, *id*. Because the Convention does not define those limits, it may reasonably be argued that such limits relate, *inter alia*, to the obligation not to cause appreciable harm to other riparian states.

[41] *See* International Law Association, *Principles of Law and Recommendations on the Uses of International Rivers*, 56 (1959).

[42] Resolution on the Utilization of Non-Maritime International Waters (Except for Navigation), adopted by the Institute of International Law at its Session at Salzburg, September 11, 1961, 49

Salzburg Resolution show marked differences from the provisions of the Madrid Declaration, perhaps due to the changing economic and political circumstances since the Madrid Declaration was issued 50 years earlier. For example, the preamble to the Resolution recognizes the fact that "the economic importance of the use of waters is transformed by modern technology and that the application of modern technology to the waters of a hydrographic basin which includes the territory of several States affect in general all these States, and renders necessary its restatement in juridical terms." The preamble also recognizes that "maximum utilization of available natural resources is a matter of common interest," but confirms the obligation of riparian states not to cause unlawful harm to other riparians, and calls this obligation one of the basic general principles governing neighborly relations. Although the Resolution confirms the rights of every state to utilize the waters that traverse or border its territory, it subjects this right to two limitations: the limits imposed by international law and the right of utilization of other states. Article 3 of the Resolution deals with cases where there are disagreements among the riparian states over the scope of their rights of utilization and stipulates that settlement would take place "on the basis of equity, taking particular account of their respective needs as well as other pertinent circumstances." This is, in essence, a reference to the concept of equitable utilization, although not with the necessary details needed for addressing the concept. The Resolution includes detailed provisions for works on international waters that may seriously affect the possibility of utilization of the same waters by other states, and requires prior notification of such states.[43] In case of objection, the matter should be resolved by negotiations. The Resolution recommends that the states in disagreement should have recourse to technical experts, and if the parties still fail to reach an agreement, they should submit the dispute to judicial settlement or arbitration.[44] This was certainly a major improvement over the Madrid Declaration, which required the consent of other affected riparians.[45]

Annuaire de l'Institut de Droit International 370 (1961); *see* also, 56 *American J. International Law* (1962), at 737.

[43] The Salzburg Resolution, Article 5. It should be noted that, unlike the Madrid Declaration, which requires consent of other riparians, the Salzburg Resolution requires only notification of such riparians. As such, the Salzburg Resolution follows the approach adopted by the Geneva Convention. *See supra* note 41.

[44] The Salzburg Resolution, Article 8. It is worth adding that this Article gives the state proposing works on an international watercourse the right to proceed with such works, subject to its responsibility, if the state objecting to such works refuses to submit to judicial settlement or arbitration. However, the proposing state is still bound by its obligation not to cause appreciable harm to other riparians.

[45] It is also worth noting that the Salzburg Resolution is in line with a decision of the Arbitral Tribunal in the *Lake Lanoux* case where the Tribunal held that "the rule that states may utilize the hydraulic power of international watercourses only on condition of a *prior* agreement between the States concerned cannot be established as a custom, even less as a general principle of law." *See supra* note 26, at 130. The use of the term "watercourses" by the Arbitral Tribunal in 1957 is quite noteworthy. During the 1950s and 1960s, and indeed prior to that, the terms used most frequently were "river," "waterway" and "drainage basin." The term "watercourse," which is more inclusive than any of the other terms, was introduced earlier by the Madrid Declaration in 1911 (*supra*

Another noteworthy Resolution of the Institute of International Law is on the pollution of rivers and lakes and was adopted in Athens in 1979.[46] The Resolution confirms the sovereign right of the states to exploit their own resources pursuant to their own environmental policies. However, the Resolution subjects the states' right to exploit their own resources to the duty to ensure that their activities cause no pollution in the waters of international rivers and lakes beyond their boundaries.[47] Any breach of this obligation would result in liability under international law. The Resolution prescribes two means for compliance with this obligation: (i) enactment of necessary laws and regulations, and adoption of efficient and adequate administrative measures and judicial procedures for the enforcement of such laws and regulations; and (ii) cooperation in good faith with the other states concerned.

In 1997 at its meeting in Salzburg, the Institute adopted three resolutions that deal with the environment. They are entitled "the Environment," "Responsibility and Liability for Environmental Damage under International Law" and "Procedures."[48] The term "environment" is defined in the first resolution to include "abiotic and biotic natural resources, in particular air, water, soil, fauna and flora, as well as interaction between these factors." Article 4 states that international law shall determine the basic models and minimum rules required for the protection of the environment. This wide definition of "environment" would subject all uses of international watercourses to environmental law rules enunciated in those resolutions, without recognition of the fact that shared water resources require different sets of rules from other components of the environment for regulating their use and protection. Articles 6 and 9 of the first resolution emphasize the need that actions of the states "entail no harmful consequences," and that the state whose activity might be linked with damage to the environment should ensure that "such damage does not arise."

The Madrid Declaration and the subsequent Salzburg and Athens Resolutions adopt in clear terms the principle of limited territorial sovereignty by subjecting the right of the riparian state over the international river to the duty of such state not to cause unlawful harm to other riparians. However, it should be added that such prohibition is not absolute, as it applied only to serious damage, or damage that affected the possibility of utilization by other riparians. Although the Salzburg Resolution

---

note 14), and was also used by the International Law Association in the Helsinki Rules *(see infra* note 57), but was not defined in either document. The search for a definition of the term started with the work of the International Law Commission on the UN Convention in the 1970s. The United Nations General Assembly used the term "watercourses" in Resolution 2669 of December 8, 1970; *see supra* note 10.

[46] Resolution on "The Pollution of Rivers and Lakes and International Law" adopted by the Institute of International Law, September 12, 1979, 58 *Annuaire de l'Institut de Droit International* (1979), at 196, also known as the "Athens Resolution"; *see* also Harald Hohmann, *Basic Documents of International Environmental Law,* Vol. 1 (London: Graham & Trotman, 1992), at 256.

[47] *Id.*, Article II. Article 1 of the Resolution defines pollution as any physical, chemical or biological alteration in the composition or quality of waters which results directly or indirectly from human action and affects the legitimate uses of such waters, thereby causing injury.

[48] *See* 67 *Annuaire de l'Institut de Droit International* (1997), at 217.

included references to the principle of equitable utilization, the work of the Institute of International Law, particularly the three 1997 Resolutions on the environment, clearly emphasize the obligation of the riparian states not to cause unlawful harm to other riparians. This contrasts sharply with the work of the International Law Association, which is based on the principle of equitable and reasonable utilization, as discussed below.

4. Contribution of the International Law Association

The International Law Association started working on international water resources law in 1954 following the establishment of the Committee on the Uses of the Waters of International Rivers.[49] In 1956 the International Law Association issued its first set of principles entitled "A Statement of Principles upon which to Base Rules of Law Concerning the Uses of International Rivers," also known as the Dubrovnik Statement.[50] The Statement of Principles confirms the sovereign control each state has over the international river within its own boundaries but requires such state to exercise such control with due consideration for its effects upon other riparian states.[51] Paragraph V of the Statement established a number of factors that should be taken into consideration by states in reaching agreements, or by tribunals in settling disputes. Although the Statement did not use the term "equitable and reasonable utilization" or any of its equivalent formulation, it has certainly laid down the foundation for the development of this principle.[52] As such, the International Law Association not only rejected the principle of absolute territorial sovereignty, but also carried the principle of limited territorial sovereignty to its logical end by adopting the principle of equitable utilization.[53] The Dubrovnik meeting did not

---

[49] For a detailed account of the work of the International Law Association in this field, *see* Charles Bourne, "The International Law Association's Contribution to International Water Resources Law," *Natural Resources Journal* 36 (1996), at 155. *See* also Patricia Wouters, ed., *International Water Law: Selected Writings of Professor Charles Bourne* (London: Kluwer Law International, 1997), Chapter 3, at 83. *See* also Slavko Bogdanovic, *International Law of Water Resources: Contribution of the International Law Association* (London: Kluwer Law International, 2001). The Committee on the Uses of the Waters of International Rivers was also known as the "Rivers Committee."

[50] International Law Association, Report of the Forty-Seventh Conference, Dubrovnik, 1956, at 241. The intention of the Rivers Committee was not to state rules of law, but only to lay down principles on which rules of law could be formulated. *See* Bourne, *supra* note 49, at 159-160.

[51] *See* paragraph 3 of the Dubrovnik Statement, International Law Association, Report of the Forty-Seventh Conference, Dubrovnik, 1956, at 241-242.

[52] The Statement specified the following five factors that should be taken into consideration in reaching an agreement on the uses of the waters of the international river: "(i) The right of each to reasonable use of the water; (ii) The extent of the dependence of each state upon the waters of that river; (iii) The comparative social and economical gains accruing to each and the entire river community; (iv) Pre-existent agreements among the states concerned; (v) Pre-existent appropriation of water by one state." *See* Paragraph V of the Dubrovnik Statement, *id.*, at 241-242.

[53] Equitable utilization has been defined as "...the division of the waters of an international river among the co-riparian states in accordance with the legitimate economic and social needs of each, in such a manner as to achieve the maximum benefits for all with a minimum of detriment to

clearly label the essence of its Statement, but the matter was addressed in 1958 at the International Law Association meeting in New York with the adoption of the New York Resolution.[54] Article 2 of the Resolution states that each co-riparian state is entitled to a reasonable and equitable share in the beneficial uses of the waters of the drainage basin.[55] The principle of equitable utilization was the essence of discussions at the Tokyo meeting of the International Law Association in 1964.[56]

In 1966, the International Law Association adopted the Helsinki Rules on the Uses of the Waters of International Rivers.[57] The Rules incorporated and elaborated the previous principles and resolutions adopted successively at Dubrovnik, New York and Tokyo. Like the previous principles and resolutions, the Helsinki Rules have no formal standing. Yet until the adoption of the UN Convention 30 years later, they remained the single, most authoritative and widely quoted set of rules for regulating the use and protection of international watercourses. As noted by Professor Bourne, the Helsinki Rules were soon accepted by the international community as customary international law.[58]

Although the title of the Rules refers to international rivers only, Article 1 states that the Rules are applicable to the use of the waters of an international drainage

---

each." See Jerome Lipper, *supra* note 27, at 63. Equitable utilization is based on the theory that each riparian state has an equality of right with every other riparian state to utilize the waters of the international river in a reasonable and beneficial manner. It should be emphasized, however, that equality of rights does not necessarily mean an equal division of the waters of the international river. See *id.,* at 63.

[54] International Law Association, Report of the Forty-Eighth Conference, New York, 1958, at 28. The New York Resolution codified the provisional principles included in the Dubrovnik Statement.

[55] Article 2 of the New York Resolution states that a reasonable and equitable share should be determined in light of all the relevant factors in each particular case. However, the Resolution did not include any such factors.

[56] International Law Association, Report of the Fifty-First Conference, Tokyo, 1964, at 167. In elaborating on the concept of equitable utilization, the International Law Association observed: "Any use of water by a riparian State, whether upper or lower, that denies an equitable sharing of uses by a co-riparian State conflicts with the community of interests of all riparian States in obtaining maximum benefit from the common source. Thus uses of waters by a riparian State that cause pollution resulting in injury in a co-riparian State must be considered from the overall perspective of what constitutes an equitable utilization." As such, the obligation not to cause significant harm was brought within the concept of equitable utilization, thus expanding the boundaries of the concept.

[57] International Law Association, Report of the Fifty-Second Conference, Helsinki, 1966, at 486.

[58] See Bourne, *supra* note 49, at 215. The Helsinki Rules have been referred to or adopted by a number of cases. For example, the Asian-African Legal Consultative Committee, Sub-committee on International Rivers, adopted in 1973, in its meeting in New Delhi, India, the principle of reasonable and equitable share and included, to a large extent, the factors specified in Article V of the Helsinki Rules as the factors for determining such share; see Asian-African Legal Consultative Committee, Report of the Fourteenth Session, from January 18-19, 1973 (New Delhi, India). "The Protocol on Shared Watercourse System in the Southern African Development Community," which was concluded on August 23, 1995 (*supra* note 3), is based largely on the Helsinki Rules, and the Protocol makes clear references to such Rules. When India and Bangladesh argued their

basin. Such drainage basin is defined as "a geographical area extending over two or more States determined by the watershed limits of the system of waters, including surface and underground waters, flowing into a common terminus."[59] The Helsinki Rules have clearly established the principle of "reasonable and equitable utilization" of the waters of an international drainage basin among the riparian states as the guiding principle of international water law. For that purpose, the Helsinki Rules specified a number of factors for determining what is reasonable and equitable share for each basin state.[60] The Rules devote a separate chapter to pollution, navigation

---

case on the dispute over the Ganges River before the United Nations, both relied heavily on the Helsinki Rules (*infra*, Chapter 7). Some of the bilateral treaties also made specific reference to the Helsinki Rules such as the 1992 "Agreement between the Government of Namibia and the Government of the Republic of South Africa on the Establishment of a Permanent Water Commission." *See* Treaties Concerning the Non-Navigational Uses of International Watercourses – Africa, 61 FAO Legislative Study 214 (1997).

[59] Helsinki Rules, Article II. It is worth noting that the definition of drainage basin includes both "surface and underground waters, flowing into a common terminus." This is the first time that groundwater was included in any resolution or rules, although the Comment on "Agreed Principles on International Law" of the Forty-Eighth conference of the International Law Association held in New York in 1958, brought underground water to the discussion, and highlighted the need "to consider the interdependence of all hydrological and demographic features of the drainage basin." *See* International Law Association, Report of the Forty-Eighth Conference, New York, 1958, *supra* note 54, at 100.

[60] Article V of the Helsinki Rules states that the relevant factors to be considered include, but are not limited to:
 (a) the geography of the basin, including in particular the extent of the drainage area in the territory of each basin state;
 (b) the hydrology of the basin, including in particular the contribution of water by each basin state;
 (c) the climate affecting the basin;
 (d) the past utilization of the waters of the basin, including in particular existing utilization;
 (e) the economic and social needs of each basin State;
 (f) the population dependent on the waters of the basin in each basin State;
 (g) the comparative costs of alternative means of satisfying the economic and social needs of each basin State;
 (h) the availability of other resources;
 (i) the avoidance of unnecessary waste in the utilization of waters of the basin;
 (j) the practicability of compensation to one or more of the co-basin States as a means of adjusting conflicts among uses; and
 (k) the degree to which the needs of a basin state may be satisfied, without causing substantial injury to a co-basin State.
Paragraph 3 of Article V states that the weight to be given to each factor is to be determined by its importance in comparison with that of other relevant factors. *See* Helsinki Rules, *supra* note 57. Those factors are a major elaboration of the five factors that the International Law Association established in the Dubrovnik Statement; *see supra* note 52. The factors elaborated in the Helsinki Rules have been used widely, including in inter-states water disputes. The United States Supreme Court, in the case involving a dispute over the waters of the North Platte River (*Nebraska v. Wyoming*, 325 U.S. at 618, 1945), listed a number of factors for determining equitable apportionment. The Court stated, "Priority of apportionment is the guiding principle. But physical and climatic conditions, the consumptive use of water in the several sections of the river, the character and rate of return flows, the extent of established uses, the availability of storage water, the practical effect of wasteful uses on downstream areas if a limitation is imposed on the former – these are all relevant factors. They are merely an illustrative, not exhaustive, catalogue. They indicate the nature of the problem of apportionment and the delicate adjustment of interests which must be

and timber floating.[61] They also include a chapter on procedures, not only for settlement but also for the prevention of disputes. The latter part of the chapter deals with notification of any proposed construction or installation that would alter the regime of the basin or give rise to a dispute, to any basin state whose interests may be substantially affected by such construction.[62] The Rules include an Annex on "Model Rules for the Constitution of the Conciliation Commission for the Settlement of a Dispute." As such, the Helsinki Rules cover a wide range of issues, including both navigational and non-navigational uses of international watercourses.[63]

In this context, it is worth noting that while the Madrid Declaration and Salzburg Resolution emphasize the obligation not to cause appreciable harm to other riparians, equitable utilization of the waters of the international drainage basins has been the guiding principle in the work of the International Law Association, particularly after the elaboration and clarifications of the Helsinki Rules. It should be mentioned that the Helsinki Rules do not include a separate reference to the obligation not to cause harm, but rather specify the injury that may result from the use of the river by one riparian as one of the elements in determining equitable utilization.[64] Another element that needs to be considered in determining equitable utilization is past utilization of the waters of the basin, including in particular existing utilization.[65] The Helsinki Rules have, in this regard, incorporated the notion of "prior appropriation," which basically means "first in time, first in right." Taken in an absolute sense, the application of this notion would mean the predominance of the obligation not to cause injury to other riparian by interfering with existing uses. However, the Helsinki Rules treat prior appropriation as one element in determining equitable utilization, and not as a freestanding obligation protecting the *status quo* which may not necessarily be reflective of equitable utilization.[66]

---

made." *See id.* The similarities between the two lists of factors and the conclusion that those factors are neither exclusive nor absolute are both worth noting.

[61] It is noteworthy that instead of the term "drainage basin," the Chapter on "Navigation" refers to rivers and lakes, whereas the Chapter on "Timber Floating" uses the term "watercourse." Indeed, the term international drainage basin, as defined under the Helsinki Rules, is too broad for dealing with navigation and timber floating. Moreover, the term "watercourse" is not defined in the Rules. As we have seen, the Madrid Declaration, *supra* note 35, included the term "watercourses" in its title, but again the term "watercourses" was not defined. For other discussion of the use of the term "watercourse," *see* also *supra* note 45.

[62] The Salzburg Resolution of the Institute of International Law (*supra* note 42) includes similar provisions on the notification requirement.

[63] It should be pointed out, however, that Article VI of the Helsinki Rules confirmed the decline of the primacy of navigation by stating that "A use or category of uses is not entitled to any inherent preference over any other use or category of uses." The Article, as such, equates all uses of international drainage basins.

[64] Article V (2) of the Helsinki Rules enumerates as one of the factors for determining equitable utilization "(k) the degree to which the needs of a basin state may be satisfied, without causing substantial injury to a co-basin State."

[65] *Id.*, paragraph (d).

[66] It should be pointed out that Article 2 of the Geneva Convention (*supra* note 19) required, in

The International Law Association's work on international water law did not taper off after the issuance of the Helsinki Rules. In 1972 the Association issued its Articles on Flood Control,[67] and in 1976 the Rules on Administration of International Watercourses were adopted.[68] In 1980, the Belgrade Conference of the Association adopted two sets of rules. The first set dealt with the regulation of the flow of the water of international watercourses, and the other dealt with the relationship of international water resources to other natural resources' environmental elements.[69] Separate articles on water pollution in an international drainage basin were adopted at the Montreal Conference in 1982.[70] In all the International Law Association rules and resolutions, the supremacy of the Helsinki Rules has been underscored. Each was subjected to the requirement of being consistent either with the Helsinki Rules or with the principle of equitable utilization, which is itself the foundation of the Rules.

In 1986 at its Seoul conference, the International Law Association adopted the "Complementary Rules Applicable to International Water Resources."[71] The articles of the Complementary Rules were intended to clarify certain elements with regard to the application of the Helsinki Rules. The Complementary Rules dealt with three issues: substantial injury to co-basin states, the installation of works or the use of water resources in the territory of co-basin states, and notification procedures, all of which were addressed earlier under the Helsinki Rules. In addition, the Seoul Conference dealt with transboundary groundwater. The definition of an international drainage basin under the Helsinki Rules includes underground waters that are connected to surface waters. As such, the definition does not extend to what is known as "confined groundwater," that is groundwater not connected to surface water. Realizing this lacunae, the International Law Association adopted additional rules for international groundwater in 1986.[72] These Rules extend the application of the Helsinki Rules to an aquifer intersected by the boundary between two or more States that does not contribute water to, or receive water from, surface waters of an international drainage basin. Finally, the Seoul Rules also dealt with the protection of groundwater and urged the riparian states to consider the integrated management of their international groundwaters, including conjunctive use with surface waters. Those Rules should also be seen as complementary to the Helsinki Rules on groundwater.

---

the development of hydraulic power involving international investigation, that such investigation should pay due regard to "…any works existing, under construction, or projected."

[67] International Law Association, Report of the Fifty-Fifth Conference, New York, 1972, at 46.

[68] International Law Association, Report of the Fifty-Seventh Conference, Madrid, 1976, at 213-266.

[69] International Law Association, Report of the Fifty-Ninth Conference, Belgrade, 1980, at 362-373, and 273-375.

[70] International Law Association, Report of the Sixtieth Conference, Montreal, 1982.

[71] International Law Association, Report of the Sixty-Second Conference, Seoul, 1986, at 275-294, and 298-303.

[72] *Id.*, at 238-274.

In summary, the work of the International Law Association has been quite extensive and has addressed a wider array of issues of international water law, focusing largely on, and expounding, the concept of "equitable and reasonable utilization." It is indeed this work, together with that of the Institute of International Law, that paved the way for the work of the International Law Commission.

5. Contribution of the International Law Commission: The UN Convention

The work of the Institute of International Law and the International Law Association, as well as the two conventions adopted under the auspices of the League of Nations, namely the Barcelona and the Geneva Conventions, have contributed immensely to the evolution of the law of international watercourses. By the time the International Law Commission started working on the United Nations Convention on the Law of the Non-Navigational Uses of International Watercourses in the early 1970s, a number of resolutions, rules, regulations and conventions were in place. The preamble to the UN Convention acknowledges the valuable contribution of international organizations, both governmental and non-governmental, to the codification and progressive development of international law in this field.[73]

The UN Convention is a *framework convention* that aims at ensuring the utilization, development, conservation, management and protection of international watercourses and promoting optimal and sustainable utilization thereof for present and future generations.[74] The decision to opt for a framework convention was quite realistic given the varying and competing interests of the different riparian states. These also include the competing interests of the upper and lower riparians.[75] They also include the interests of the states that believe in pre-eminence of historical or estab-

---

[73] *See* generally, Recital 10, preamble to the UN Convention; for discussion of the Convention, *see* Aaron Schwabach, "The United Nations Convention on the Law of Non-Navigational Uses of International Watercourse: Customary International Law, and the Interests of Developing Upper Riparians," *Texas International Law Journal* 33 (1998), at 257; Attila Tanzi, "Codifying the Minimum Standards of the Law of International Watercourses: Remarks on Part One and a Half," *Natural Resources Forum* 21 (1997), at 109; John R. Crook and Stephen C. McCaffrey, "The United Nations Starts Work on a Watercourses Convention," *Am. J. International L.* 91 (1997), at at 374; Stephen C. McCaffrey and Mpazi Sinjela, "The 1997 United Nations Convention on International Watercourses," *Am. J. International L.* 92 (1998), at 97; Stephen C. McCaffrey, "The UN Convention on The Law of The Non-Navigational Uses Of International Watercourses: Prospects and Pitfalls," in *International Watercourses, Enhancing Cooperation and Managing Conflict, supra* note 10 (1998), at 22. Attila Tanzi and Maurizio Arcasi, *The United Nations Convention on the Law of International Watercourse* (London: Kluwer Law International, 2001). See also McCaffrey, Stephen C., *The Law of International Watercourses: Non-Navigational Uses* (Oxford University Press, 2001).

[74] *See* generally, preamble to the UN Convention.

[75] The three countries that voted against the Convention (Burundi, China and Turkey) are all upper riparians. Similarly, most of the 27 countries that abstained are upper riparians. This could lead to the conclusion, adopted by some upper riparian countries, that the Convention is biased in favor of lower riparian countries. However, it should be stressed that not all upper riparian countries have abstained, nor are all the countries that abstained upper riparians. Moreover, not all the countries that have signed and/or ratified or acceded to the Convention thus far (*infra* note 86) are upper riparians.

lished rights, and hence the no-harm rule, and those states that believe in the principle of equitable and reasonable utilization.[76] There are states that had entered into treaties, and did not want any changes or adjustments to those treaties, and those which either did not enter into treaties, or were left out.[77] There are also states that had not concluded any treaties and did not want their hands tied in any future negotiations over international watercourses by any detailed convention prescribing for them what such treaties may and may not include. The issue of dispute settlement procedures and mechanisms, and the role of third parties, have also been viewed differently by different states. For any convention to be acceptable to the majority of the states, those competing and varying interests have to be taken into account, and the conflicting concerns have to be addressed. The only way for addressing those varying interests and concerns is through a framework convention that would be complemented with detailed agreements between the watercourse states, taking into account their concerns and the particularities and the special characteristics of each watercourse. It is not surprising that it took more than a quarter of a century for the Convention to be adopted. Indeed, the adoption was made possible because it is a

---

[76] It is interesting to note how the language of the articles of the Convention on the relationship between the principle of equitable and reasonable utilization on the one hand, and the no harm rule on the other, were negotiated during discussion of the draft UN Convention. The attempt to reconcile the views of the participants on those two principles, as noted by Caflisch (*supra* note 15, at 13) resulted in the replacement of the words "taking into account" in Article 7 (2) of the Convention (dealing with the obligation not cause significant harm), with the expression "having due regard for." As such, the new Article 7 (2) reads: "Where significant harm nevertheless is caused to another Watercourse State, the State whose use cause such harm shall, in the absence of agreement to such use, take all appropriate measures, *having due regard for* the provisions of Articles 5 and 6, in consultation with the affected State, to eliminate or mitigate such harm, and where appropriate, to discuss the question of compensation." As Caflisch noted, "This new formula was considered by a number of lower riparians to be sufficiently neutral not to suggest a subordination of the no-harm rule to the principle of equitable and reasonable utilization. A number of upper riparians thought just the contrary, that the formula was strong enough to support the idea of such subordination." *See* Caflisch, *supra* note 15, at 15.

[77] With regard to existing watercourse agreements, Article 3 (1) of the Convention states that "In the absence of an agreement to the contrary, nothing in the present Convention shall affect the rights and obligations of a watercourse State arising from agreements in force for it on the date on which it became a party to the present Convention." On the other hand, Article 3 (3) of the Convention stipulates that "Watercourse States may enter into one or more agreements, hereinafter referred to as 'watercourse agreements' which apply and adjust the provisions of the present Convention to the characteristics and uses of a particular international watercourse or part thereof." The Helsinki Rules extend the application of the Rules to the use of an international drainage basin, "except as may be provided otherwise by convention, agreement, or binding custom among the basin States." *See* Article 1 of the Helsinki Rules, *supra* note 56. With regard to the number of existing watercourse agreements, the World Commission on Dams states "Since AD 805 approximately 3,600 water related treaties were signed between nations. Although the majority of these related to navigation and national boundaries, approximately 300 are non-navigational and cover issues related to water quantity, water quality and hydropower." *See* World Commission on Dams, *Dams and Development – A New Framework for Decision-Making* (The Report of the World Commissions on Dams, 2000), at 174. The existence in force of such a large number of watercourse agreements shows clearly that the approach adopted by the Convention toward such agreements is realistic and prudent. Any attempt to have the provisions of the

framework convention.[78] Any other attempt would have been futile, and would have likely been a failure.

The UN Convention is divided into seven parts and consists of 37 articles. In addition, it includes an Annex on arbitration that consists of 14 articles. It asserts in Article 1 (2) that the uses of international watercourses for navigation are not within the scope of the Convention, except insofar as other uses affect navigation or are affected by navigation. It should be noted, however, that Article 10 of the Convention states that in the absence of an agreement or custom to the contrary, no use of an international watercourse enjoys inherent priority over other uses. Although it does not list any specific uses, the Article was originally conceived, according to one of the Special Rapporteurs of the International Law Commission, to indicate that navigational uses no longer enjoy inherent priority over non-navigational uses.[79] The Convention defines the term "watercourse" to include both surface water and groundwater that is connected to surface water.[80] It embraces the principle of equitable and reasonable utilization, and lays down certain factors and circumstances that should be taken into account for determining such equitable and reasonable utilization.[81] The Convention also deals with the obligation not to cause

---

Convention override such agreements would have resulted in confusion, if not chaos. However, one should hasten to add that such an attempt would have been rejected by the vast majority of the members of the United Nations General Assembly who adopted the Convention originally.

[78] It is worth noting that the Helsinki Rules were also described as a "framework" in connection with the proposal to add a new article on navigation during the New Delhi Conference, *see* International Law Association, Report of the Fifty-Sixth Conference, New Delhi, 1975, at 118.

[79] *See* Stephen McCaffrey, "The UN Convention on The Law of the Non-Navigational Uses Of International Watercourses: Prospects and Pitfalls," in *International Watercourses, Enhancing Cooperation and Managing Conflict, supra* note 10, at 22 (1998). The approach adopted by Article 10 of the Convention is in line with Article VI of the Helsinki Rules, which equates all uses of an international drainage basin; *supra* note 63.

[80] Article 2 (a) of the Convention defines the term "watercourse" as "a system of surface waters and groundwater constituting by virtue of their physical relationship a unitary whole and normally flowing into a common terminus." Article 2 (b) defines international watercourse as "a watercourse, parts of which are situated in different states." For the full text of the Convention, *see* 36 I.L.M. 700 (1997), *see* also *International Watercourses, Enhancing Cooperation and Managing Conflict, supra* note 10, at 173 (Annex 1). Like the Helsinki Rules, the definition of watercourse includes only groundwater connected to surface water, and does not extend to confined groundwater. It may be recalled that the Seoul Rules of the International Law Association addressed this lacuna, *see supra* note 64. The International Law Commission, after completing the work on the UN Convention in 1994, passed in the same year a "Resolution on Confined Transboundary Groundwater" to address the fact that the definition of the term watercourse in the Convention does not include such transboundary groundwater. The Resolution commends states to be guided by the principles contained in the UN Convention, where appropriate, in regulating transboundary groundwater. For the International Law Commission Resolution, *see* Yearbook of the International Law Commission, 1994, Vol. 2 (1997), at 135. For discussion of the issue, *see* Stephen McCaffrey, "International Groundwater Law: Evolution and Context," in *Groundwater: Legal and Policy Perspectives*, Salman M. A. Salman, ed. (1999), at 139; *see* also Raj Krishna and Salman M. A. Salman, "International Groundwater Law and the World Bank Policy for Projects on Transboundary Groundwater," in *Groundwater: Legal and Policy Perspectives, id.,* at 163.

[81] Article 6 (1) of the Convention states that utilization of an international watercourse in an

significant harm, and requires the watercourse states to take all appropriate measures to prevent the causing of significant harm to other watercourse states. Although the two principles (equitable and reasonable utilization and the obligation not to cause significant harm) have been referred to in the Convention, the prevailing view is that the Convention has, indeed, subordinated the no-harm obligation to the principle of equitable and reasonable utilization. This conclusion is based on a number of reasons. Article 5 of the Convention enumerates a number of factors for determining what is reasonable and equitable utilization. Those factors include (i) "the effects of the use or uses of the watercourse in one watercourse State on other watercourse States" and (ii) "existing and potential uses of the watercourse." The same factors will also need to be used, with other factors, to determine whether significant harm is caused to another riparian. Moreover, Article 7 (1) of the Convention obliges watercourse states, when utilizing an international watercourse in their territory, to take all appropriate measures to prevent the causing of significant harm to other watercourse states. When significant harm nevertheless is caused to another watercourse state, then Article 7 (2) of the Convention obliges the state causing the harm to "take all appropriate measures, having due regard to Articles 5 and 6, in consultation with the affected State, to eliminate or mitigate such harm, and where appropriate, to discuss the question of compensation." Articles 5 and 6 of the Convention deal with equitable and reasonable utilization. As such, Article 7 (2) requires giving due regard to the principle of equitable utilization when significant harm has nevertheless been caused to another watercourse state. The paragraph also indicates that the causing of harm may be tolerated in certain cases such as when the possibility of compensation may be considered. Accordingly, a close reading of Articles 5, 6 and 7 of the Convention should lead to the conclusion that the obliga-

---

equitable and reasonable manner within the meaning of Article 5 requires taking into account all relevant factors and circumstances, including:
 (a) Geographic, hydrographic, hydrological, climatic, ecological and other factors of a natural character;
 (b) Social and economic needs of the watercourse States concerned;
 (c) Population dependent on the watercourse in the watercourse State;
 (d) The effects of the use or uses of the watercourses in one watercourse State on other watercourse States;
 (e) Existing and potential uses of the watercourse;
 (f) Conservation, protection, development and economy of the water resources of the watercourse and the cost of measures taken to that effect;
 (g) Availability of alternatives, of comparable value, to a particular planned or existing use.
In comparing the factors under Article V of the Helsinki Rules (*supra* note 59), with the factors under Article 6 (1) of the UN Convention, it can be concluded that the factors under the UN Convention are based largely on those of the Helsinki Rules. In particular, (i) factor (a) above lumps together factors (a), (b) and (c) of the Helsinki Rules, (ii) factors (b), (c) and (e) above are almost the equivalents of factors (e), (f) and (d), respectively, of the Helsinki Rules, (iii) factors (d) and (g) above are based largely on factors (k) and (h), respectively, of the Helsinki Rules, and (iv) factor (f) above is based to some extent on factor (i) of the Helsinki Rules. The only major difference is that factor (j) of the Helsinki Rules on "the practicability of compensation to one or more of the co-basin States as a means of adjusting conflicts among uses" does not have an equivalent in the factors specified in the UN Convention. This is perhaps due to the fact that international trade in water may still be an anathema for most of the developing countries.

tion not to cause harm has indeed been subordinated to the principle of equitable and reasonable utilization.[82]

Other basic obligations under the Convention include the obligation to cooperate through, inter alia, the establishment of joint mechanisms or commissions and the regular exchange of data and information, and through notification of other riparian states on planned measures with possible significant adverse effects.[83]

Planned Measures are dealt with in Part III of the Convention. This is the longest part of the Convention and includes nine articles that deal with a number of aspects, including notification, period for reply, obligations of the notifying state during the period for reply, reply for notification, absence of reply for notification, consultations and negotiations concerning planned measures, procedures in absence of notification and urgent implementation of planned measures.[84]

---

[82] *See* McCaffrey, *supra* note 79, at 22. Moreover, the International Court of Justice in its judgment in the *Gabcikovo-Nagymaros* case, in which the decision was issued in September 1997, four months after adoption of the Convention by the UN General Assembly (Hungary/Slovakia) General List No. 92 (1997) (*reprinted in* 37 I.L.M. 162; 1998), emphasized the importance that "…the multi-purpose program, in the form of a coordinated single unit, for the use, development and protection of the watercourses is implemented in an equitable and reasonable manner." No reference to the obligation not to cause harm was included in the judgment. *See id.*, paragraph 150, at 202. The Court stated further that the adoption of the Convention strengthened the principle of community of interest for non-navigational uses of international watercourses; *see id.*, paragraph 85. The Court also quoted Article 5, paragraph 2 of the Convention on the right of watercourse states to participate in the use, development and protection of the international watercourse in an equitable and reasonable manner, and the duty of such a state to cooperate in the protection and development of such a watercourse. *See id.*, paragraph 147. The *Gabcikovo-Nagymaros* case arose out of a dispute between Hungary and Czechoslovakia over whether to build two barrages over the Danube River, as envisaged under a Treaty concluded in 1977 between the two countries. Construction began in the late 1970s, but in the mid-1980s, environmental groups in Hungary claimed negative environmental impacts of the barrages and began protesting the project, forcing the Hungarian government to suspend work in 1989. Czechoslovakia insisted that there were no negative environmental impacts, and decided to proceed unilaterally with a provisional solution consisting of a single barrage on its side, but requiring diversion of a considerable amount of the waters of the Danube to its territory. Czechoslovakia claimed that this was justified under the 1977 Treaty. As a result of the unilateral action of Czechoslovakia, Hungary decided to terminate the 1977 Treaty. The situation became more complicated with the split of Czechoslovakia in December 1992 into two countries (the Czech Republic and the Slovak Republic, or Slovakia), and the agreement that Slovakia would succeed in owning the Czechoslovakian part of the project. By that time Slovakia had already dammed the Danube and diverted the waters into its territory. The two countries agreed in April 1993, basically because of the pressure from the Commission of the European Community, to refer the dispute to the International Court of Justice. The Court ruled in September 1997 that Hungary was not entitled to suspend or terminate the work on the project in 1989 on environmental grounds, and that Czechoslovakia, and later Slovakia was also not entitled to operate the project based on the unilateral solution it developed without an agreement with Hungary. The Court further ruled that Hungary was not entitled to terminate the 1977 Treaty on the grounds of ecological necessity, and thus concluded that the Treaty is still in force. The Court concluded that "Hungary and Slovakia must negotiate in good faith in the light of the prevailing situation, and must take all necessary measures to ensure the achievement of the objectives of the Treaty of 16 September 1977, in accordance with such modalities as they may agree upon."

[83] *See* Article 8 and 9 of the Convention.

[84] The work of the Institute of International Law (particularly the Salzburg Resolution), and the

The Convention also includes detailed provisions on the environment, dealing with the protection, preservation and management of international watercourses.[85] Article 33 and the Annex to the Convention deal with dispute settlement mechanism and procedures.[86]

---

[85] International Law Association (particularly the Helsinki Rules (1966), has contributed significantly to the thinking of the International Law Commission in the area of Planned Measures. It should also be pointed out that the concept of notification can be attributed to some international legal instruments. Article 74 of the United Nations Charter, which deals with "good neighborliness," reads: "Members of the United Nations also agree that their policy in respect of the territories to which this Charter applies, no less than in respect of their metropolitan areas, must be based on the general principle of good-neighborliness, due account being taken of the interests and well-being of the rest of the world, in social, economic and commercial matters." The Charter of Economic Rights and Duties of States (*supra* note 23) requires cooperation and prior consultation in the exploitation of natural resources shared by two or more countries. Similarly, Article 3 (2) of the United Nations Declaration on the Right to Development adopted by the General Assembly on December 4, 1986 states that "the realization of the right to development requires full respect for the principles of international law concerning friendly relations and co-operation among States in accordance with the Charter of the United Nations." *See* Resolutions and Decisions adopted by the General Assembly during its Forty-First Session (16 September – 19 December 1986) Supplement No. 53 (A/41/53) (1987). The World Bank Policy for Projects on International Waterways has benefited considerably from the work of the Institute of International Law and the International Law Association and the early work of the International Law Commission in the field of planned measures, and in turn has contributed to the evolution of the procedural rules in this field. The Bank policy, for example, introduced the possibility of the Bank notifying the other riparians on behalf of the borrower if the latter does not want to carry out the notification itself. Article 30 of the UN Convention addresses the same situation by proposing indirect procedures. The Bank policy has also introduced the notion of "opinion of independent experts" in case of objection to the project by one of the riparians. This notion has the advantages of (i) not giving one of the riparians a veto power over the decision of whether to proceed with the project, and (ii) injecting an element of objectivity in the process of reviewing and deciding on the likelihood that the proposed project may have adverse impact on other riparians. For discussion of the World Bank Policy for Projects on International Waterways, see Raj Krishna, "Evolution and Context of the Bank Policy for Projects on International Waterways," in *International Watercourses: Enhancing Cooperation and Managing Conflict, supra* note 10, at 31. The World Commission on Dams has gone beyond the existing standards when it proposed that "Where a government agency plans or facilitates the construction of a dam on a shared river in contravention of the principle of good faith negotiations between riparians, external financing bodies withdraw their support for projects and programmes promoted by that agency." *See* the Report of the World Commission on Dams, *supra* note 77, at 251. The withdrawal of support is not only for the planned dam, but for projects and programs promoted by that agency. This proposal will certainly enliven the debate in this delicate area, and is likely to put pressure on the financing agencies not only to refrain from financing controversial dams, but to withhold financing to agencies promoting construction of dams in contravention of good faith negotiations. It should be added that Article 30 of the Convention which deals with indirect procedures, is included in Part V of the Convention "Harmful Conditions and Emergency Situations." However, this Article is quite relevant to the part on Planned Measures, as there are likely to be situations where the state planning the measure and one or more of the other riparian states may not have the necessary diplomatic relations to allow direct contacts.

[85] Article 21 (1) of the UN Convention defines pollution as "any detrimental alteration in the composition or quality of the waters of an international watercourse which results directly or indirectly from human conduct." This definition is based largely on the definition proposed by the Institute of International Law in Article 1 of its Athens Resolution of 1979 on "Pollution of Rivers and Lakes and International Law" (*supra* note 46).

[86] The mechanism for settlement of disputes, according to Article 33, includes the use of good

Despite divergent views on the UN Convention, the Convention, building on the work of the Institute of International Law and the International Law Association, has, no doubt, brought international water law a long way. The Convention has codified a number of customary international water law principles, including the principle of reasonable and equitable utilization, the obligation not to cause significant harm, the notification requirement for planned measures and the provisions relating to the protection of the environment.[87] It may take some time before the Convention receives the required number of instruments of ratification to enter into force and effect.[88] However, even if it fails to do so, the Convention will continue to provide influential guidance in this field.[89]

---

offices of, or mediation or conciliation by a third party, or the use of any joint watercourse institution that has been established by them, as well as impartial fact-finding procedures. It also includes, subject to the parties declaring in a written instrument, arbitration or the agreement to submit the dispute to arbitration or to the International Court of Justice. The Annex to the Convention lays down detailed procedures on arbitration.

[87] *See* McCaffrey, *supra* note 79, at 26.

[88] The Convention opened for signature from May 21, 1997 to May 20, 2000. According to Article 36, the Convention shall enter into force on the ninetieth day following the date of deposit of the thirty-fifth instrument of ratification, acceptance, approval or accession with the Secretary General of the United Nations. As of May 20, 2000, the closing date for signing the Convention, sixteen countries signed the Convention. Those countries are Cote d'Ivoire, Finland, Germany, Hungary, Jordan, Luxembourg, Namibia, the Netherlands, Norway, Paraguay, Portugal, South Africa, Syrian Arab Republic, Tunisia, Venezuela and Yemen. Out of those countries, six have ratified the Convention. Lebanon acceded to the Convention without signing it, bringing the number of ratification/accession to seven. Although the date for signing the Convention (May 20, 2000) has already passed, states can still accede to or accept the Convention, and the Convention will enter into force when it receives the required number of instruments of ratification/accession. It may be contended that the pace of signing and ratifying the Convention seems quite slow. However, it is not unusual for important and perhaps controversial conventions to take some time to enter into force. For example, the United Nations Convention on the Law of the Sea was approved by the General Assembly of the United Nations on December 10, 1982, but did not enter into force until November 16, 1994.

[89] As noted (*supra* note 82), the International Court of Justice referred to the Convention in its judgment in the *Gabcikovo-Nagymaros* case in which the decision was issued in September 1997, four months after the Convention was adopted by the United Nations General Assembly in May 21, 1997. The Protocol on Shared Watercourse Systems in the Southern African Development Community (SADC) Region that was signed on August 23, 1995, has been, after it entered into force and effect on September 29, 1998, revised to incorporate the main principles enunciated by the Convention. The Revised Protocol on Shared Watercourses in the Southern African Development Community (SADC) has been signed by 13 of the 14 members of SADC on August 7, 2000 (*see supra* note 3). *See* also, Salman M. A. Salman, "Legal Regime for Use and Protection of International Watercourses in the Southern Africa Region: Evolution and Context," *Natural Resources Journal* 41, at 981. The World Commission on Water in the 21st Century concluded that the basis for consensus in the management of shared waters "would be strengthened by the reactivation and follow-up of the currently stalled work of the United Nations Convention on Non-Navigable (*sic*) Uses of International Watercourses." *See* Global Water Partnership, *Towards Water Security: A Framework for Action* (2000), at 32. However, a clearer statement of endorsement of the Convention was delivered by the Sovereignty Panel of the World Commission on Water in the 21st Century when it proposed "the ratification of the UN Convention on the Law of the Non-Navigational Uses of International Watercourses." The Panel added that "This would not only contribute to the universal application of the principles of equitable utilization and the

III. Scope of the Study

On the South Asian Sub-continent, international water law rules have been interpreted and used differently, as will be discussed during the course of this study. Elements of the principles of absolute territorial sovereignty and absolute territorial integrity could be detected in the countries' claims and counter claims. Although the countries have, in their disputes and negotiations, often invoked the principle of equitable utilization as well as the obligation not to cause significant harm, the concepts were understood by the countries to include different sets of rights and obligations, and were interpreted differently. Similarly, the principle of established and historic rights has been invoked, but again with different interpretations. The variations in the understanding and comprehension of the principles of international water law, with regard to the protection of the interests of those countries, were reflected in the manner in which those countries reacted to the UN Convention. For instance, whereas Bangladesh and Nepal voted for the Convention, India and Pakistan abstained, albeit for different reasons.[90] A wider, and perhaps better, comprehension of those differences will be discernible in the discussion of the various aspects of the conflict and cooperation on South Asia's international rivers in subsequent chapters of this study.

The international norms and rules related to international watercourses have had a relatively paced evolution. Even now, the bulk of the rights and obligations that are applicable still emanate from customary international water law. An interesting and immediate observation is that in parallel to the discussions regarding evolution of international water law, including the several declarations and resolutions, the Helsinki Rules and the UN Convention, countries in the South Asian Sub-continent were carrying out delicate negotiations pertaining to their own waters in an attempt to resolve some of their difficult disputes. Interestingly, the negotiations in the South Asian Sub-continent were not different in substance and reflected principles similar to those being discussed during the progressive development of international water

---

obligation not to cause significant harm, but would be a gesture of goodwill and indicate a high level of dedication to resolving the question of international watercourses." *See* Green Cross International, *National Sovereignty and International Watercourses* (Geneva: 2000) at 60. Along the same lines of endorsement, the World Commission on Dams stated that "The Commission views the principles of the UN Convention as an emerging body of customary law and considers that States will reduce the possibility of conflict if they are prepared to endorse and adhere to them." In clear, unequivocal words, the Commission added: "The principles embodied in the 1997 UN Convention on the Law of the Non-Navigational Uses of International Watercourses warrant support. States should make every effort to ratify the Convention and bring it into force." *See* World Commission on Dams, *supra* note 77, at 252–253.

[90] Pakistan indicated that it had reservations regarding Article 2 (definitions, with regard to inclusion of groundwater), Article 7 (obligation not to cause significant harm) and 23 (protection and preservation of marine environment). India, on the other hand, had reservations with regard to Article 3 (watercourse agreements), Article 5 (equitable and reasonable utilization and participation), Article 32 (non-discrimination) and Article 33 (settlement of disputes); *see* United Nations Press Release GA/9248, General Assembly Adopts Convention on Law on Non-Navigational Uses of International Watercourses, 21 May 1997.

law. The tension among those countries was related, by and large, to the creation of a balance between the applicability and choice of such different principles. This study therefore also attempts to analyze the parallelism between the principles of international water law and the different approaches the South Asian countries have taken in the search for the applicable regimes for rivers shared between them.

This study covers four countries within the quadrangle of the South Asian Sub-continent (Bangladesh, India, Nepal and Pakistan) and focuses on the hydro-politics and legal regime of international water in the Sub-continent. For methodological clarity and organization, the bilateral aspects of relations in this study are covered in three main parts, each one dealing with the treaty regime of a particular country vis-a-vis India. India is an upper riparian vis-a-vis Pakistan on the Indus River and vis-a-vis Bangladesh on the Ganges. On the other hand, India is a lower riparian vis-a-vis Nepal with regard to the Kosi, Gandaki and Mahakali River Basins. Therefore India is the central actor in this study.

Part Two focuses on dispute resolution, an excellent example of which is found in the Treaty pertaining to the Indus Rivers system between India and Pakistan. In this context, this part also reviews the legacy of the dispute that emanated from the political changes after the partition of the Indian sub-continent and the resultant contested water rights. This part also discusses the role of the World Bank in the resolution of the dispute.

Part Three focuses on the integrated approach to watercourse management and reviews three agreements related to the Kosi, Gandaki and Mahakali River Basins that India and Nepal have entered into, each one with its own typical sociopolitical and technical characteristics. In order to facilitate the discussion and provide an understanding of the evolutionary features of the cooperative forces involved in developing those agreements, each chapter in this part briefly describes the political climate that existed between India and Nepal prior to the conclusion of each agreement. The political climate clearly illustrates the dilemma faced by countries that are significantly different in size, interests, perspectives and priorities. Due to the specific and diverse nature of the problems addressed by those agreements, this part dwells more in content analysis of the agreements than other parts.

In contrast, Part Four deals with the Indo-Bangladesh relations that pertain largely to the Ganges River and delves into their different water-sharing problems and the successive modalities and approaches they used to deal with such problems. In this context, this part also reviews the unpredictable, and to a certain extent inevitable, dynamics of relations between India and Bangladesh—from a phase of excessively overt friendship to a phase of extreme tension, to the current phase of anxiety and apprehension over the implementation of the recent Treaty.

Finally the last part, while providing a recapitulation of the issues discussed in the study, reviews some common elements and problems regarding the shared water resources. This part also endeavors to draw some lessons and to project the prospects for future cooperation on the international rivers of the South Asian Sub-continent.

PART TWO

India-Pakistan Relations

Chapter 2

The Indus River

I. Introduction and History of the Indus Dispute

The conclusion in 1960 of the Indus Waters Treaty between India and Pakistan was, no doubt, a remarkable achievement.[1] After a long period of negotiations carried out under the auspices and mediation of the World Bank, the Indus Waters Treaty brought to an end the long-standing dispute between India and Pakistan on the use of the waters of the Indus River systems for irrigation and hydropower.[2] This chapter briefly discusses the history and politics surrounding the dispute as well as the present treaty regime applicable to the waters of the Indus Rivers system.

The Indus is located in Northwest India and Pakistan and is one of the most important rivers in the world. The main river Indus is about 2,000 miles long. Its two principal tributaries from the West, the Kabul River and the Kurram River, together are more than 700 miles long. The five main tributaries from the East, the Jhelum, the Chenab, the Ravi, the Beas and the Sutlej, have an aggregate length of more than 2,800 miles.[3] From their origin in the Himalayan Snow Belt to their end into the Arabian Sea, the Indus Rivers carry 90 x 106 acre-feet of water and cover a drainage area of 450,000 square miles. The Indus and the eastern-most tributary, the Sutlej, both rise in the Tibetan plateau. The Kabul and the Kurram rise in Afghanistan. Most of the Indus Basin lies in Pakistan and India, with about 13 percent of the total catchment area of the basin situated in Tibet and Afghanistan.[4]

The Indus system comprises the main river Indus and its major tributaries: the Kabul, the Swat and the Kurram from the West; and the Jhelum, the Chenab, the Ravi, the Beas and the Sutlej from the East. The main river of the system, the Indus, rises north of the Himalayas. Originating near Lake Mansarovar, the Indus flows in Tibet for about 200 miles before it enters the southeastern corner of Kashmir at about 14,000 feet. Skirting Leh in Ladakh (India), the river flows on toward Gilgit and after 35 miles toward the southwest enters Pakistan, long before it emerges out

---

[1] The Treaty was signed at Karachi, Pakistan, September 19, 1960; *see,* 419 U.N.T.S. 126.

[2] *See* Foreword by Sir William Iliff, in Niranjan D. Gulhati, *Indus Waters Treaty: An Exercise in International Mediation* (Bombay: Allied Publishers, 1973); for discussions on the role of the World Bank, *see* generally, Edward S. Mason and Robert E. Asher, *The World Bank Since Bretton Woods* (Washington, DC: Brookings Institution, 1973), at 610-627.

[3] *See* Gulhati, *supra* note 2, at 18.

[4] *See* Gulhati, *supra* note 2, at 18; for detail on the physical geography of the Indus Basin, *see* generally, Undala Z. Alam, "Water Rationality: Mediating the Indus Waters Treaty," unpublished Ph.D. Thesis, (University of Durham, U. K., 1998), at 42-49.

of the hills near Attock (at 1,100 feet), where it receives the waters of the Kabul-Swat system. For several miles after this, the Indus assumes the character of a many-channeled, braided river rather than a meandering, volume-variable one, before it falls into the Arabian Sea near Karachi.[5]

The Indus system of rivers had been used for irrigation since civilization began in the area.[6] Sporadic conflicts were not uncommon, but were resolved through locally available means.[7] Things started to change in the middle of the nineteenth century due to sizable works on the waters of the Indus system. The dispute on the Indus waters began long before the independence of India and Pakistan.[8] The dispute started in the form of inter-state differences between the Punjab, Sind, Bahawalpur and

---

[5] See Gulhati, *supra* note 2, at 25. It is also worth noting that the Governor General of India, on March 13, 1843, had declared the navigation of the Indus free for the vessels of all nations. See Bela Vitanyi, *The International Regime of River Navigation* (Alphen aan den Rijn, The Netherlands: Sijthoff and Noordhoff, 1979), at 99.

[6] However, the several small-scale projects irrigated only a relatively limited land area. This situation started to change from the middle of the nineteenth century when, in 1859, the Upper Bari Doab Canal was completed. It was meant to irrigate about one million acres of land between the Ravi and the Beas Rivers with the water from the Ravi. See Asit K. Biswas, "Indus Water Treaty: The Negotiating Process," in *Water International* 17 (1992), at 202.

[7] Indeed while disputes over sharing of water were not uncommon, the then-central government of India acted as a neutral third party to facilitate resolution through negotiations and, if the negotiations failed, appointed independent commissions to arbitrate. The first major dispute was settled through arbitration by the Anderson Commission in 1935, the second through arbitration by the Rau Commission in 1942, and the third through negotiations between the provinces in 1945. The Indus system, as such, had a sound system to address water disputes and establish and protect rights of all canal systems of the basin. See Syed Kirmani and Guy Le Moigne, *Fostering Riparian Cooperation in International River Basins: The World Bank at its Best in Development Diplomacy,* World Bank Technical Paper No. 335 (Washington, DC, 1997) at 3; *see also*, Biswas, *supra* note 6, at 201-202; *see also*, Patricia Wouters, ed., *International Water Law: Selected Writings of Professor Charles B. Bourne* (London: Kluwer Law International, 1997), at 46.

[8] In October 1939, for instance, Sind had formally complained to the Governor-General about a project initiated by Punjab (the Bhakra Project). As the provinces were now separate and irrigation was a provincial matter, a special commission (Indus Commission) with quasi-judicial powers was appointed by the government of India in September 1941. The Commission comprised two engineers and was headed by Justice B. N. Rau. A report was presented by the Commission in July 1942. See Alam, *supra* note 4. The central government, after appointing the Commission, made no representations to it, and left Sind and Punjab to discuss their claims to the waters of the Sutlej. Sind tried to use the Commission as a forum in which to have Punjab prevented from encroaching on what Sind regarded as its share of the river. Thus Sind not only complained about projects that had already been built or were being considered, but also tried to guess which projects the Punjab might try to build in the future. Punjab admitted to having further plans for using the Sutlej, but on a much smaller scale than Sind had suggested. See Alam, *supra* note 4. The Indus Commission's findings essentially acknowledged the damage that would occur to Sind's inundation canals if the Bhakra Dam were constructed. To protect these canals, the Commission recommended the construction of two barrages across the river Indus flowing through Sind (the Gudu and the Hajipur barrages), and suggested that Punjab contribute to the costs of these works. But neither Punjab nor Sind accepted the Indus Commission's findings, and both appealed to the central government. Some informal meetings were held under the auspices of the central government officials, without reaching any final accord. In 1947 the Government of India referred the case to the Secretary of State for India in Whitehall. However, the events of partition overwhelmed the dispute momentarily. It was re-opened later as an international conflict between India and Pakistan.

Map 1: The Indus River Basin

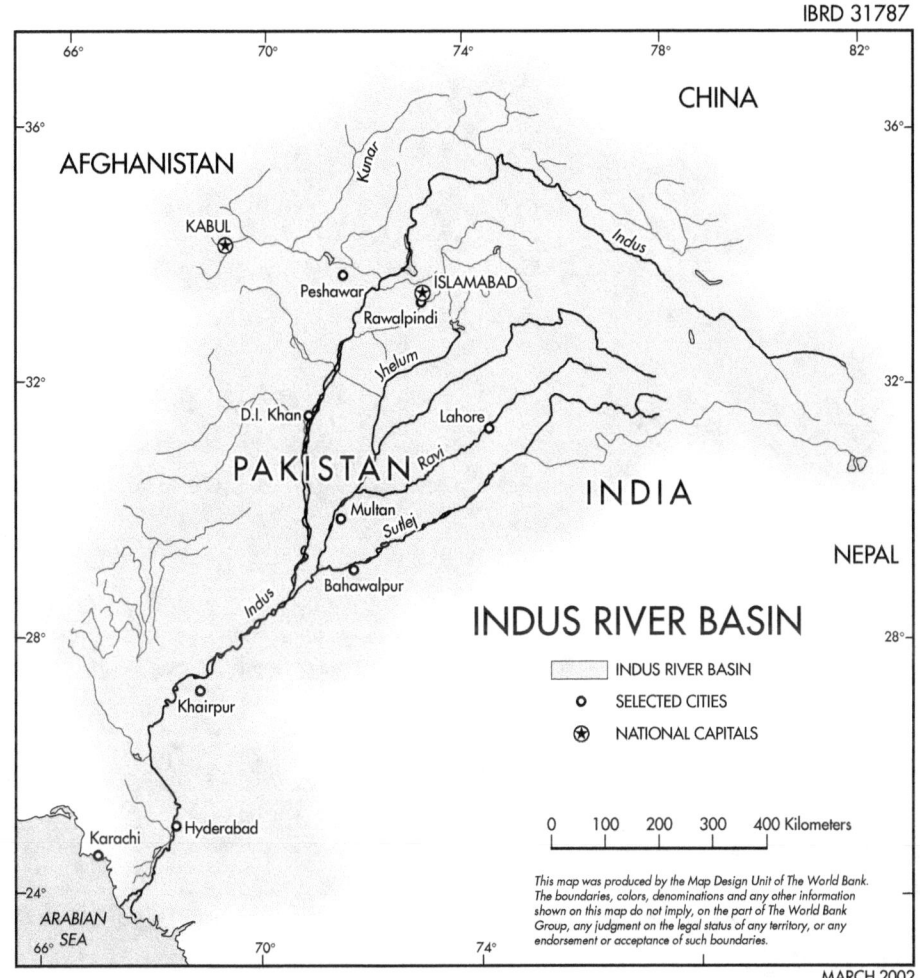

Bikaner.[9] After the creation of Pakistan in 1947, the dispute became an international issue between East Punjab (in India) and West Punjab (in Pakistan),[10] and was exacerbated by the fact that the political boundary between the two countries was drawn right across the Indus Basin, leaving India the upstream and Pakistan the downstream riparian on five of the six rivers in the Indus system.[11] Most of the water-rich headwater went to India, and Pakistan was left as the water-short lower riparian.[12] Moreover, two important irrigation headworks, one in Madhopur on the river Ravi and one at Ferozepur on the river Sutlej, on which two irrigation canals in West Punjab had been completely dependent for their supplies, were left in Indian territory. India was therefore given the physical capacity to cut off vital irrigation water from large and valuable tracts of agricultural land in West Pakistan.[13] India, which had large areas that needed irrigation, claimed the right to devote to its own use the waters from all six of the rivers as long as they were flowing outside Pakistan territory. Even if India's claim were not to be enforced to the prejudice of Pakistan's historic use, the quantum of water available to Pakistan for the development of new uses would be substantially curtailed.[14]

The partition of India and Pakistan had not dealt with the waters of the Indus. Indeed, when the British Act of Parliament was passed on July 18, 1947, the bound-

---

[9] As early as 1919, a tripartite agreement between Punjab, Bikaner and Bahawalpur was signed and had paved the way for sanction and construction of the Sutlej Valley Project. However, the Agreement did not specify any right of the downstream Indus riparians: Kharipur State and Sind. See Aloys Arthur Michel, *The Indus Rivers: A Study of the Effects of Partition* (New Haven: Yale University Press, 1967), at 99; *see also* Gulhati, *supra* note 2, at 1.

[10] Following partition, the State of Punjab was divided between India and Pakistan, as per the decision dated August 1947, of the Arbitral Commission presided over by Lord Radcliffe. *See* Georges Fischer, "La Banque Internationale pour la Reconstruction et le Developpement et l'Utilisation des eaux du Bassin de l'Indus," in *Annuaire Français de Droit International* (1960), at 43. Clearly, the Arbitral Commission handed down decisions predicated on continued supplies of water for irrigation. For detail on the partition and the different alternatives contemplated, *see* Michel, *supra* note 9, at 134-194.

[11] However, technically, the Indus dispute started as a dispute on the river Sutlej when the East Punjab government stopped the supply of water to West Punjab on April 1, 1948 (*see infra*). The action was meant to establish legal right to the water flowing through its territory in the absence of an agreement with West Punjab. This dispute technically needs to be treated as separate from the pre-partition provincial dispute between undivided Punjab and Sind, even though this too was based upon Sutlej.

[12] *See* G. T. Keith Pitman, "The Role of the World Bank in Enhancing Cooperation and Resolving Conflict in International Watercourses: The Case of the Indus Basin," in *International Watercourses: Enhancing Cooperation and Managing Conflict*, Salman M. A. Salman and Laurence Boisson de Chazournes, eds. (1998), at 155. In terms of annual availability of water, however, a clarification is needed. The Indus and Sutlej both rise in Tibet within 80 km of each other but do not meet until they reach Pakistan. The three Eastern Rivers (Sutlej, Beas and Ravi) carry approximately 20 percent of the water of the basin, and the three Western Rivers (Indus, Jhelum and Chenab) carry approximately 80 percent.

[13] *See* Chaudhri Muhammad Ali, *The Emergence of Pakistan* (New York: Columbia University Press, 1967), at 318-319.

[14] *See* Foreword by Sir William Iliff, in Gulhati, *supra* note 2.

ary between the two new dominions was not demarcated[15] and so it was impractical to deal with the allocation of waters. To remedy the legal vacuum created by the partition, the chief engineers of East Punjab (India) and West Punjab (Pakistan) signed a Standstill Agreement on December 20, 1947 providing, *inter alia*, that until the end of the current *rabi* crop, on March 31, 1948, the status quo would be maintained with regard to water allocation in the Indus Basin irrigation system.[16] The authorities in East Punjab refused the renewal of the agreements upon expiration and on April 1, 1948, halted the supply of water to several canals in Pakistan territory.[17] The real reason for the misunderstanding is hard to determine, but deliberately or inadvertently, West Punjab, until the expiry date of the agreement on March 31, 1948 had not taken initiative to negotiate any further agreement.[18] On April 1, India discontinued the delivery of water from the Ferozepur headworks to Dipalpur Canal and to the main branches of the Upper Bari Doab Canal.[19] While Pakistan criticized the incident and called India's action "Machiavellian duplicity," India relied on the fact that the agreements had simply lapsed[20] and stated that the proprietary rights in

---

[15] *See* for detail, R. R Baxter, "The Indus Basin," in *The Law of International Drainage Basins* (Garretson et al, eds. 1967), at 449-457. It should be noted that Radcliffe in his deliberation did acknowledge the importance of the Indus system to both countries, but did not make any explicit recommendation other than to hope that they would work together in finding a solution.

[16] In the effort to solve the problem and at the invitation of the East Punjab government, engineers from West Punjab had met their counterparts at Simla in April 1948. As a result of the meeting, two Standstill Agreements were signed on April 18, 1948 (also referred to as the Simla Agreements), in connection with the Central Bari Doab canal and the Dipalpur canal, to take effect upon ratification by India and Pakistan. But the West Punjab government refused to ratify them. If the agreements had been ratified, they would have provided an immediate supply of water. The first Standstill Agreement, which dealt with the Central Bari Doab canal, restored the *status quo* until September 30, 1948. The second Standstill Agreement, which related to the non-perennial Dipalpur canal's supplies from the Ferozepur headworks and other canals in West Punjab and Bahawalpur offtaking from the Sutlej, was to expire on October 15, 1948. However, in the absence of ratification, none of the agreements became applicable. *See* Alam, *supra* note 4, at 57.

[17] East Punjab declared that it would not restore the flow of water in these canals, "unless West Punjab recognized that it had no right to the water." *See* Stephen C. McCaffrey, "Water, Politics and International Law," in *Water in Crisis: A Guide to the World's Fresh Water Resources*, Peter H. Gleick, ed. (Oxford University Press, 1993), at 95; *see also*, F. J. Fowler, "The Indo-Pakistan Water Dispute," in *Yearbook of World Affairs* Vol. IX (London: 1955), at 101. The legal rationale, typical of an upper riparian, was to try to establish a claim that waters that flow through one's territory before downstream utilization became a prescriptive right. *See* Jagat S. Mehta, "The Indus Water Treaty: A Case Study in the Resolution of an International River Basin Conflict," *Natural Resources Forum* 12 (1988), at 72. However, it should also be noted that the decision was that of the East Punjab government, made without official knowledge of the Central government. Prime Minister Nehru, who was sensitive to the moral and international implications, is recorded as having chastised the government of East Punjab for its action. *See* Jagat Mehta, *supra* at 72.

[18] As a result of India's action, about 5.5 percent of the sown area (and almost 8 percent of the culturable commanded area) in West Pakistan was without water at the beginning of the critical *kharif*-sowing phase. The city of Lahore was simultaneously deprived of the main source of municipal water, and incidentally, distribution to West Pakistan of power from the Mandi Hydroelectric Scheme was also cut off. *See* Michel, *supra* note 9, at 196.

[19] *See* Ali, *supra* note 13, at 319-320.

[20] Some scholars have noted that India had other politico-economic motives for discontinuing the

the waters of the rivers in East Punjab continued to be vested in East Punjab (India), and that West Punjab (Pakistan) could not claim rights to any share of those waters.[21] In this situation, one option for Pakistan was war, and there were many who advocated for it, but it would have been an error for Pakistan because it could hardly use the Bari Doab, where all the strategic advantages were held by India. Authors have noted that a declaration of war by India might have led to the extinction of the new State. Pakistan could not face the *kharif* season without water for 5.5 percent of its cropland. So Pakistan opted for negotiations and decided to send its delegation to New Delhi to negotiate for restoration of the canal waters. India remained firm and wanted recognition of their rights to all of the waters in the Eastern Rivers (Sutlej, Beas and Ravi) and they wanted Pakistan to pay for such water supplied by the Indians until such time as Pakistan could find replacement. India proclaimed its purpose to use all the water in the Eastern Rivers, but because this was not immediately possible, Pakistan would have time to develop alternative supplies. Moreover, India claimed that Pakistan's agreement to pay water dues in the Standstill Agreement of December 1947 was tantamount to recognition by Pakistan of India's proprietary rights. Pakistan, on the other hand, insisted that these payments had been for the costs of operating and maintaining the irrigation works, not payment for water that belonged to Pakistan by right of prior allocation.[22]

Following extensive discussions in an Inter-Dominion conference held in New Delhi on May 3-4, 1948, a new agreement was signed (commonly called the Delhi Agreement) on May 4, 1948. Under the terms of that Agreement, East and West Punjab recognized the necessity to resolve the issues in the spirit of goodwill and friendship. Without prejudice to its own rights, the government of East Punjab granted to West Punjab the assurance that it would not suddenly withhold the supply of water without providing sufficient time for West Punjab to develop alternate sources.[23] The agreement also provided for the gradual diminishing of supply of water to Pakistan, and for Pakistan to tap alternative resources.[24] West Punjab con-

---

delivery of water. The motives were: (i) to put pressure on Pakistan to withdraw the "volunteers" from Kashmir; (ii) to use every means at its disposal to wreck Pakistan's economy and demonstrate that it could not succeed as its own nation, therefore bringing it back to India; (iii) and to retaliate for Pakistan's imposition of an export duty on raw jute, leaving East Bengal for processing in the jute mills of West Bengal. For detail, *see* Biswas, *supra* note 6, at 203; *see also* Michel, *supra* note 9, at 196-197.

[21] *See* Pitman, *supra*, note 11, at 158. In its arguments, India was asserting, at least by implication, the doctrine of "upstream riparian proprietary rights," which had no historical basis. In effect, India was saying that partition and independence had created a new situation, and that it could proceed from any *a priori* basis it chose. It could, on one hand, maintain that it had succeeded to the rights of British India as a sovereign state. On the other hand, India could assert that because there was no sovereign Pakistan before 1947, there could be no responsibilities of a successor state toward Pakistan. For detail, *see* Michel, *supra* note 9, at 200.

[22] *See* Michel, *supra* note 9, at 202; *see also*, Mason and Asher, *The World Bank Since Bretton Woods*, *supra* note 2, at 611.

[23] *See* Fischer, *supra* note 10 at 671; *see also* Biswas, *supra* note 6, at 204.

[24] Inter-Dominion Agreement between the Government of India and the Government of Pakistan

tinued to stress the need for reasonable time to develop alternative resources. Contrary to the expectation, the agreement could not stay intact for long and on issues relating to the interpretation of the agreement, the dispute continued.[25] Although the Inter-Dominion Agreement did not settle many of the issues, it at least blocked out the arguments and provided a *modus vivendi* until 1960, when it was formally superseded by the Indus Waters Treaty.[26]

Consistent with the conflicting rationales of the two countries, the combination of a series of decisions and actions by India and Pakistan precipitated a dispute that led to Pakistan's formal denouncement of the agreement in 1950. Pakistan proposed that the issue be submitted to the International Court of Justice or the UN Security Council,[27] but India categorically rejected third-party involvement in dispute resolution and urged that the Inter-Dominion Agreement be made permanent.[28]

The stalemate in negotiations was reversed by the visit of David Lilienthal, former Chairman of the Tennessee Valley Authority, and of the United States Atomic Energy Commission, to India and Pakistan in February 1951. Following his visit, Lilienthal wrote an article in which he made a series of recommendations pertaining to the Indus system of rivers. Among others, the recommendations included that the Indus Basin be treated, exploited, and developed as a single unit[29]; that financing be provided by India, Pakistan and the World Bank; and that the Indus be administered by an Indo-Pakistan mixed body or a multinational body.[30] In fact, Lilienthal's proposal was based on a return to a pre-partition premise for the Indus Basin irrigation system. At that time Mr. Lilienthal believed that the waters from the basin were sufficient to support the needs of the two countries, a belief that would not be confirmed by later studies. But regardless of future studies, Lilienthal's pro-

---

on the canal water dispute between East and West Punjab, signed at New Delhi, May 4, 1948, 54 U.N.T.S 45; *see* also B.C. Upreti, *Politics of Himalayan River Waters: An Analysis of the River Water Issues of Nepal, India and Bangladesh* (Delhi: Nirala Publication, 1993), at 86-87.

[25] *See* Fischer, *supra* note 10, at 671; *see* also for detail, Gulhati, *supra* note 2, which deals with the issue in a comprehensive fashion.

[26] *See* Michel, *supra* note 9, at 205.

[27] *See* Fischer *supra* note 10, at 671. On Pakistan's proposal for submission of the Indus problem to the International Court of Justice, two years later Lilienthal (*see infra*) had commented that even though the legal position of Pakistan might bring a decision in Pakistan's favor (if India agreed to submit the case), it would be inadequate for the great issues of maintaining peace and providing sufficient food for the people of the Indus Basin. According to Lilienthal, such a decision would antagonize India and certainly would not facilitate active partnership between the two countries in developing their common resource on the six rivers. *See* for detail, Michel, *supra* note 9, at 221.

[28] *See* Michel, *supra* note 9, at 219.

[29] The problem of Indus, according to Lilienthal, was not a religious or political problem, but a feasible engineering and business problem for which there were plenty of precedents and experiences. But this objective could not be met by the countries working separately. *See* Michel, *supra* note 9, at 222.

[30] *See* Fischer, *supra* note 10, at 672; *see* also, for detail, Biswas, *supra* note 6, at 205; *see* also, Ali, *supra* note 13, at 326; it should also be noted that the Indus Basin irrigation system that irrigated some 37 million acres of land was conceived originally as a unified system and considered

posal had two notable advantages. It provided a new avenue of negotiations that could be based on technical and engineering data, and it introduced a third party in the negotiations process that was also a potential source of financial assistance.

Eugene Black, the President of the World Bank at the time, acquiesced to Lilienthal's recommendations and decided to react positively to the opportunity.[31] Upon his decision, the World Bank offered its good offices for discussion of the dispute and negotiation of a settlement, and proposed that a solution to the problem be looked for based purely on technical and engineering grounds. On November 18, 1951, the President of the World Bank proposed the establishment of a working group of engineers which, building on Mr. Lilienthal's recommendations, would deal with the problem of Indus as a single unit without taking into account any past negotiations or political considerations. The World Bank made a clear distinction between the "functional" and "political" aspects of the Indus dispute and asserted that it could most realistically be solved if the functional aspects of disagreement were negotiated apart from political considerations. The World Bank noted that it was important to assess how best to utilize the waters of the Indus Basin while leaving aside questions of historic rights or allocations. India's previous objections to third-party arbitration were remedied by the World Bank's insistence that it would not adjudicate the conflict, but instead work as a conduit for agreement.

Through an understanding dated March 10, 1952, India and Pakistan welcomed the good offices of the World Bank and committed that they would not reduce the supply of water for the other country's actual use until mediation was carried out.[32] While at times both parties failed to comply with their commitments, provisional understandings made it possible to contain the conflict. Each party appointed a Special Commissioner to follow up the implementation of the provisional understandings and to settle any differences. In case settlement was impossible, negotiations would resume in Washington and each of the two governments could call upon the World Bank to intervene.

The World Bank proposed a comprehensive plan for the joint development of the waters of the basin, but the plan failed to take into account all the sensitive issues

---

one of the most extensive and highly developed irrigation systems of the world. *See* Yunus Khan, "Boundary Conflict Between India and Pakistan," *Water International* 15 (1990), at 195.

[31] *See* for detail, Wouters, ed., *supra* note 7, at 16-17. In this context it is also important to note that in 1949, when matters were still undecided between India and Pakistan, India had approached the World Bank for loans for the construction of the Bhakra-Nangal Multipurpose Project on the Sutlej and the Damodar Valley Project in the State of Bihar. Pakistan had cited the water controversy in its objections to the Indian Bhakra-Nangal Project proposal to the Bank. Only a few weeks before the Lilienthal article appeared, India had also objected to a Pakistani request for financing a barrage at Kotri on the Indus. The Bank was aware of the already strained relations between India and Pakistan and was reluctant to make loans for projects that involved any unresolved disputes, not only because the investment was risky, but also because once built, these projects could exacerbate the existing dispute. *See* Alam, *supra* note 4, at 97; *see also*, Mason and Asher, *The World Bank Since Bretton Woods*, *supra* note 2, at 612.

[32] *See* Michel, *supra* note 9, at 227.

and was not endorsed by either party.[33] The World Bank's expectation for a quick resolution to the Indus dispute was premature. Although the Bank had expected that the two sides would come to an agreement on the allocation of waters, neither India nor Pakistan seemed willing to compromise their positions. While Pakistan insisted on its historical right to waters of all the Indus tributaries, India argued that the previous distribution of waters should not determine future allocation. Instead, India set up a new basis of distribution, with the waters of the western tributaries of the Indus allocated to Pakistan and the eastern tributaries allocated to India. The substantive technical discussions that were hoped for were stymied by the political considerations.

In the meetings in Karachi in November 1952 and in Delhi in January 1953, the two countries could not agree on a common approach to developing the waters of the Indus system. The World Bank suggested that both countries prepare their own plans. The two countries' water use and allocation plans were submitted to the World Bank on October 6, 1953.[34] They differed significantly. According to the Indian plan, of the 119 million acre-feet (MAF) of total usable water, 29 MAF would be allocated to India and 90 MAF to Pakistan. But according to the Pakistan plan, which estimated 118 MAF of total usable water, 15.5 MAF would be allocated to India and 102.5 MAF to Pakistan.

Obviously, it was difficult to reconcile the two plans. After some discussions and concessions from both parties, the plans were modified. According to the modified Indian proposal, 7 percent of the waters of the Western Rivers and all waters of the Eastern Rivers were to be allocated to India, whereas 93 percent of the waters of the Western Rivers and no water from the Eastern Rivers were to be allocated to Pakistan. But Pakistan's modified proposal was different. It allocated 30 percent of the waters of the Eastern Rivers and none of the Western Rivers to India, and 70 percent of the Eastern Rivers and all of the Western Rivers to Pakistan.[35]

From the proposals and counter-proposals, it became apparent that political sovereignty and the joint development and use of water resources of a river basin as a single unit were not compatible at all.[36] The only formula that was likely to provide an acceptable basis for settlement was the quantitative division of waters between the two countries, leaving each of the two countries free to carry out its own development independently of the other, and in accordance with its own plans. Indeed, this was the basis for the Bank's revised proposal. It is interesting to note that the Bank's revised proposal signified a complete departure from Lilienthal's proposal to develop the water resources of the Indus Basin as a single unit through the construction of storage dams and other facilities. In fact, the Bank went in the opposite direction in its proposal to divide the water resources of the basin between the two

---

[33] *See* generally for detail, Gulhati, *supra* note 2.
[34] *See* Biswas, *supra* note 6, at 206.
[35] *See, id.*
[36] *See* Kirmani and Le Moigne, *supra* note 7, at 4.

countries on the basis of political boundaries. The Bank envisaged no cooperative development. The justification for this approach was that after transfer works were completed, each country would be independent in the operation of its supplies and avoid the complexities that would arise if the supplies from particular rivers were shared by the two countries.[37] The Bank also explained that its formula of sharing the waters was no mere averaging of the demands of each party, but rather resulted from the Bank's engineers' analysis of the usable supplies on each of the six Indus Rivers.[38]

This new formula, proposed by the World Bank on February 5, 1954, was in principle endorsed, albeit with a few reservations.[39] In fact, India accepted the proposal on March 25, 1954, but Pakistan questioned the proposal's premise that there was enough surplus water in the Western Rivers to replace its irrigation uses on the Eastern Rivers. Pakistan contended that a system of link canals would not be adequate to meet all uses without including storage reservoirs in the replacement works. The Bank agreed to examine Pakistan's contention, and carried out its own independent studies to examine the issues in dispute and to prepare an adequate system of works to replace Pakistan's uses on the Eastern Rivers.[40] The studies confirmed that there was not enough surplus water in the Western Rivers, particularly in the critical crop periods, to replace Pakistan's uses and that storage reservoirs were necessary to meet the shortages. At this juncture, the Bank issued an aide memoire on May 21, 1956 that modified its original proposal and included storage dams in the system of replacement works.[41] Pakistan accepted the modified proposal in 1958, but India disputed the need for storage dams and insisted that its liability should be limited to the original Bank proposal. Recognizing the impossibility of resolving the dispute without additional financing for the huge cost of replacement works, and the fact that neither India nor Pakistan were in a position to bear the costs of the replacement works, the Bank decided to mobilize funds from bilateral donors.[42] At this point, the issue pending in the dispute was practically resolved.

After almost two years of negotiations on many complex technical, operational and legal issues—the complexity of which are exemplified by the eight annexures

---

[37] *See* for detail, Ali, *supra* note 13, at 328. However, one should also note that in terms of treatment of a river basin as an integrated whole, the Indus Treaty is a success. It embraces to a greater degree the waters falling within the basins of the Indus River and has been successful in providing exact definition of the notions employed. *See* Vitanyi, *supra* note 5, at 208.

[38] *See* Michel, *supra* note 9, at 239.

[39] Pakistan's acceptance seems to have been possible particularly because of the *coup d'etat* that had recently occurred in Pakistan. For detail of the Bank plan, *see* Alam, *supra* note 4, at Appendix 5; *see* also Michel *supra* note 9, at 235.

[40] See Kirmani and Le Moigne, *supra* note 7, at 4.

[41] The *Aide Memoire* recognized that the flow surpluses in the Western Rivers would not be sufficient to meet even the replacement needs in early and late *kharif*, unless storage was provided. *See* generally Michel, *supra* note 9, at 244. The text of the *Aide Memoire* reproduced in Alam, *supra* note 4, at Appendix 6; *see* also, Mason and Asher, *supra* note 2, at 619.

[42] *See infra*, Section II, Part 4 of this chapter.

the Treaty required—an agreement was finally reached between the parties. On September 19, 1960, the Indus Waters Treaty was signed at Karachi by Field Marshall Mohammad Ayub Khan, then President of Pakistan, and Mr. Jawaharlal Nehru, then Prime Minister of India. For the purpose of some specific articles, Sir W. A. B. Iliff of the World Bank also became a signatory.[43] As noted by some purists, the legal status of the World Bank as a party to the Indus Treaty is not equal to that of India and Pakistan.[44] However, the World Bank, as shall be discussed later, played a crucial role in the Treaty, much more from a functional rather than a normative perspective.

II. The Indus Treaty Regime

The Indus Treaty is a complex instrument whose basic approach was to increase the amount of water available to the two parties and to apportion the water resources of the Indus equitably between them.[45] It is indeed a complete Treaty in view of its objectives. It has normative as well as functional values as it contains, in addition to the substantive rules regarding the regime of the Indus system of rivers, provisions regarding the implementation of an administrative and institutional mechanism and the management of the basin resources. These two categories of rules aim at resolving the dispute and maintaining peace between the two countries through contributing to their development.

The Governments of India and Pakistan desired the most complete and satisfactory utilization of the waters of the Indus system of rivers.[46] The primary objective was to fix and delimit the rights and obligations of each country's use of the waters in relation to the other. With its preamble, followed by 12 articles and eight annexures (including appendices), the Indus Treaty attempts comprehensively to deal with the issues of water allocation and the flow of water. Crafted by technicians and engineers rather than lawyers and diplomats, the Indus Treaty, is complex and prolix, despite its apparent brevity. The complexity was perhaps inevitable, but some articles are of unusual length.[47]

---

[43] Along with the Indus Waters Treaty, on September 19, 1960, two other agreements were concluded. The first agreement, the Indus Basin Development Fund Agreement, was between Australia, Canada, Federal Republic of Germany, New Zealand, Pakistan, the United Kingdom and the United States of America, and the International Bank for Reconstruction and Development. The second one, pertaining to the implementation of the Indus Basin Project, was a Loan Agreement between Republic of Pakistan and the International Bank For Reconstruction and Development (Loan No 266 PAK); *see* also, Mason and Asher, *supra* note 2, at 626.

[44] *See* Fischer, *supra* note 10, at 675; *see* also Yvon-Claude Accariez, "Le Regime Juridique de l'Indus," in *The Legal Regime of International Rivers and Lakes,* Ralph Zacklin and Lucius Caflisch, eds. (The Hague: Marinus Nijhoff, 1981), at 61.

[45] *See* Stephen C. McCaffrey, "Water, Politics and International Law," *supra* note 17, at 95; It is also worth noting that one interesting aspect of the Treaty is that it only refers to distribution of waters, but remains silent on the issue of navigation.

[46] *See* preamble to the Treaty.

[47] For instance, Article 10 on "emergency" consists of two sentences that contain 33 lines. This style of treaty drafting often leads to ambiguity.

The eight Annexures are quite elaborate and deal with issues that are technical in nature. While Annexure A, written in the form of exchange of notes, specifies the extinction, on April 1, 1960, of the May 4, 1948 Agreement, Annexure B deals with the use of certain tributaries of the Ravi by Pakistan for agricultural purposes. Similarly while Annexure C provides details regarding the use of the Western Rivers by India, Annexures D and E respectively deal with the supply by India of hydropower from some Western Rivers and with the stocking by India of water from such Western Rivers. Annexures F and G of the Treaty deal respectively with the appointment of neutral experts and the constitution of an arbitral tribunal. Finally, Annexure H provides details on specific transitional measures.

1. Principle of Water Sharing: Eastern and Western Rivers

Briefly put, the waters of the three Eastern Rivers (the Ravi, Beas, and Sutlej) were allocated to India, subject to a duty during a transition period of 10 years to supply a certain quantum of water to Pakistan while Pakistan was carrying out the necessary construction works on the Western Rivers to replace its Eastern Rivers sources.[48]

Pakistan received the flow of the Western Rivers (the Indus, Jhelum and Chenab), subject to the right of India to use some of the water for irrigation, the generation of hydroelectric power, and other designated purposes before the rivers crossed into Pakistan.[49] Pakistan was to refrain from any interference with the waters of the Sutlej Main and Ravi Main and of their tributaries until the rivers had finally flowed into Pakistan, but was permitted by way of exception to take water for domestic use, non-consumptive use and certain limited agricultural use.[50] Similarly, India was to refrain from any interference with the waters of the Indus, the Jhelum and the Chenab, except for domestic use, non-consumptive use, and certain limited agricultural use and power generation.[51]

During the 10-year transitional period,[52] India was to limit its withdrawals for agricultural use, to limit its abstractions for storage, and to make deliveries to Pakistan from the Eastern Rivers.[53] The period of transition could be extended for further periods up to a total of three years if Pakistan required additional time to secure replacement waters, but was in no event to terminate later than March 31, 1973.[54] Elaborate provisions governed the supply of water during the period of transition.[55] Water was to be supplied from the Ravi for the Central Bari

---

[48] Article II of the Treaty; *see* also for detail, Baxter, *supra* note 15, at 467.

[49] Article III.

[50] Article II (2) through (4).

[51] Article III (2). For detailed mechanism, *see* Annexures C and D.

[52] Beginning on April 1, 1960 and ending March 31, 1970, or if extended, the date up to which it has been extended, but in any manner not later than March 31, 1973.

[53] Article II (5).

[54] Annexures H, part 8, and Article II (6).

[55] Annexure H. It should be noted that historically, a supply of 8.27 MAF was being delivered

Doab Channels, which prior to August 14, 1947 formed part of the Upper Bari Doab Canal System.[56] India was to limit its withdrawals from the Sutlej Main and the Beas component at Ferozepore in *kharif* during the first phase of transition, running from 1960 to 1965.[57] From 1965 through the remainder of the period of transition, India had to furnish designated quantities of water in *kharif*.[58] During *rabi,* India was likewise under an obligation to provide at Ferozepore water from the Sutlej and Beas, in quantities specified in the Treaty, for use in the Pakistan Sutjej valley canals.[59] Pakistan was to compensate India for its proportionate share of the working expenses for headworks, such as those at Madhopur and Ferozepore, and carrier channels relied upon for the furnishing of waters to Pakistan.[60] But if Pakistan were to request extension, it would have to pay graduated charges for the water itself.

Every conceivable safeguard that Pakistan's engineers and lawyers could suggest was included to prevent India from altering the amount or the timing of its water supplies to Pakistan during the transition period. The portions of the "distributable supply" that India was to furnish to the Central Bari Doab Channels are specified not only for *rabi* and *kharif,* but for six intervals within these periods. Provisions are made for India to reduce supplies if the "distributable supply" falls below certain levels, if closures are necessary for safety, operations or maintenance, or if Pakistan has completed the highest links (Rasul-Quadirabad and Quadirabad-Balloki). With regard to the Sutlej Valley canals, the transition period is divided into two phases: Phase I up to a point between March 31, 1965 and March 31, 1966, and Phase II from the end of Phase I to the end of the transition period.[61]

Because Pakistan was no longer to have water from the Eastern Rivers, a system of works was required in order to transfer water from the Western Rivers to the canal system of Pakistan.[62] These works would confer a number of benefits on Pakistan. They would permit substantial additional irrigation development, develop 3,000,000 kW of hydroelectric potential, contribute to soil reclamation and drainage by lowering water levels in water-logged and saline areas, and give some protection from floods.[63] Eight link canals, nearly 400 miles in length, were to be constructed

---

during *kharif* at Madhopore and Ferozepore for use in Pakistan canals. In Phase I, this supply was to be reduced by 4.7-5.0 MAF and with the beginning of Phase II, it was to be reduced further by about 2.5 MAF. *See* Statement of the Indian Minister of Irrigation and Power, Fortnightly News Digest (New Delhi), 7:No.21:605-6, India, Lok Sabha Secretariat, (November 1-15, 1960), at 606.

[56] Annexure H part 2.

[57] Annexure H part 3.

[58] Annexure H part 4.

[59] Annexure H part 5.

[60] Annexure H part 7.

[61] *See* Michel, *supra* note 9, at 256.

[62] *See* generally Baxter, *supra* note 15, at 468.

[63] *Id.*

or remodeled in order to transfer 14 million acre-feet of water. An earth-fill storage dam was to be built on the Jhelum River (Mangla Dam) with a live reservoir capacity of 4.75 million-acre feet. On the Indus, another earth-fill dam (Tarbela) would permit live storage of 4.2 million-acre feet. Together, the dams would compensate for seasonal fluctuations in supplies of water and would permit the irrigation of additional areas in Pakistan. Additional works would be needed in order to integrate the existing system with the new link canals that were to be constructed. Three barrages (Qadirabad, Ravi River, and Sutlej River) were designed to carry canals across rivers. Five existing barrages and eight existing canals were to be modified. At the Jhelum Dam, there was to be a power station with a capacity of more than 300,000 kW.[64] It is interesting to note that the Treaty allows each country to develop hydropower independently. From this angle, the Treaty is an example of water trade-off, rather than water-sharing.[65]

2. Principle of Cooperation Between the Parties

The Indus Treaty acknowledges that both India and Pakistan have an interest in the optimum development of the rivers, and to that effect provides for cooperation and collaboration between the two countries. At the request of either party, the two parties may, by mutual agreement, cooperate in undertaking engineering works of the rivers. The formal arrangements, in each case, shall be as agreed upon between the parties. The Treaty also provides for exchange of data. Both countries agreed to monthly exchanges of data on the subjects of: (i) daily gauge and discharge data relating to flow of the rivers at all observation sites; (ii) daily extractions for or releases from reservoirs; (iii) daily withdrawals at the heads of all canals operated by government or any agency thereof, including link canals; (iv) daily escapages from all canals, including link canals; and (v) daily deliveries from link canals.[66] These data were to be transmitted monthly by each party to the other as soon as the data for a calendar month have been collected and tabulated, but not later than three months after the end of the month to which they relate.[67]

If either party plans to construct any engineering work that would cause interference with the waters of any of the rivers and, in its opinion, that would affect the other party materially, it shall notify the other party of its plans and shall supply such data relating to the work as may be available and as would enable the other party to inform itself of the nature, magnitude and effect of work. If a work would cause

---

[64] *See id.*

[65] C. K. Sharma, *A Treatise on Water Resources of Nepal* (Sangeeta Sharma, 1997), at 436.

[66] *See* Article VI.

[67] An article by a Pakistani official in the early 1990s pointed out that India has not complied with some of its obligations under the Treaty. India has, *inter alia*, failed to share data, has developed new hydroelectric projects on Western Rivers, has constructed the Wuller Barrage and carried out storage works on the Jhelum Main without informing Pakistan, and created a live storage capacity behind the barrage far in excess of Treaty allowance. *See* M. Y. Khan, "Boundary Water Conflict between India and Pakistan," 15 *Water International*, at 195, abstracted in Transboundary Resources Report, 5 (1), Spring 1991, International Transboundary Resources Center.

interference with the waters of any of the rivers but would not, in the opinion of the party planning it, affect the other party materially, the party planning the work shall nevertheless, on request, supply the other party with such data regarding the nature, magnitude and effect of the work as may be available.

In addition to the above details, the Treaty also contains certain technical, procedural and institutional provisions designed to promote cooperation and problem solving. Among others, the provisions specify that the two parties would continue to maintain the equipment so as not to prejudice the other party and that they would avoid polluting the waters of the Indus system of rivers. Also Pakistan was required to maintain the actual capacity of the drainage system, and if India asked for enlargement or additional digging of the drainage canals, Pakistan would carry out the works with Indian finance. In this connection a provision of the Treaty recognizes the common interest in the optimum development of the rivers and stresses the intention of the parties to cooperate fully.[68]

3. Dispute Resolution Mechanism and the Permanent Indus Commission

The Indus Treaty establishes a complex system for dispute settlement. The Permanent Indus Commission examines all disputes, in first instance. From there onward, two procedures are envisaged depending on the nature of the conflict: disputes that are purely technical in nature, and disputes that are of a grave and serious nature that cannot be examined by a neutral expert.

A Permanent Indus Commission consisting of two Commissioners (one appointed by India and another by Pakistan) was to establish and maintain cooperative arrangements for the implementation of the Indus Treaty. The commission was to promote cooperation between the parties in the development of the waters of the rivers, and in particular to study matters referred to it to help resolve questions concerning the interpretation or application of the Treaty, and to make tours of inspection.[69] It may be noted that the Indus Commission was inspired by the International Joint Commission established by the United States and Canada.[70] The Commissioner, unless either government decides to take up any particular question directly with the other government, is the representative of his government for all matters arising out of the Treaty and serves as the regular channel of communication on all matters relating to the implementation of the Treaty.

The Commission is required to meet at least once a year, alternately in India and Pakistan. The Commission shall also meet when requested by either Commissioner.

---

[68] For detail on notification, exchange of information, and cooperation, *see* Article VII.

[69] *See* for detail Article VIII; *see* also Baxter, *supra* note 15, at 471; *see* also Statement of the Minister of Irrigation and Power, *supra* note 46, at 605; it should also be noted that the original intent of the Bank's plan was to avoid the establishment of any continuing joint administration of the Indus Basin irrigation system. However, a permanent commission was desired later to oversee the implementation of the Treaty and to settle any questions that might arise thereunder. *See* Michel, *supra* note 9, at 260.

[70] *See* Baxter, *supra* note 15, at 471.

The programs of meetings are generally finalized in a meeting of the Commission. As the Commission comprises the two commissioners who are the representatives of their governments, the decision on a matter can only be taken by agreement. There is no voting involved as the two commissioners have to agree or disagree in regard to a particular matter after discussion. The two Commissioners are assisted by their advisers. There is no restriction on the number of advisers required to assist a Commissioner in a meeting. No participation by the public at any phase of the decision-making is envisaged in the Treaty. The Treaty also does not provide for any contact of the Commission as a body with governmental authorities, agencies or departments of member countries at the national, regional or local level.[71]

The Commission as a body does not have funds of its own. The respective governments bear the expenses of the organization headed by its Commissioner and also bear the expenses of the Commission meetings in its country. To enable the Commissioners to perform their functions in the Commission, each government has agreed to accord to the Commissioner of the other government the same privileges and immunities as are accorded to representatives of member states to the principal and subsidiary organs of the United Nations.[72] The Commission is required to submit to the two governments, before June 1 every year, a report on its work for the year ending on the preceding March 31, and may submit to the two governments other reports at such times as it may think desirable.[73]

Elaborate provisions concerning the settlement of differences and disputes are included in the Treaty. The task of dealing with disputed questions in the first instance falls to the Permanent Indus Commission.[74] If the Commission cannot agree, either Commissioner may, by certifying that the matter falls within one of 23 designated areas, have the "difference" deferred to a neutral expert who is to be a highly qualified engineer.[75] How the matter is to be laid before the neutral expert and how it is to be resolved by him are the subjects of detailed provision. If the "difference" does not fall under one of the 23 categories or the neutral expert decides that the "difference" should be treated as a "dispute," the governments are to negotiate with the assistance of mediators if they so desire. Finally, the "dispute" may be laid before a Court of Arbitration if the parties agree to do so or at the request of either party if the dispute is not likely to be resolved by negotiation or meditation or one party or the other considers that the other is "unduly delaying the negotiations." A Court of Arbitration is to consist of seven members, two to be designated by each of the parties, and the other three to be selected by agreement of the parties or, failing that, by designated individuals. The three neutral "umpires" are to be respectively a person qualified to be chairman of the Court of Arbitration, an engineer, and

---

[71] *See generally,* the Indus Treaty; *see* also, Khan, *supra* note 67, at 196-197.

[72] *Id.,* at 197.

[73] *Id.,* at 197.

[74] Article IX (1).

[75] Article IX (2), in conjunction with Annexure F.

an international lawyer.[76] The parties were to endeavor to put together a Standing Panel of Umpires, from whom the selections might be made. The constitution and procedure of the Court of Arbitration were spelled out in an Annexure to the Treaty.[77] It is noteworthy that the applicable law includes the Treaty, and for purposes of the interpretation and application of the Treaty, and in order, (i) the international conventions establishing the rules explicitly recognized by India and Pakistan, and (ii) the customary international law.

4. Principle of Basin Administration: Indus Basin Development Fund

In the context of maintaining an ever-lasting peace, and in addition to the general scope of responsibilities pertaining to the administration of the Indus Basin assumed by the Permanent Indus Commission, the Indus Treaty also envisages assistance in basin administration from bilateral and multilateral organizations, including and in particular the World Bank. In order to carry out a series of work in the basin, and recognizing that the sizable work was not in the capacity of Pakistan to finance, the World Bank had been instrumental in the creation of an Indus Basin Development Fund. Financial contribution for the Fund was provided by several countries, including in addition to the World Bank itself, Australia, Canada, Germany, New Zealand, Pakistan, the United Kingdom and the United States of America. These countries agreed to contribute grant money to the establishment and functioning of the Indus Basin Development Fund.[78]

In consideration of the fact that the purpose of part of the system of works to be constructed was the replacement of supplies that had hitherto come from the Eastern Rivers (allocated to India pursuant to the Treaty), India agreed to pay a fixed contribution of 62,060,000 Sterling Pounds toward the cost of the works.[79] The payment was to be made in 10 equal annual installments on November 1 each year.[80] In addition, two loans to Pakistan (from the United States of America and from the World Bank) were also provided. Pakistan also agreed to provide a contribution to

---

[76] *See* generally Article IX and Annexure G.

[77] *Id*.

[78] During the negotiations of the Treaty, the World Bank had made a distinction between works needed to replace water when the basin was divided between India and Pakistan, and the development works desired to enhance water use by both countries. In this connection, to address the financial liability question, the World Bank had determined the principle of "beneficiary pays," which meant that works would be paid for by the country that benefited. India was willing to pay for the replacement works in Pakistan, but not development works. Pakistan, on the other hand, insisted that there was no distinction to be made because the development works were based upon pre-partition plans, and thus it was logical for India to also pay for the development works in Pakistan. By applying the "beneficiary-pays" principle and establishing the Indus Basin Development Fund, the World Bank was able to overcome this financial obstacle. *See* generally, Syed S. Kirmani, "Water, Peace and Conflict Management: The Experience of the Indus and Mekong River Basins," in *Water International* 15 (1990), at 201-202.

[79] Article V (1).

[80] Article V (2).

the Indus Basin Development Fund. The World Bank was designated administrator of the Fund.

The Indus Basin Development Fund consisted approximately of 900 million dollars to finance the construction of irrigation and other works in Pakistan, made up of 640 million dollars provided by participating governments, 174 million dollars payable by India and 80 million dollars loan from the World Bank. The program for construction work in Pakistan included *inter alia* eight link canals nearly 400 miles long for transferring water from the Western Rivers to areas formerly irrigated by the Eastern Rivers; two storage dams, one on the Jhelum and the other on the Indus; power stations; 2,500 tubewells; and other works to integrate the whole river and canal system.[81]

The Indus settlement also envisaged the construction of a storage dam on the Beas River in India which, together with the Bhakra Dam on the Sutlej and the Rajasthan canal, was to irrigate new areas in India. However, it is appropriate to note that the works to be carried out in India did not come within the scope of the Indus Basin Development Fund.

In the context of the administration of the basin, it is important to stress the role of the World Bank. Indeed, the World Bank played an important role in the resolution of the Indus dispute.[82] As mentioned earlier, the signatories to the Treaty were not only India and Pakistan, but also the World Bank. The World Bank representative signed the Treaty only for the purposes of Article V (Financial Provisions) and Article X (Emergency Provision), and the Annexures F, G and H (on Neutral Expert, Court of Arbitration, and Transitional Arrangements, respectively). The provisions of the Treaty specify the role of the World Bank. For instance, if, at the request of Pakistan, the transition period was extended, the World Bank was required to pay to India, out of the Indus Basin Development Fund, amounts specified in the Agreement.[83]

If at any time the execution of works is unfavorably affected by hostilities beyond Pakistan's control, the World Bank would provide its good offices, with a view to reaching mutual agreement as to whether any modifications of the provisions of the Treaty are appropriate and advisable under the circumstances.[84] The World Bank is also required to inform India and Pakistan of the eventual completion of the work prior to the end of the transition period.[85] If in the course of the work, the junction canals suffered from damage due to flood, the two permanent Commissioners would consult and would call upon the good offices of the World Bank in order to introduce provisional modifications to the work program.[86] Finally, the World Bank was

---

[81] *See* Ali, *supra* note 13, at 330.

[82] Statement of the Minister of Irrigation and Power, *supra* note 55, at 606.

[83] *See* Article V (5).

[84] *See* Article X.

[85] *See* Annexure H, paragraph 66.

[86] *See* Annexure H, paragraph 65.

also vested with responsibilities to designate the Neutral Expert, fix the remuneration, and to nominate the President of the Court of Arbitration.[87]

The role of the World Bank as Administrator of the Indus Basin Development Fund is also noteworthy. Twice a year, the Bank furnishes the reports to the parties to the Indus Basin Development Fund agreement (which, it needs to be emphasized, excludes India). Also, notification to the parties would be sent by the World Bank if unexpected events affected the completion of the Project by Pakistan, funds were considered insufficient, and Pakistan failed to fulfill its obligations. In case there was breach of obligation by Pakistan, the Bank also reserved the right to suspend all disbursements. In connection with the Indus Basin Development Fund, the disputes were to be settled by a single arbitrator, and in case that became impossible, by the Secretary General of the United Nations.

The establishment of the Indus Basin Development Fund and the role played by the World Bank therein are particularly noteworthy illustrations of the potential role of international financing organizations that are able to mobilize expertise and sizable international financial resources for development.[88] At various stages, the World Bank could politely impose its independent proposals.[89] Pakistan, being a lower riparian, was not prepared to risk breakdown of negotiations for that reason. India's own second five-year plan depended on massive economic aid from the World Bank and from the developed World Bank member countries. These exogenous factors enhanced the effective role of the World Bank in the negotiations.[90] Indeed, the World Bank did not have political power but its ability to bring together several countries with the financial commitment was a kind of quasi-imperial third-party inducement to the successful resolution of the dispute.[91] The Herculean effort by the World Bank in bringing India and Pakistan to the mediating table and keeping them there until the Treaty was signed, is also a testimony to the Bank's commitment to resolving international water disputes.[92] Overall, the role of the World Bank, as noted by some scholars, has been proactive, neutral, pragmatic and fair.[93] The World Bank was pragmatic enough to give up its ideal of the unified development of the basin and propose a workable solution based on the division of rivers.[94]

---

[87] *See* Article IX, Annexures F and G.

[88] Wolfgang Friedman et al., *International Law: Cases and Material* (St. Paul: West Publishing, 1969), at 628.

[89] *See* Mehta, *supra* note 17, at 75.

[90] *Id.*

[91] *Id.*

[92] *See* Alam, *supra* note 4, at 179.

[93] *See* Kirmani and Le Moigne, *supra* note 7, at 5.

[94] *Id.*

III. Conclusion

The Indus Treaty is an excellent example of the settlement of riparian issues and one of the few examples of a successful settlement of a major international river basin conflict.[95] Also it is the first dispute regarding water use in which an international organization played a successful mediating role in resolution. Even if it was far from an optimum economic solution and failed to cover vital drainage issues, the Treaty is regarded as a major achievement as it has been able to divide the Indus and its tributaries unambiguously between the riparians.[96] The fact that there were six rivers in the system offered the simple solution of the three Western Rivers (the Indus, Jhelum and Chenab) being reserved for consumptive use by Pakistan, and the three Eastern Rivers (the Ravi, Beas and Sutlej), being reserved for consumptive use by India. The Treaty's originality has contributed importantly to its success. The allocation of the waters of the three rivers to India and three to Pakistan is in the nature of a territorial division.[97] Since the Treaty was signed, the two parties have not had to deal jointly with water administration other than to enforce the Treaty's terms and iron out some practical difficulties.[98] The Treaty has also set an optimistic tone. Thanks to protracted negotiations, the dispute that had brought the two countries to the brink of war was resolved with the emergence of an effective Treaty.[99] Also noteworthy is the fact that the critical discussions were taken at a political level, but the protracted and complex negotiations were between senior professional engineers. India's chief negotiator was always an irrigation engineer and Pakistan was represented for some time by an engineer who was replaced by a senior administrative civil servant.[100] It follows then that in delicate issues involving rivers shared among nations, the decision-makers at the highest level of government must be brought into the process.

One can also assume that the growing realization of a common and mutual interest in the Indus Basin Project provided the real basis for the agreement.[101] Indeed, some amount of dissatisfaction was noted by the parties. In India, it was widely felt

---

[95] See Mehta, *supra* note 17, at 69; *see also* Alam, *supra* note 4, at 1 (Introduction).

[96] Opinions have been expressed that the agreement was a triumph of the lesser evil. In terms of optimum gains that could be derived from the total waters of the Indus Basin, by treating the basin as an ecological and economic unity, one must at least hypothetically recognize the great opportunity costs in repudiating the investment in the existing network of irrigation canals. But in the circumstances in the Sub-continent, the Treaty was the most politically feasible solution. *See* Mehta, *supra* note 17, at 69-70.

[97] Harald D. Frederiksen et al., *Water Resources Management In Asia* (Vol. I), World Bank Technical Paper No. 212 (1993), at 23.

[98] *Id.*; it should be noted that after almost four decades the Treaty does not include China and Afghanistan, which also share part of the Indus.

[99] *See* Jayanta Bandyopadhya and Dipak Gyewali, "Ecological and Political Aspects of Himalayan Water Resources Management," in *Water Nepal* (Ajaya Dixit, ed. September 1994), Vol 4. No.1, at 20.

[100] *See* Mehta, *supra* note 17, at 74.

[101] *See* New York Times (Editorial), March 2, 1960.

that Pakistan obtained a better position from the Treaty for potential development. Seventy-nine percent of the total volume of waters (the statistical average of the three rivers) was made available to Pakistan, whereas the Eastern Rivers earmarked for India equalled only the balance of 21 percent.[102] On the other hand, Pakistan had its own complaints pertaining to additional commitment for storage of water. Pakistan was able to obtain this additional storage, in 1964, through a supplemental agreement on the storage project at Tarbela on the Indus.[103]

From the standpoint of international water law, the finalization of the Treaty confirms the resolution that international disputes are not necessarily a problem linked only with the interpretation of existing rules, but also with the drafting of new rules. To that extent, the dispute often may not necessarily be resolved by the usual judicial or arbitral methods.[104]

The Treaty, in accordance with Article 12, was deemed to have entered into force retroactively on April 1, 1960. This was, it should be emphasized, not only prior to the date of exchange of instruments of ratification (which occurred on January 12, 1961), but prior to the date of the execution of the Treaty. This element should indeed be noted because it is a practice rarely found in conventional international law.[105]

The Indus Waters Treaty is one of the most shining examples of dispute resolution because it contributes not only to the solution of an international dispute but also to the development of a scheme. The scheme compensates Pakistan for the diversion to Indian usage of certain river waters that irrigated parts of what is now Pakistan prior to partition. In that sense, it is not "development aid" for Pakistan but "replacement aid" following one of the exigencies of partition.[106]

As noted by an eminent scholar, the Indus settlement was reached not merely by agreement on a solution of the dispute but by change in the factual situation that had

---

[102] See Mehta, *supra* note 17, at 73.

[103] In connection with this, some scholars argue that the fact that Pakistan had become a United States ally in the CENTO and SEATO gave Pakistan an intangible political advantage and diplomatic leverage. It is still important to note that the overriding consideration that propelled the World Bank and its developing partners to satisfy the demand of Pakistan was the fear of an Indo-Pakistan war precipitated by non-resolution of the Indus Waters Dispute. See Mehta, *supra* note 17, at 73.

[104] Charles Rousseau, "Inde et Pakistan: Conclusion du traité du 19 septembre 1960 relatif à l'utilisation des eaux de l'Indus," in *Revue générale de droit international public* (1961), at 376.

[105] *Id.*, at 375. One reason for parties to agree on a retroactive application of the Treaty (as of April 1, 1960) was that the transition period started on that date, as per Article II (6) of the Treaty. The retroactive effect of the Treaty was meant to serve this practical purpose. During negotiations, indeed, the 10-year transition period (see *supra* note 52 and accompanying text) was already agreed to have begun on April 1, 1960. It was therefore important for the Treaty to become applicable as of that date. India, it should be noted, was to continue to supply Pakistan with water in the Central Bari Doab Channels and in the Sutlej Valley systems during the transition period.

[106] See I. M. D. Little and J. M. Clifford, *International Aid: A Discussion of the Flow of Public Resources From Rich to Poor Countries* (Chicago: Aldine Publishing, 1968), at 225.

formed the basis of the dispute.[107] Instead of a limited and insufficient quantity of water to quarrel over, the supply of water would be increased to a level that would permit the needs of both parties to be met sufficiently. From the perspective of international law, there is reason to applaud the novel approach. All the existing rights and obligations were wiped clean to start discussions afresh. The negotiated settlement terminated any claims that India, the upper riparian, had to the waters of the Indus on the basis of prior appropriation.[108]

Several key factors contributed to the successful conclusion of the Indus Treaty. The fact that an international organization got involved as a third party to help resolve the dispute, the fact that a solution based on well-known principles of developing water resources of a river basin as a single hydrological unit was dropped, and that a unique solution based on the division of rivers was proposed, and the fact that when the solution proved too costly for India to finance, the third party mobilized the needed resources, are the most notable factors.[109] A third party or parties (whether countries or organizations) are often very useful in mediating conflicts or disputes as they influence the belligerent's behavior by exploiting the strength of their own position. The third-party mediators can use their leverage. However, the Indus settlement provides the example of an opposite technique: the rewarding of cooperation. By providing Pakistan with the resources needed to control its own water supply, the World Bank in effect bought one party its objective, while relieving the other, India, of the burden of the dispute.[110] Indus was thus a settlement

---

[107] See Baxter, *supra* note 15, at 476.

[108] While the Treaty has achieved, as expected by the negotiators and the mediator, equitable apportionment of Indus waters, the Treaty itself, in Article 11 (paragraph 2), expressly provides that nothing it contains is to be construed by the parties as in any way establishing any general principle of law or precedent. Due to this provision, Professor McCaffrey believes that the two countries could presumably revert to their fundamental legal postures in any future water disputes that was not governed by the Indus Treaty. See Stephen C. McCaffrey, *Water, Politics and International Law*, *supra* note 17, at 95. But Professor Baxter views this provision differently, and thinks that despite the stated intention of the Treaty, a provision of this nature cannot keep others from looking to the settlement as a precedent or from deriving what general principles they choose from the terms agreed upon. See Baxter, *supra* note 15, at 476. Along those lines, Professor Lipper, citing this attempt "...expressly to negate any precedential value (the Treaty) might otherwise have," commented that "Of course, if the general thesis were to be accepted that treaties were mere bargains without international law-making effect, a major source of international law would be eliminated. Fortunately, no such thesis has found its way into international legal practice." See Jerome Lipper, "Equitable Utilization," in *The Law of International Drainage Basins* (Garretson et al.), at 35. A similar approach was adopted in another Treaty between the United States of America and the United States of Mexico pertaining to the "Distribution of the Water of Rio Grande" dated May 21, 1906. Article IV of said Treaty states that "The delivery of water [as herein] provided is not to be construed as a recognition by the United States of any claim on the part of Mexico to the said waters..." see *Treaties and Other International Agreements of the United States of America*, 1776-1949 (compiled under the direction of Charles I. Bevans), 1972.

[109] See Kirmani and Le Moigne, *supra* note 7, at 5.

[110] This is, however, not to suggest that money was the only problem and reason that allowed the Indus Treaty to be signed. But, with hindsight, one can safely note that in the final stage of the negotiations, when almost everything but the resources issue was settled, it would have been risky to prolong the negotiations by discussing which country should pay for the work. So clearly the resource aspect was also one piece of the puzzle, albeit not the most important.

in which both parties were able to realize their goal with the aid of outside intervention.[111]

The brief overview of the treaty regime permits us to draw three instructive conclusions.

The first conclusion relates to the issue of exclusive appropriation of water by one riparian state. Under the theory of exclusive appropriation (more commonly known as the Harmon doctrine), which is based on the notion of absolute territorial sovereignty, an upper riparian, in a successive watercourse, enjoys an exclusive status. In the case of the Indus, India tried its best to use this thesis to support its arguments.[112] In addition to the Harmon doctrine, India also invoked the thesis of its economic development needs to justify its claims on the waters of the Indus. Coupled with the Harmon doctrine, the argument based on economic needs brought a third notion according to which the waters of an international river should be reasonably and equitably utilized. This notion, based on the principle of limited territorial sovereignty, recognizes the existence of reciprocal rights and obligations of riparian states, and from that emerged the duty to compensate.

The second conclusion relates to the issue of compensation. The solution proposed in the Indus Treaty recognizes the notion of compensation. In 1947, India had claimed an amount of Rs.150,000,000 from Pakistan to compensate for the loss of water due to the canals built under the British rule.[113] A year later, India accepted the principle of payment of compensation in favor of Pakistan for the deviation of water in the Indian Territory. Finally the Treaty provides for a financial contribution of India, for the development of the Indus Basin, which was essentially meant to be for carrying out works in Pakistan territory. India contributed to the investment in

---

[111] *See* J. G. Merrils, *International Dispute Settlement* (Cambridge: Grotius Publication Ltd., 1991), at 37.

[112] Similar efforts were made by several countries in the past, such as Austria in its dispute against Hungary and Bavaria in the beginning of the twentieth century, USA in its dispute against Mexico in connection with the Rio Grande, and Canada against the USA in connection with the North American border waters.

[113] Under British rule, Bikaner State had to pay seigniorage charges to the Punjab for supplying water, and proportionate maintenance costs for the Ferozepur headwork and the feeder canal located in Punjab territory. East Punjab, based on this precedent, claimed that West Punjab must pay similar costs. Whether reluctant or not, West Punjab agreed to pay seigniorage charges, proportionate maintenance costs, and interest on a proportionate amount of capital. However, at the Inter-Dominion conference Pakistan challenged the calculation by which the seigniorage charges and capital cost of the Upper Bari Doab Canal for interest charge were made. The West Punjab government agreed, in turn, to pay seigniorage charges for the cost of transporting water through canals in East Punjab, and give its share of any maintenance costs. As the dispute over the calculation of seigniorage remained unresolved, the portion that was held in dispute was decided to be held in escrow. This amount would be decided by the Indian Prime Minister. It was also agreed that further talks would be held to achieve a mutually acceptable solution. This issue of disputed seigniorage charges had dominated bilateral discussions between India and Pakistan and had reached an impasse by the time the World Bank came to intervene. In the meantime, both countries continued to construct works that would safeguard their water supply, either existing or planned. The matter of the seigniorage charges was only resolved in 1960, in the final stages of the drafting of the Indus Waters Treaty. *See,* for detail, Alam, *supra* note 4, at 63-65.

Pakistan so that benefit flows could be secured as per schedules.[114] The acceptance of compensation also meant that the country endorsed the notion of limited sovereignty of the riparian state. Acceptance also implied the rejection of the prior use notion, and more importantly meant that in order to serve the reciprocal interests best, it was important to effectively apply the principle of equitable water sharing and the theory of equitable utilization.[115]

The third conclusion thus is related to water sharing between riparian states. The fact that the Indus Treaty does not specify the quantity of water allocated has led some scholars to believe that the Treaty effectively provides for a territorial type of sharing.[116] The Treaty merely reaffirms the territorial sovereignty of each state on the different watercourses. It does not modify the boundary between the two countries but traces a fictitious line East-West that divides the basin and limits the sovereign rights of use of each state to one half of the river system, and grants quasi-exclusive rights on the other half. In fact it is neither a territorial nor quantitative division, but a division that concerns only the use of the water, an excellent example in contemporary international law of rivers. This kind of division is what explains the predominantly political and economic, not legal, reasoning behind the Treaty.

---

[114] *See* Kamala Prasad, "Priority and Institutional Development," in *Water Nepal* (Ajaya Dixit, ed. September 1994), Vol 4., No.1, at 220.

[115] *See* Vitanyi, *supra* note 5, at 346.

[116] *See* Accariez, *supra* note 44, at 68.

PART THREE

India-Nepal Relations

Chapter 3
The Kosi River

I. Introduction and History of the Kosi Project

Four separate river systems, each with its headwaters in the Tibetan plateau, flow through Nepal. The Sapta-Kosi River system flows from the eastern mountains, the Gandaki River system flows from the central mountains, and the Karnali and the Mahakali River systems flow from the far western mountains. With four large rivers (Kosi, Gandaki, Karnali and Mahakali) and their tributaries fed by snow and glacier melt and monsoon rainfall accounting for nearly 90 percent of the country's surface water, Nepal is endowed with significant water resources. This remarkable endowment is supplemented by the flow of smaller rivers that drain the lower mountains and foothills, bringing the average annual run-off up to 200 billion cubic meters.[1] These major river basins are within the larger Ganges Basin that Nepal shares with China, India and Bangladesh. Most of the rivers in Nepal are inherently linked to potential international water rights issues with Nepal's upstream and downstream neighbors because all of the rivers flow in or out of the country. The rivers that flow from Nepal to India account for a large volume of water resources in the region.

1. The Political Constraints

Although the potential for water resources development between India and Nepal is considerable, the cooperation between these two countries on the issues related to water has not been easy and forthcoming, in particular because of the extreme sensitivities and divergent interests and approaches of the political parties. Their bilateral relations have been heavily influenced by politics. The vested interests and inward-looking dynamics of the political actors in both countries, rather than technical discussions related to water, have influenced the decision-making. To appreciate the ramifications of the problems with water resources between these two countries, it is imperative to acknowledge the political underpinnings of their bilateral relations.

India and Nepal have a long history of political relations. The political relations had been regularized, in the form of a Peace Treaty, as early as 1815, when India was still a British colony, and almost a century and a half later, on July 31, 1950,

---

[1] See Surya Nath Bastola, *Water Resources Development of the Mighty Himalayan Rivers* (Kathmandu: Sunil Bastola, 1997), at 121; Generally speaking, the waters from more than 6,000 rivers and rivulets in Nepal ultimately flow toward the Ganges. However, more specifically, the Indo-Nepal river system can be classified into seven river systems that range from east to west: Mahananda, Kosi, Kamla Balan, Bagmati, Burhi Gandaki, Gandak and Ghaghra. All these rivers and their major tributaries originate in Nepal and after traversing various distances in Nepal, enter Indian Territory and join the Ganges. For detail, see A. R. Rao and T. Prasad, "Water Resources

through a new Treaty of Peace and Friendship between Nepal and newly independent India.[2] Also signed with the 1950 Treaty of Peace and Friendship was a Side Letter that formed an integral part of the Treaty. While the 1950 Treaty and its Side Letter generally aimed at strengthening and developing the ties between India and Nepal, it also established special relations between the two countries. In particular, it provided for equal and reciprocal treatment of the citizens of both countries, and dealt with the issue of importation of equipment and armaments, by Nepal, from or through the territory of India, necessary for the security of Nepal. While the special relations aspect may have been quite justifiable in the early 1950s, it imposed a number of restrictions on Nepal, particularly in its dealings with countries other than India (since the early 1960s the Treaty has been disavowed by Nepal, but nothing formal was done). A detailed analysis of the Treaty remains beyond the scope of this study, but it is important to note that it continues to influence the bilateral relations between these two countries in all spheres of cooperation. Water resources are no exception.

2. The Kosi River and the Scheme

The Kosi, Nepal's largest river, originates in Tibet. The river is called Sapta Kosi after the Tribeni confluence, from which point it starts its southwesterly journey. The basin is oval-shaped with a protruding projection in the Sapta Kosi area of Chatra. The Kosi Basin is 270 km N-W, S-E long and about 145 km N-E, S-W wide with a catchment area of about 25,600 sq. km.[3] With seven main tributaries, it is the largest tributary of the Ganges. It drains an area of 92,538 square km, of which 30,800 square km are in Tibet, 41,333 square km are in Nepal, and 20,405 square km are in India. The Kosi flows through a narrow gorge for 10 km before entering the plains at Chatra. After another 25 km, it enters India near Hanumangarh, and 20 km further downstream it joins the Ganges near Khursela in the State of Bihar. The Kosi is the wildest river with the most devastating effects in the Indian State of Bihar. For this reason, the Kosi is also referred to as the "sorrow of Bihar." Because of the seasonal damage it caused, a scheme to attenuate the effects of the Kosi was deemed necessary. The Prime Minister of India Jawaharlal Nehru emphasized the importance of such a scheme. Referring to the strategy at the time of its initiation, Pandit Nehru stressed: "[I]t is my opinion that the Kosi Project is very necessary and should be somehow constructed. We must make a start even though it may take a few years to complete because, as you know, in some parts of Bihar every year a strange difficulty arises, bringing disaster and ruin."[4]

Development of the Indo-Nepal Region," *Water Resources Development* 10, (1994), at 160-161.

[2] Treaty of Peace between the Honourable East India Company and Maharaja of Nepal, December 2, 1815, in A. S. Bhasin, *Documents on Nepal's Relations with India and China, 1949-1966* (New Delhi: Academic Books, 1970), at 12-14; Treaty of Peace and Friendship, July 31, 1950, in *id.*, at 32-34.

[3] For detail, *see* C. K. Sharma, *A Treatise on Water Resources of Nepal* (Kathmandu: Sangeeta Sharma, 1997), at 47-48.

[4] See the speech "Planning and Development," delivered in Hindi on June 19, 1951 (Selected

Map 2: The Kosi River Basin

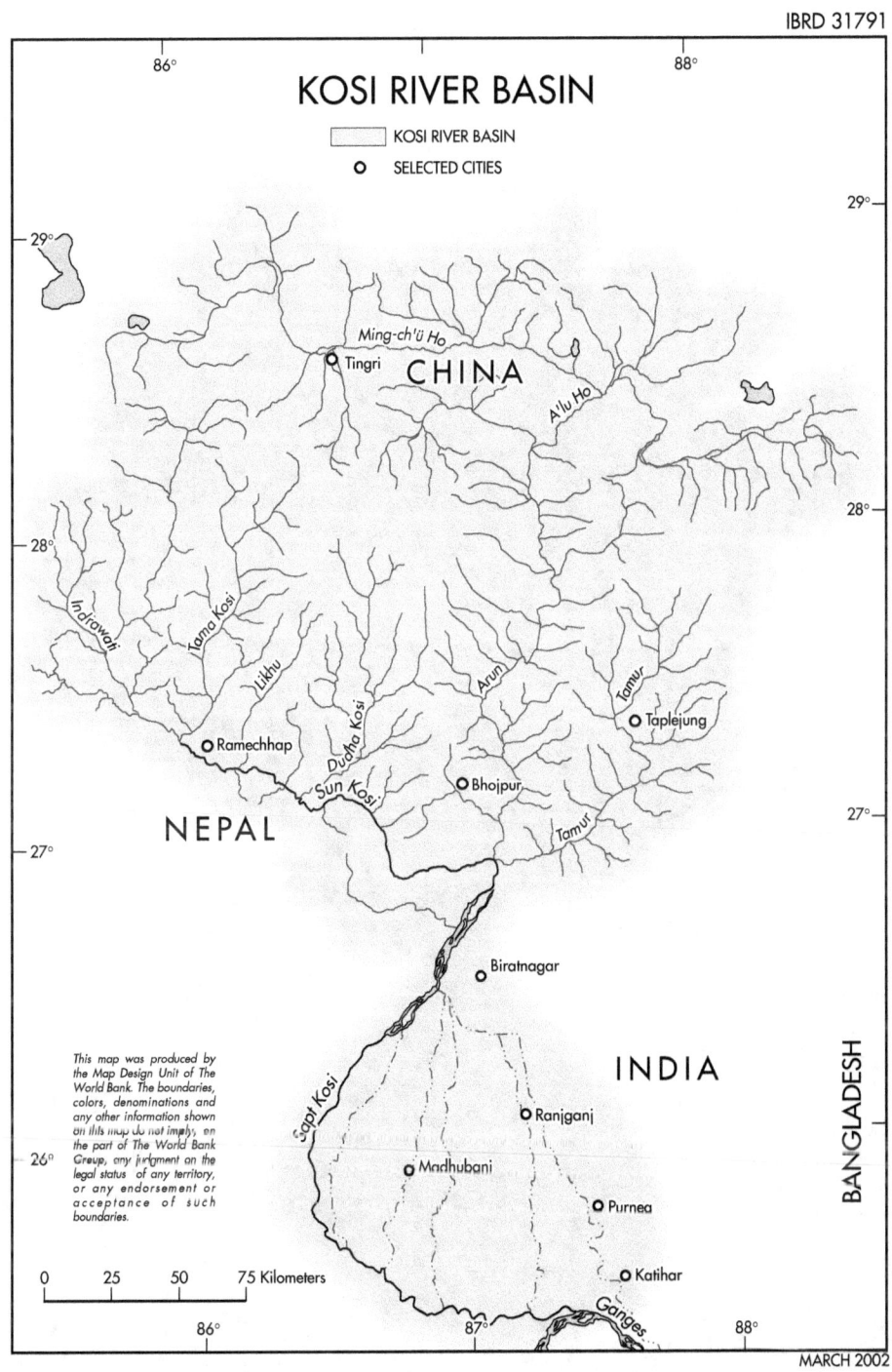

In post-1950 Nepal,[5] the Kosi Project became the first development Project in an international river presented as mutually benefiting both India and Nepal.[6] It is a multipurpose scheme that includes flood control, hydropower generation and irrigation. Historically, the idea of tapping the waters of the Kosi had been discussed in India as early as 1896,[7] but because of the absence of serious feasibility studies no immediate decision was made. This idea resurfaced in the 1930s, but again because of political uncertainties in both India and Nepal, no concrete decision was made. In 1951, after the overthrow of the Rana oligarchy, a new government was installed in Nepal and more focused attention was directed to the Kosi project. The Central Water and Power Commission of the Government of India prepared a scheme for harnessing the Kosi River that received the sanction of the Government of India in 1953. Thereafter, the scheme was endorsed by the Nepalese Government, following which the 1954 Kosi Agreement was negotiated and signed.[8]

Despite its so-called multipurpose ambit, the Kosi Project was conceived essentially to yield flood control benefits, and to reduce the recurrent flood devastation in the two countries.[9] In this connection, a 1,150-meter barrage was built in Bhimnagar, 5 km upstream of Hanuman Nagar (8 km inside Nepal).[10] The barrage is intended to serve as a gradient control measure for containing the meandering behavior of the river. Two canals take off from either side of the barrage. The Eastern Main Canal, which is entirely in the Indian Territory, provides irrigation to 612,500 hectares of

---

Works of Jawaharlal Nehru; March 1, 1951 to June 30, 1951), edited by S. Gopal, Second Series, Volume 16, Part I, pp. 17-30), cited in Arvind Panagariya, *Consensus Building and Nehru*.

[5] In 1951, the Rana's hereditary premiership, which had prevailed in the country for about a century, was put to an end and Monarchy was re-established. The change was politically significant and the era after the change is commonly referred to as the new era. The present study uses this date as a reference merely for purposes of methodological simplicity.

[6] U. K. Verma, "Socioeconomic Renaissance through Dynamic Indo-Nepal Cooperation in Water Resources Development," in *Water Nepal* (Ajaya Dixit, ed., 1994) Vol.4, No.1, at 140.

[7] P. C. Rawat, *Indo-Nepal Economic Relations* (New Delhi: National Publishing House, 1974), at 205.

[8] B. C. Upreti, *Politics of Himalayan River Waters: An Analysis of the River Water Issues of Nepal, India and Banagladesh* (Delhi: Nirala Publication, 1993), at 96; *see* also for detail on the origin of the Kosi Project, Dinesh Kumar Mishra, "Refugees of the Kosi," in *Himal South Asia*, August 2000: *See* also, Agreement on the Kosi Project, Kathmandu, April 25, 1954 signed by Gulzari Lal Nanda (India) and Mahabir Shumsher (Nepal) (hereinafter 1954 Agreement). For the text of the Agreement, *see*, Bhasin, ed., *supra* note 2, at 152-156.

[9] *See* B. G. Verghese and Ramaswamy R. Iyer, eds., *Harnessing the Eastern Himalayan Rivers: Regional Cooperation in South Asia* (Delhi: Konark, 1994), at 201; *see* also, Dipak Gyewali and Ajaya Dixit, "Mahakali Impasse and Indo-Nepal Water Conflict," *Economic and Political Weekly*, Vol. XXXIV, No. 9 (February 27, 1999), at 553.

[10] The original plan was to build the dam in the foothills of the Siwalik range, but because of high cost and especially the fear of losing control over the management and operation of the barrage due to extended distance, India abandoned the idea and a site near the Indo-Nepal border was chosen for the barrage with its several sluice gates. *See*, for detail, Aditya Man Shrestha, *Bleeding Mountains of Nepal* (Kathmandu: Ekta Books, 1999), at 157.

agricultural land in India.[11] A power house with an installed capacity of four units of 5,000 kW each is located along the canal at a distance of 11 km from the barrage and generates power by making use of the head drop of the canal.

The Western Main Canal traverses a distance of 35 km in Nepal before entering the Indian Territory, and provides irrigation water to 11,300 hectares of agricultural land in Nepal and 356,610 hectares of agricultural land in India. Flood control works in Nepal consist of a western afflux bund about 2 km long and a 40-km embankment along the eastern bank of the river. Extensive embankments, about 220 km long, were built on either side of the river in the Indian territory to confine the river flow and protect the land beyond from flooding.

The estimated cost of the Project was Rs 45.0 crores,[12] but because of siltation problems and the shifting nature of the Kosi River, additional works were required that raised the cost to 54.5 crores.[13] The barrage and the Eastern Main Canal were completed in 1962. The construction of the Western Main Canal started in 1972 and it became operational in 1982.

II. The Kosi Treaty Regime

As mentioned previously, the international rights and obligations of India and Nepal regarding the Kosi River were first spelled out with the signing of the Kosi Agreement on April 25, 1954.[14] But soon after its conclusion, the 1954 Agreement was sternly criticized by the opposition political parties in Nepal. Critics asserted that the Project did not benefit Nepal in any manner whatsoever, and that it granted extraterritorial rights to India for an indefinite period without providing Nepal with adequate compensation. Nepal would receive only a minute proportion of the total irrigated land and India would benefit more from the power resources developed by Nepal. Also alleged was that Nepal had to lose its fertile land without equivalent gains in exchange of it, and that the scheme was actually designed for the furtherance of India's own interests without paying proper attention to the well being of the Nepalese people.[15] Without detailing the arguments and counter-arguments, it should be noted that there was widespread Nepalese resentment about the Project.[16]

During the early 1960s when the political relations between India and Nepal had deteriorated severely[17] and criticism against the Kosi Agreement had intensified,

---

[11] See Bhekh B. Thapa and Bharat B. Pradhan, *Water Resources Development, Nepalese Perspective*, IIDS, 1995 (Bombay: Konark Publishers, 1995), at 201.

[12] See Upreti, *supra* note 8, at 96.

[13] *Id.;* and see also Rawat, *supra* note 7, at 206.

[14] See *supra* note 8.

[15] For more detail, *see* Upreti, *supra* note 8, at 98; *see* also Leo E. Rose, *Nepal Strategy for Survival* (Oxford University Press, 1971), at 199.

[16] *See* generally Upreti, *supra* note 8, at 99; *see* also Verghese and Iyer, *supra* note 9, at 164-165.

[17] This was particularly due to a serious political change in Nepal whereby, in 1960, the then King dismissed the democratically elected government, disbanded political parties, dissolved the

pressure was put on the Indian Government to revise the Agreement. The Indian Power and Irrigation Minister, Mr. K. L. Rao, visited Nepal during 1962-63 and expressed India's readiness to amend the Agreement in light of the complaints lodged by Nepal. The Indian authorities were then asked to suspend the execution of work pending further discussions for the revision of the Agreement. In 1965, during his visit to Nepal, Premier Lal Bahadur Shastri further assured the Nepalese Government of India's readiness for revision. The agreement was amended in 1966.[18] Because each and every provision of the 1954 Agreement had been subjected to criticism, the modification of said agreement was extensive. The present rights and obligations actually stem from the 1966 revised Agreement[19] which replaced the earlier 1954 Agreement, and which entered into force immediately after the signature. The following paragraphs review the 1966 Agreement in comparison, as and when appropriate, with the 1954 Agreement. This comparative approach is warranted not only to appreciate the evolutionary aspect of the treaty regime itself, but also to comprehend the rationale for contentions surrounding the several provisions of the Treaty.

1. Contentions Regarding the Execution of the Kosi Project

The Kosi Project consists of the construction of a barrage, head-works and other appurtenant works about three miles upstream of Hanuman Nagar town on the Kosi River with afflux and flood banks, and canals and protective works, on land lying within the territories of Nepal. The purposes of the Kosi Project were flood control, irrigation, generation of hydroelectric power and prevention of erosion of Nepal areas on the right side of the river, upstream of the barrage.[20] It is worth noting that following the conclusion of the 1954 Agreement, various works in respect of the Project were already carried out by the Government of India. For works that remained in various stages of completion, the Nepalese Government had agreed to afford necessary facilities. This intention was later reflected in the 1966 revised Agreement which stressed that "Nepal had suggested revision of the said Agreement in order to meet the requirements of the changed circumstances," and India, "with a view to maintaining friendship and good relation subsisting between Nepal and India," had agreed to the revision of the 1954 Agreement.[21]

---

parliament and imposed a new system in which the king would hold absolute power. A lot of internal as well as external opposition to the act surfaced, which had also become an irritant to the Indo-Nepalese relations.

[18] For detail, *see* Upreti, *supra* note 8, at 100-101.

[19] Revised Agreement on The Kosi Project, Kathmandu, December 19, 1966, signed by Shriman Narayan (India) and Y. P. Pant (Nepal) (hereinafter referred to as the 1966 Agreement or the revised Agreement). For the text of the Agreement, *see* Bhasin, *supra* note 2, at 156-163.

[20] *See* preamble, 1966 Agreement.

[21] *See* preamble to the 1966 Agreement. It seems appropriate to note that the use by the Agreement of some terms give the impression that the Agreement was not entered into between two states with equal status. For instance, one party (India) is referred to as "the Union" and the

Hence the dynamic nature of the Project preparation necessitated that the revised Agreement take into account the new developments of the Kosi Project. The general layout of the barrage, the areas within afflux banks, flood embankments, and other protective works, canals, power house and the lines of communication were accordingly modified prior to the signing of the revised Agreement and a detailed plan was annexed thereto.[22] It was also agreed through an exchange of Letters between the two governments[23] that the land on which the Nepal Link Bund is situated would be surrendered by India to Nepal, but Nepal agreed to permit the Government of India to maintain and operate the existing waterways in this Bund.

Focusing on bilateral consultation, the Agreement further provided that any construction and other undertaking by India in connection with the Project needed to be planned and carried out in consultation with the Government of Nepal, and that works and undertakings which, pursuant to the Agreement required prior approval of the Nepalese Government, would only be implemented after securing such approval.[24]

The 1966 revised Agreement delineates quite clearly the responsibilities of India and Nepal in the execution of the Kosi Project. The Government of the Indian State of Bihar is designated Chief Engineer. When it considers any survey or investigation in connection with the Kosi Project to be required, the Nepalese Government provides necessary facilities to the concerned Indian officers or persons acting under their orders to undertake such surveys and investigations.[25] Such surveys and investigations may comprise aerial and ground surveys, hydraulic, hydrometric, hydrological and geological surveys, including construction of drill holes for surface and sub-surface exploration, investigations for communications and for materials of construction, and all those necessary for the proper design, construction and maintenance of the barrage and any work connected with the Project.[26] The Chief Engineer may also undertake surveys and investigations of storage dams or detention dams on the Kosi, soil conservation measures such as check dams, afforestation, and so forth, required for a complete solution to the Kosi problems in the

---

other party (Nepal) is referred to as "the Government." Due to this, arguments that the Agreement undermines the sovereign status of Nepal have been forwarded by some intellectuals. *See* Aditya Man Shrestha, *supra* note 10, at 157. However weak this argument may be in treaty-law, it certainly comes out as a political stain for Nepal. Curiously indeed, one notes that in some other agreements between the same two countries during the same time period, the terms "Government of India" and "Government of Nepal" have been used. For instance, the Treaty of Peace and Friendship, dated July 31,1950 (see *supra*), signed a few years prior to the Kosi Agreement, an important Treaty which bore heavily on the Indo-Nepal relations for decades, and the Extradition Treaty dated October 2, 1953, both refer to "Government of India" and "Government of Nepal," not to "Union of India" and "Government of Nepal."

[22] 1966 Agreement, Article 1.

[23] Signed and confirmed on December 19, 1966. For the text of the Letter, *see* Bhasin, *supra* note 2, at 163.

[24] 1966 Agreement, Article 1 (iii).

[25] 1966 Agreement, Article 2.

[26] *Id.*, Article 2 (i).

future.[27] While the previously noted surveys and investigations are to be carried out in cooperation with the Nepalese Government,[28] those deemed necessary for the general maintenance and operation of the Project may be conducted by India after due intimation to the Government of Nepal.[29]

The Agreement also includes provisions regarding the authority for execution of works and use of land and other property.[30] When any major construction work not envisaged in the amended plan required prior approval of the Nepalese Government, it is to be granted as and when the Project or a part of the Project receives the Indian Government's sanction and notice has been given by India to Nepal. In this context, Nepal is required to permit access by the engineer and all other officers, servants, and nominees of India, with such men, animals, vehicles, plant, machinery, equipment and instruments as may be necessary for the direction and execution of the respective constructions, to all such lands and places, and to permit the occupation, for such period as may be necessary, of all such lands and places as may be required for the proper execution of the respective constructions.[31] Moreover, the Nepalese Government, upon prior notification, is to authorize Indian officers to enter on land outside the limits or boundaries of the barrage and its connected works in case of any accident happening or being apprehended to any of the said works and to execute works that may be necessary for the purpose of repairing or preventing such damage.

It is clear that the Project did not give priority to consensus in decision-making. Practically all decisions regarding the Project execution can be taken by India, a *modus operandi* criticized by the Nepalese, although no formal complaint was ever lodged. However, the findings of the surveys and investigations remain an issue, particularly for Nepal. Under the Agreement all data, maps, specimens, reports and other results of surveys and investigations carried out by or on behalf of India in Nepal are to be made available to Nepal freely and without delay. In turn, Nepal is to make available to India all data, maps specimens, reports and other results of surveys and investigations carried out by or on behalf of the Nepalese Government in Nepal in respect to the Kosi River.[32] It should be noted that while each country is required to give to the other the data resulting from its surveys and investigations on the "Kosi in Nepal," there is no provision about the exchange of data on the "Kosi in India."

Amid these contentions, an effort to ease the possible tension in the execution of the Kosi Project has been made through the provision of a Joint Indo-Nepal Kosi Project Commission, envisaged under the Treaty framework. The 1954 Agreement provided for a Coordination Committee for Kosi Project, meant to be a forum for

---

[27] *Id.*, Article 2 (ii).

[28] *Id.*, Article 2 (iii).

[29] *Id.*, Article 2 (i).

[30] *Id.*, Article 3.

[31] *Id.*, Article 3 (i).

[32] *Id.*, Article 2 (iv).

discussion of problems of common interest in connection with the Project. Almost immediately after the Agreement was signed, this committee was established and had started to function. Thus, it was important for the revised Agreement to ensure continuity to the activities of the committee. The 1966 revised Agreement has indeed quite pragmatically succeeded in ensuring such continuity. It chose to maintain a similar body, but with a name change. Instead of Committee, the body was called Indo-Nepal Kosi Project Commission. The Commission was vested with the responsibility of facilitating cooperation and coordination between the governments with regard to any matter covered in the Agreement. The rules for the composition and jurisdiction of the said Commission were to be mutually agreed upon. Until the constitution of the Joint Commission, the "Coordination Committee for the Kosi Project" was to continue to function with: (a) four representatives from each country to be nominated by the respective governments; and (b) the Chair of the Committee to be assumed by a Minister of Nepal and the Secretariat to be assumed by the Administrator of the Kosi Project. The Commission was mandated to consider matters of common interest that concerned the Project, such as land acquisition by Nepal for lease to India, rehabilitation of displaced population, and among others, maintenance of law and order.[33]

2. Contentions Regarding Land Ownership and Sovereignty

All infrastructure development works involve acquisition or redirecting of lands that are owned by individuals, communities or government. Compensation in obtaining such lands becomes a major issue and Kosi was no exception.

The land required for the purposes of the Project was to be acquired by Nepal, and compensation was to be paid by India.[34] Compensation, in every case, was to be tendered through the Government of Nepal to the owner of the land. The methodology regarding compensation for land is spelled out in the revised Agreement.[35] For the purpose of assessing the cash compensation, lands required for the execution of various works and submerged lands were divided into four classes to include: (i) cultivated lands, (ii) forest lands, (iii) village lands and houses and other immovable property standing on them, and (iv) waste lands. All lands registered in the cadastre in the territory of Nepal actually cultivated were deemed to be cultivated lands.[36]

---

[33] The Commission has met 17 times since the inception of the Project. The last meeting was held in February, 1991. The issues considered in the meetings include: (i) acquisition of land and payment of compensation; (ii) quarrying; (iii) supply of timber by Nepal; (iv) compensation for forest land and waste land and for assets falling within the embankments and in the submergence area in Nepal; (v) soil erosion prevention measures in Nepalese territory; (vi) rehabilitation arrangement for population living within the embankments; (vii) crop compensation on lands acquired; (viii) compensation for damage of crops due to breach of embankments; (ix) income tax exemption to the Nepalese contractors working in the Indian territory; (x) additional cross drainage works in Kosi western canal; and (xi) protection of areas on both banks of Kosi River. *See* for detail Thapa and Pradhan, *supra* note 11, at 205-206.

[34] *See* Article 8 of the Agreement.

[35] *Id.*, Article 8 (i) (a).

[36] *Id.*, Article 8 (i) (b).

India was also to compensate Nepal for the loss of land revenue as at the time of acquisition in respect of the area acquired, and to whomsoever it may be due for the lands, houses and other immovable property acquired for the Kosi Project and leased to India. The methods of assessment of such compensation and the manner of payment were to be determined by mutual agreement, and all lands required for the purposes of the Kosi Project were to be measured by the duly authorized officers of the Nepalese and Indian Governments respectively.[37]

An Exchange of Letters[38] between the two countries, also signed on December 19, 1966, further clarified the provision regarding compensation. India would pay the compensation annually at the rate of Nepalese Rupees five per Nepali Bigha[39] for all lands that were already acquired for the Kosi Project. For lands to be acquired in the future, and especially for the Western Kosi Canal, the existing provision would be applicable, under which loss of land revenue is to be determined on the basis of the land revenue payable as at the time of acquisition of the land.

Despite the previously noted detailed provisions, land ownership became one of the most sensitive and controversial issues emanating from the 1954 Agreement. It conferred on India the ownership of all lands acquired by Nepal and subsequently transferred to India for Project purposes. The 1954 Agreement read: "The Union shall be the owner of all lands acquired by the Government [under the provisions of clause 3 hereof] which shall be transferred by them to the Union and of all water rights secured to it under clause 4(i). Provided that the sovereignty rights and territorial jurisdiction of the Government in respect of such lands shall continue unimpaired by such transfer."[40]

The revised Agreement changed "ownership" to a "lease."[41] Indeed, it provides for Nepal to acquire land required for the construction of the Project and lease it to India after payment of compensation. In accordance with Article 5, all the lands acquired by Nepal are to be leased to India for a period of 199 years from the date of the signing of these amendments (the revised Agreement) at an annual nominal rate. The rent and other terms and conditions on which lands for Western Kosi Canal are to be leased by Nepal to India would be similar. The terms and conditions of any other land to be leased, are to be fixed by mutual agreement. At the request of India, Nepal is to grant renewal of the lease on mutually agreed terms and conditions. The Agreement further confirms that the Nepalese sovereign rights and territorial jurisdiction, including the application and enforcement of the laws of Nepal on and in respect of the leased land, continues unimpaired by such lease.

---

[37] *Id.*, Article 8 (iii).

[38] Exchange of Letters dated December 19, 1966, *supra* note 23.

[39] One Bigha is equal to 0.6772 hectare.

[40] *See* Article 5.

[41] Article 5 (i) of the 1966 Agreement.

It is worth noting that this duration of the lease far exceeds what is usual in treaties of this sort. Nonetheless, with regard to the renewal of the lease after 199 years, a Letter exchanged[42] provides assurances that the Government of India would be reasonably compensated in case the Project properties are taken over by Nepal at the end of the lease period. The compensation would include the cost borne to date and to be incurred in the future by India. In that case the depreciation in the value of the Project materials would also be taken into account.

3. Contentions Regarding Water and Power Use

The issues regarding the use of water and power by Nepal had also been problematic under the 1954 agreement. A literal comparison between the relevant articles of both agreements may help explain the nature of the contention. Article 4 of the 1954 Agreement stated: "(i) Without prejudice to the right of Government [of Nepal] to withdraw for irrigation or any other purpose in Nepal such supplies of water, as may be required from time to time, the Union [India] will have the right to regulate all the supplies in the Kosi River at the Barrage site and to generate power at the same site for the purposes of the Project." Moreover, sub-paragraph (ii) of the 1954 Agreement stated: "The Government shall be entitled to use up to 50 percent of the hydroelectric power generated at the Barrage site Power House on payment of such tariff rates as may be fixed for the sale of power by the Union in consultation with Government."

The revised Agreement not only changed the tone of the provision but also improved the Nepalese situation by affirming Nepal's right to withdraw water from the Kosi River for irrigation or for any other purposes and from the Sunkosi River or within the Kosi Basin from any of the Kosi tributaries. Article 4 (i) of the revised agreement states: "HMG [His Majesty's Government] shall have every right to withdraw for irrigation and for any other purpose in Nepal water from the Kosi River and from the Sunkosi River or within the Kosi Basin from any other tributaries of the Kosi River as may be required from time to time. The Union shall have the right to regulate all the balance of supplies in the Kosi River at the barrage site thus available from time to time and to generate power in the Eastern Canal."

Article 4 (ii) further states "HMG shall be entitled to obtain for use in Nepal any portion up to 50 percent of the total hydroelectric power generated by any Power House situated within a 10-mile radius from the barrage site and constructed by or on behalf of the Union, as HMG shall from time to time determine and communicate to the Union. However, HMG shall communicate to the Union any increase or decrease in the required power supply exceeding 6,800 kW at least three months in advance."

In addition to these changes, the revised Agreement also added that if any power to be supplied to Nepal is generated in a power house located in Indian territory, the Indian Government would construct the necessary transmission line or lines to a point at the Nepal-Indian border that shall be mutually agreed upon, and the tariff

---

[42] Exchange of Letters dated December 19, 1966, *supra* note 23.

rates for electricity to be supplied to Nepal would be fixed mutually.[43] It further provided for Nepal to receive 50 percent of the total hydroelectric power generated by any powerhouse situated within a 10 miles radius of the barrage site.[44] However, in spite of a provision regarding power, the Agreement failed to determine (i) the installed capacity of the power house, (ii) the quantum of power available to Nepal, and (iii) the cost and benefits of the Project. Similarly, it failed to specify (i) the quantum of water that will flow along the irrigation canals, (ii) the land area that will come under the command of these canals, and (iii) the respective irrigation benefits for the countries, which resulted in added ambiguity to the Agreement.

The power and other materials used for the purpose of the Project are not provided for free. They yield royalties for Nepal. In respect to power generated and utilized in the Indian-Union, according to the 1966 Agreement, the Government of Nepal is entitled to receive royalty at rates to be settled by agreement. No royalty is to be paid on the power sold to Nepal.[45]

Nepal is also entitled to receive royalty from India in respect of stone, gravel and ballast obtained from the Nepalese territory and used in the construction and future maintenance of the barrage and other connected works. Such rates are to be settled by agreement.[46] The Indian Government can use and remove clay, sand and soil without let or hindrance from land leased by Nepal to India. Besides, Nepal would not levy customs or any duty during construction and subsequent maintenance on any articles and materials required for the purpose of the Project or the work connected to it.[47] The use of timber from the Nepalese forests required for construction work is also permitted on payment of compensation. Compensation is not payable for quantities of timber necessary for the use in the spurs and other river training works required for the prevention of caving and erosion on the right bank in Nepal. Similarly, no compensation is payable for timber obtained from the forestlands leased by Nepal to India.

In this context, it was also agreed that Nepal would provide land to India, against payment of compensation, for purposes of construction and maintenance of roads, tramways, railways, ropeways, and so forth. Such construction, if outside the Project area, would require prior approval of the Nepalese Government.[48] Any restrictions, required in the interest of construction, maintenance and proper operation of the Project, regarding the use of the roads, and so forth by commercial or private vehicles would be agreed upon mutually.[49] In case of threatened breach or

---

[43] 1966 Agreement, Article 4 (iii).

[44] *Id.*, Article 4 (ii).

[45] *Id.*, Article 6 (i).

[46] Under Article 3 (iv), 1966 Agreement, Nepal also permitted India to quarry the construction materials required for the Project from the various deposits at Chatra, Dharan Bazar or other places in Nepal.

[47] Revised Agreement, Article 7.

[48] *Id.*, Article 9.

[49] *Id.*, Article 9 (ii).

erosion of the structures attributable to the river, the Project officials were allowed to restrict public traffic upon intimation to the Nepalese Government. Nepal also agreed to permit, on the same terms as for other users, the use of all roads, waterways and other avenues of transport and communication in Nepal for *bona fide* purposes of the construction and maintenance of the barrage and other connected works.[50]

The bridge over Hanuman Nagar Barrage (constructed under the Project) is to be generally open to public traffic.[51] India reserves the right to close the traffic over the bridge temporarily if and insofar as required for technical or safety reasons, with prior approval of the Nepalese Government, but in such cases, India has to take all measures required for the most expeditious reopening of the bridge.[52] Nepal agreed to permit installation of telegraph, telephone and radio communications in Nepal for the bona fide purposes of the construction and maintenance of the Project, on the condition that India agrees: (i) to withdraw such facilities that Nepal may in this respect provide in the future, and (ii) to permit the use of internal telephone and telegraph in the Project area to authorized Nepalese civil servants for business in emergencies without, however, hampering or interfering with the construction and operation of the Project.[53]

In addition, consistent with the usual practice in bilateral understandings, the Agreement provides for a special treatment of Nepalese labor.[54] India committed to give preference to Nepalese labor, personnel and contractors to the extent available and in its opinion suitable for the construction of the Project, but reserved the right to import labor of all classes to the extent necessary. Moreover, with the Nepalese Government's prior approval, India was allowed to establish schools, hospitals, water-supply systems, electric supply systems, drainage and other civic amenities for the duration of the construction of the Project.[55] On completion of construction of the Project, such civic amenities would, upon request by Nepal, be transferred to Nepal. In any case, all functions of public administration would be exercised by the Nepalese Government.

4. Contentions Regarding Navigational and Fishing Rights

All navigation rights in the Kosi River in Nepal rest with Nepal.[56] However, the use of any watercraft like boats, launches and timber rafts within two miles of the barrage and headworks is not allowed on grounds of safety, except by special permits to be issued by the competent Nepalese authority in consultation with the Executive Engineer of the Project. Any unauthorised water-craft found within this limit is

---

[50] *Id.*, Article 9 (iii).

[51] *Id.*, Article 9 (iv).

[52] *Id.*, Article 9 (iv).

[53] *Id.*, Article 9 (v).

[54] *Id.*, Article 12.

[55] *Id.*, Article 13.

[56] *Id.*, Article 10.

liable to prosecution. The Agreement also states that provision should be made for suitable arrangements at or around the site of the barrage for free and unrestricted navigation in the Kosi River, if technically feasible. This provision about navigation is particularly important considering Nepal's ambition for a reliable navigation route to the sea.[57] However, as it appears, this benefit is illusory and has not been realized. The obligation of India is to provide for navigation at or around the barrage, but only if technically feasible. So far no provision for navigation has been made and Nepal's apparent benefit has proven to have no substance.[58]

Like navigation, all the fishing rights in the Kosi River in Nepal rest with Nepal.[59] However, no fishing is permitted within two miles of the barrage and headworks except under special permits to be issued by the competent Nepalese authority in consultation with the Executive Engineer of the Project. While issuing the special permits within two miles, Nepal is to take into account the safety of the headwork and the permit-holders.

5. Dispute Resolution Mechanism

Any dispute or difference arising out of or in any way concerning the construction, effect or meaning of the Agreement, if not settled by discussion, is to be determined through arbitration.[60] By notice in writing, either of the parties may inform the other of its intention to refer to arbitration any such dispute or difference. Within 90 days of the delivery of such notice, each of the two parties is to nominate an arbitrator for jointly determining the dispute or difference and the award of the arbitrators is binding on the parties. In case the arbitrators are unable to agree, the parties may consult each other and appoint an umpire whose award is to be final and binding on them.

Despite the details provided by the Agreement, the arbitration mechanism appears defective in two respects. First, there is no provision for the appointment of an arbitrator if one of the states fails to nominate a member of the arbitration panel. Second, if the two arbitrators fail to agree on the disposition of the issue in dispute, the two parties then may "consult each other and appoint an Umpire whose award shall be final and binding on them." In other words there is no obligation to appoint an umpire. So a desire to submit an issue to arbitration by one party to the Agreement can easily be frustrated by the other.[61]

---

[57] Nepal is landlocked, and all means of transportation that can provide access to and from the sea remain a high priority. For detailed discussions on the problems related to landlocked states including problems faced by Nepal, *see* generally, Kishor Uprety, "Landlocked States and Access to the Sea: An Evolutionary Study of a Contested Right," *Dickinson Journal of International Law* 12, at 401-496; *see* also Verghese and Iyer, *supra* note 9, at 208.

[58] *See* Charles B. Bourne, "Nepal's International Water Resources and International Law," Report No 6/4/280696/1/1 Seq.No.492, HMG, Water and Energy Commission Secretariat, at 36.

[59] Article 11.

[60] Article 14.

[61] *See*, Bourne, *supra* note 58, at 37.

III. Conclusion

In sensitive issues like water, the perception of countries of the outcome of negotiations between them is often affected by the fact that the parties have different perspectives and priorities. Small countries have a tendency to think that they have been outsmarted, and the big countries tend to think that they have been more generous than necessary. As a result no country is ever fully contented. While a similar conclusion could be drawn from the Kosi Project with regard to India and Nepal, it also appears useful to examine cautiously the benefits and losses (merits and demerits) the parties have received under the Agreement. On the basis of the content-analysis of the Kosi Agreement, it seems quite safe to conclude that if there were significant benefits for both countries, there was also tremendous loss for Nepal, such as the submergence of fertile land.

The Agreement for the Kosi Project dealt with the fact that Nepal permitted India to build works on the Kosi River in Nepalese territory, which resulted in inundating the cultivated land and rendering it otherwise unproductive and uninhabitable. No doubt, the grant of this permission was clearly a valid exercise of Nepal's sovereignty over its territory and cannot be challenged on the grounds of its legality. Nevertheless, one may examine the terms and conditions of the Agreement from the viewpoint of their effects on Nepal's position in international law.

The matter may be considered from two aspects. First, whether Nepal received adequate compensation for the benefits it conferred on India by allowing it to build the works on and flood Nepalese territory.[62] Second, to what extent was Nepal's freedom to act in the development of the Kosi River compromised by the terms of the Agreement?

Keeping aside the issues of cost and benefits that remain for economists or engineers to decide, in the Kosi Agreement there is little evidence that the benefits that would accrue to India from the Project were carefully calculated and accounted

---

[62] One important concept that has developed in the interpretation of equitable sharing is the issue of "downstream benefits." In summary, the concept confirms that when one country takes actions to manage water resources in its territory that confer significant benefits to a downstream country, the latter must pay reasonable compensation for those benefits. This notion of "downstream benefits" was introduced by Canada as an integral part of the negotiations of the Columbia River agreement. When the United States government proposed building a dam upstream of the Columbia River in Canadian Territory, the United States Government agreed to pay for the dam but refused to pay for any other costs for the benefit of the seven million acre storage that Canada would provide. The Canadian Government argued that the State receiving the primary benefit from the proposed project was the United States (downstream country). Canada as the upstream country was enabling the United States of America to have substantial benefits including increased power production and flood control, and Canada proposed that United States of America should compensate Canada for these benefits. This proposal was rejected by the United States of America and the matter was referred to the International Joint Commission established by the two countries under the 1909 Boundary Waters Treaty (*supra* note 23, Chapter 1), which came down with a set of principles that define the downstream benefits. For detailed discussions on the Columbia Basin, *see*, Ralph W. Johnson, "The Columbia Basin," in *The Law of International Drainage Basins,* Garretson et al., eds. (Dobbs Ferry: Oceana Publications, 1967), at 167-241; *see* also generally, Patricia Wouters, ed., *International Water Law, Selected Writings of Professor Charles B. Bourne* (London: Kluwer Law International, 1997), at 343-352.

for.[63] It is true that Nepal is to receive a royalty in respect of power generated and utilized in India at rates to be fixed by agreement.[64] But it is noteworthy that if Nepal is entitled to 50 percent of the hydroelectric power generated at any power house built within a 10-mile radius from the barrage site, it must pay for this power. Furthermore, although the land needed for the Project has been granted to India on a 199-year lease, the compensation payable for it is determined by the land revenue as at the time of acquisition.[65] By the Letters exchanged on December 19, 1966, supplementary to the revised Agreement, the compensation for land already acquired was fixed at five Nepalese Rupees per Nepali Bigha, and compensation for lands to be acquired in the future, especially for the Western Kosi Canal, is to be determined by applying the same principle, that is land revenue payable as at the rate of acquisition. In other words, there is no provision for increase in the value of land by inflation or otherwise throughout the long life of the lease.

Similarly, whether the irrigation and other benefits derived by Nepal from the Project do in fact balance the benefits received by India, is a matter to be assessed by experts. But the deal has been done and can only be undone by another agreement. If the Nepalese feel seriously outsmarted, India views that the balance of advantage in the Kosi Project is merely a question of interpretation of the facts. The Indian view is interesting. Under the Project, India has an irrigation potential of 9,650,000 hectares. Indian assistance to construct infrastructure in Nepal has allowed the irrigation of 93,000 hectares in Nepal. Indeed, if looked at in those simple terms, there seems to be imbalance. But if the Indians had built the Kosi Barrage a little downstream in the State of Bihar, Nepal would have had no advantage and Indian irrigation, instead of the 9,650,000 hectares would have been 9,500,000 hectares. By constructing the barrage in Nepal, India gained only 15,000 hectares of additional potential but Nepal gained 93,000 hectares.[66]

A few comments may be appropriate with regard to the effect of the revised Agreement on Nepal's future action. It should be noted that the 1954 Agreement on the Kosi Project severely limited Nepal's freedom to develop the Kosi River system. The revised Agreement improved that situation slightly for Nepal. In the context of improving Nepal's situation, some articles were completely deleted. For instance, the 1954 Agreement contained a provision that specified that the Government of Nepal shall be responsible for the maintenance of law and order in the Project areas

---

[63] A cursory look at the sharing of costs and benefits of joint projects in international watercourses suggests that costs are proportional to benefits as a bottom line theory, although this is not always the case. As a matter of fact, the question of allocation of costs and benefits emerges only when a project is set for joint development in an international watercourse. The sharing is a fundamental issue affecting international cooperation for the development of a shared watercourse. The cost and benefit allocation principle generally dictates that each participating riparian should bear the cost of the benefit accruing from the project facilities, but models differ from one project to another.

[64] Article 6 (ii).

[65] Article 8 (ii) (a).

[66] Comment by H.E. Ambassador of India, Deb Mukharji, Face to Face Program, Reporter Club, 26 May, 2001.

within the territory of Nepal.[67] It further added that the Governments of Nepal and India would, from time to time, consider and make suitable arrangements calculated to achieve that objective. The Agreement also added that if desired by India, Nepal would establish special court or courts in the Project area to ensure expeditious disposal of cases arising within the Project area. India would bear the cost involved in the establishment of such courts, if the Nepal Government so desired.[68] The above two articles tackled the issue of sovereignty in their own subtle way, but were considered controversial and were deleted in the revised Agreement. The deletions, although sensitive, were not legally so significant. But another deleted provision that pertained to future works merits highlighting. Under Article 16 of the 1954 Agreement, the Government of Nepal consented to the work related to storage or detention dams and other soil conservation measures on the Kosi and its tributaries, if further investigations so required. Linked with Article 2 (ii) of the 1954 Agreement dealing with surveys and investigations as discussed above, this Article constituted Nepal's abandonment of control of its Kosi River water resources. The deletion was extremely useful in restoring that control.[69] One final observation regarding the Kosi Agreement is the apparent lack of any obligation on the part of India to generate any electricity in connection with the Project. Its only obligation is to provide Nepal with a percentage of any power that may be generated. Nepal's benefit from the Project is therefore illusory. In fact it has not been realized. Similarly, as already mentioned, no provision for navigation at or around the barrage has been made yet and Nepal's apparent navigational benefit has proven to have no substance.

It may be concluded that Nepal entered into the Kosi Agreement, as far as is known, under a lot of internal pressure attributable to the prevailing political instability, as well as external political pressure from India. Indeed, as the first agreement of its kind—an agreement negotiated without enough homework on the part of Nepal—mistakes were unavoidable. But the uproar generated by the conclusion of this Agreement taught Nepal to be more careful in the future on issues concerning water and the related negotiations. The Agreement helped India understand that negotiations with its tiny neighbor needed to focus more on a consensus-building approach, particularly taking into account the uneven understanding of national interests and the dynamics among the different political actors in Nepal. This careful approach can be noticed in the Gandak Agreement that India and Nepal entered into in the same decade. That Agreement is the subject of the next chapter.

---

[67] 1954 Agreement, Article 14.

[68] *Id.*, Article 15.

[69] *See* Bourne, *supra* note 58, at 35.

CHAPTER 4
The Gandaki River

I. Introduction and History of the Gandak Project

The Gandaki River, also called the Narayani, originates in the Tibetan plateau and drains the central mountains of Nepal.[1] Upon crossing the Nepalese border near Tribeni Bazar, it is called the Gandak in India, where after running a course of about 250 km, it joins the Ganges River near Patna in the State of Bihar.

Every year the Gandaki flooded, damaging crops and property and endangering people in vast areas. Indeed, the uncontrolled Gandaki was a major source of trouble to both nations. Nepal needed capital and India needed a suitable site to construct a dam for flood control and other water use. From those needs came the Gandak Project, another multipurpose undertaking by India and Nepal, aimed at benefiting both the countries with irrigation, power and flood control.

Efforts toward harnessing the large irrigation potential of the river Gandaki had been made as early as 1871, although through informal channels.[2] Formally it was initiated in 1947 with the construction of a canal in Tribeni. In 1947 Dr. Rajendra Prasad, the then Food and Agriculture Minister of India, wrote to the Government of Bihar to explore the possibilities of constructing a canal system from the Gandak for irrigation.[3] In 1951 a report was prepared in this connection and submitted to the Planning Commission of India, which accepted the proposal.[4] This proposal was later forwarded to the Government of Nepal who also endorsed it, and in December 1959, an Agreement was concluded.[5]

Similar to the Kosi Agreement, the conclusion of this Agreement sparked protests from the political parties in Nepal. The construction of the barrage in the Nepalese territory was propagated as Indian encroachment on Nepal's sovereignty and territorial integrity. Issues were raised about the Nepalese Government's lack of authority to conclude the Agreement. It was also stated that the Agreement had

---

[1] *See*, for detail, C. K. Sharma, *A Treatise in Water Resources of Nepal* (Kathmandu: Sangeeta Sharma, 1997), at 56.

[2] P. C. Rawat, *Indo Nepal Economic Relations* (New Delhi: National Publishing House, 1974), at 213.

[3] *Id.*, at 213.

[4] *See* for detail B. C. Upreti, *Politics of Himalayan River Waters: An Analysis of the River Water Issues of Nepal, India and Bangladesh* (Delhi: Nirala Publication, 1993), at 103.

[5] Agreement on the Gandak Irrigation and Power Project, Kathmandu, December 4, 1959. This Agreement came into force with effect from the date of signature. For the text of the Agreement, see A. S. Bhasin (ed.), *Documents on Nepal's Relations with India and China, 1949-1966* (Delhi: Academic Books, 1970), at 166-170.

undermined the interests of the Nepalese people in general and that they were unfairly treated.[6]

In the context of this Project, a barrage has been built at the Gandaki River near Bhaisalotan to regulate the flow of water for irrigation and power purposes. The barrage is constructed on the reach of the river, which forms the boundary between India and Nepal. Two canals take off from either side of the barrage. The main eastern canal lies in the Indian Territory but one of its branches called Don branch canal reaches the Indo-Nepal border and bifurcates into two canals. Nepal Eastern Canal constitutes one of them and traverses Bara, Parsa and Rautahat districts in Nepal. The main eastern canal serves the irrigation needs of 920,520 hectares and 37,200 hectares of agricultural land in India and Nepal respectively. The main western canal passes through a few kilometers in Nepal before entering the Indian Territory. The canal provides water to irrigate 4,700 hectares of land in Nepal and 930,000 hectares of land in India. Another canal referred to as the Nepal Western Canal takes off from the western side of the barrage and covers a command area of 16,000 hectares entirely within Nepal. Thus in the aggregate, the canals serve the irrigation needs of 57,900 hectares of land in Nepal and 1,850,520 hectares of land in India. A power house that utilizes the head drop of the canal to generate 15,000 kW of power is built at Surajpura, located on the main western canal in the Nepalese Territory.[7]

II. The Gandak Treaty Regime

The rights and obligations regarding the Gandaki stems from the Agreement entered into between the Governments of India and Nepal on December 4, 1959.[8] Along with the Agreement, a Letter was also exchanged (signed and confirmed the same day) spelling out additional operational details regarding the Project and providing for the establishment of a coordination committee.[9]

The Gandak Project consists of construction of a barrage, canal head regulators and other appurtenant works about 1,000 feet below the existing Tribeni canal head regulator. The Project also involves taking out canal systems for purposes of irrigation and development of power for India and Nepal. While the Gandak Agreement mainly highlighted the common interests and benefits of both Nepal and India, it also specified that the Project was being built by and at the cost of the Government of India.[10]

---

[6] See Upreti, *supra* note 4, at 104-106; *see* also Aditya Man Shrestha, *Bleeding Mountains of Nepal* (Kathmandu: Ekta Books, 1999), at 168.

[7] *See* generally, Bhekh B. Thapa and Bharat B. Pradhan, *Water Resources Development, Nepalese Perspective*, IIDS (Bombay: Konark Publishers, 1995).

[8] See *supra* note 5.

[9] Exchange of Letters dated December 4, 1959. For the text of the Letter, *see* Bhasin, ed., *supra* note 5, at 171-173.

[10] The total cost of the project at the time of conclusion of the agreement was estimated at Rs 50.5 crores, to be borne entirely by India.

Map 3: The Gandaki River Basin

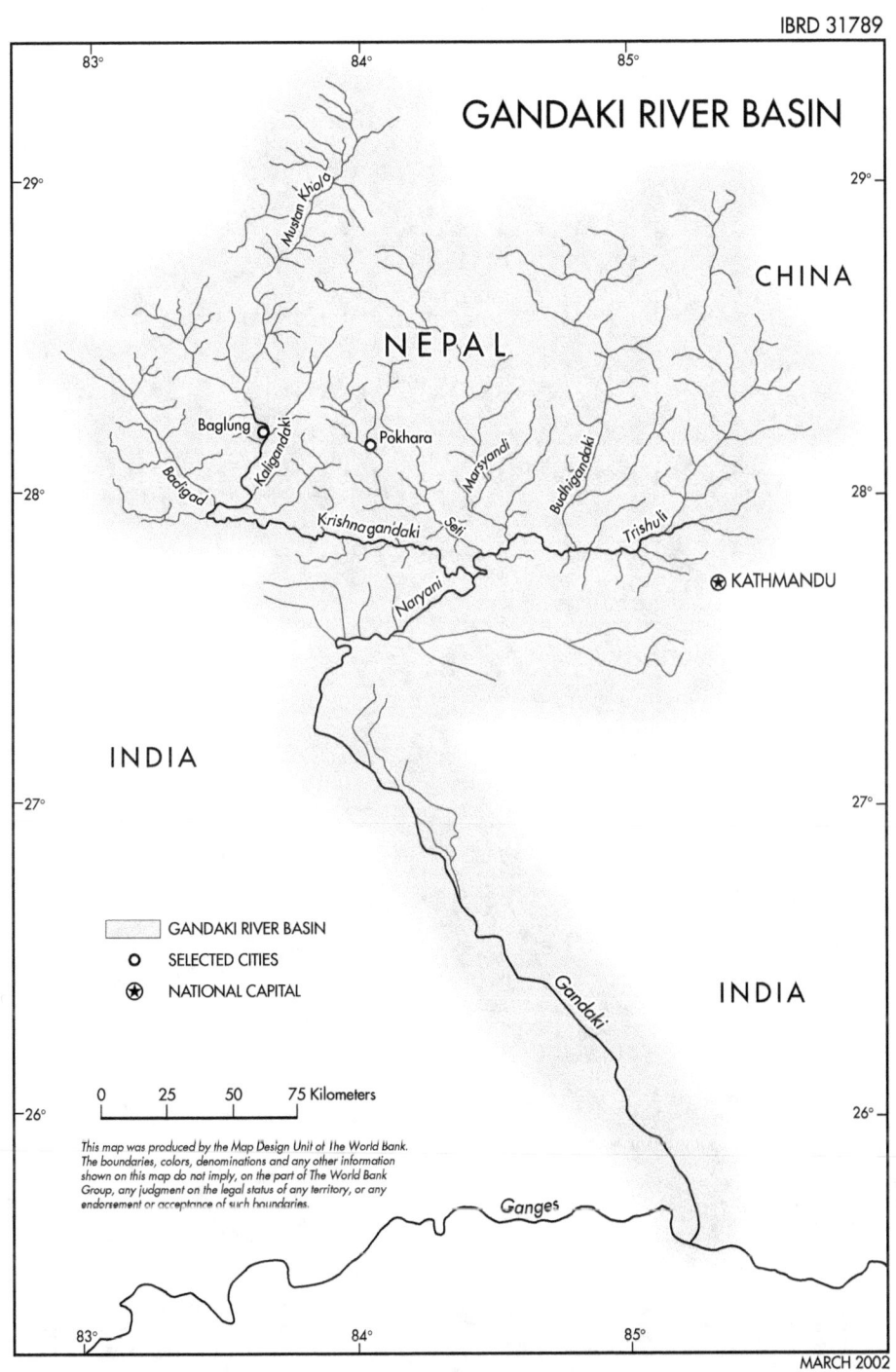

The Nepalese Government authorized the Government of India to proceed with the execution of the Project and committed to acquire all such lands as the Government of India may require and to permit the access to the movement within, and the residence in, the Project area of officers and field staff with labor force, draught animals, vehicles, plants, machinery, equipment and instruments as may be necessary for the execution of the Project, and for its operation and maintenance after its completion.

The Agreement also specified that in case of any apprehended danger or accident to any of the structures, the officers of the Government of India would execute all works that may be necessary for repairing the existing works or preventing such accidents and/or danger in the areas indicated in the plan. If any of such works had to be constructed on lands that belonged to Nepal, the Nepalese Government would authorize these works to be executed and acquire such additional lands as may be necessary for the purpose. In all such cases the Government of India would pay reasonable compensation for the lands so acquired as well as for any damage that might arise out of the execution of these works. Similarly, on payment of reasonable royalties, the Nepalese Government permitted the Government of India to quarry materials such as block stones, boulders, shingle and sand required for the construction and maintenance of the Project from the areas.[11] In this context, the Letters exchanged recorded the understanding that if suitable materials are not available from these areas in sufficient quantities the Nepalese Government would permit quarrying in other mutually agreeable areas.[12]

1. Land Acquisition and Compensation

With regard to land acquisition, the Agreement provided that the Nepalese Government would acquire or requisition all such lands as are required by the Government of India for the Project, which meant for the purpose of investigation, construction and maintenance of the Project. The Government of India was to pay reasonable compensation for such lands acquired or requisitioned. Such land would then be transferred to the Government of India.[13]

The Letters exchanged with the Agreement provided for details regarding the payment of compensation for acquisition or requisition of lands required for the Project. It was agreed that for purposes of fixation of rates of compensation the Nepalese Government would appoint an Expert Committee with which Revenue Officers of the Gandak Project would also be associated. The Committee would visit the area of the Project and fix the principles for assessment of compensation payable for such lands. The total compensation payable for the lands acquired or requisitioned would be calculated on the basis of the agreed rates fixed by the Committee. The Government of India would deposit the agreed amount of compensation to the credit of the Government in the Central Bank of Nepal. The Nepalese Government

---

[11] Article 4.

[12] *See* the Letters exchanged.

[13] Article 3 (ii).

would then make the required arrangements for payment of compensation to those persons to whom it may be due.[14]

In accordance with the Agreement, land requisitioned for the Project is to be held by the Government of India for the duration of the requisition and land acquired or transferred is to vest in the Government of India as proprietor and subject to payment of land revenue (Malpot) at the rates at which it is leviable on agricultural lands in the area. When such land vesting in the Government of India or any part thereof ceases to be required by the Government of India for the purposes of the Project, the Government of India is to reconvey the land to the Nepalese Government free of charge.

2. Canal Ownership and Operation and Maintenance

Under the Agreement, India agreed to construct at its own cost two canals. The first, the Western Nepal Canal including its distributary system down to a minimum discharge of 20 cusecs, was to provide flow irrigation in the gross commanded area estimated to about 40,000 acres. The second, the Eastern Nepal Canal from the tail end of the Don Branch Canal up to the river Bagmati including the distributary system down to a minimum discharge of 20 cusecs, was to provide flow irrigation in Nepal in a gross commanded area estimated to about 103,500 acres.[15]

The Letter exchanged provided additional explanation that this gross commanded area will be possible only on the execution of the training works on the river Bagmati for which certain proposals had already been under discussion between the two governments. The river had been taking a westward course and certain training works were required in order to divert it back into its old eastern channel to flow under the Bagmati Railway Bridge. Without the river training scheme the gross commanded area would not exceed 93,000 acres. It was estimated that an amount of rupees 15 lakhs[16] was sufficient and accordingly the Government of India agreed to make this amount available to Nepal in suitable installments according to the progress of construction.

Nepal, on the other hand, was made responsible for the construction of channels below 20 cusecs capacity for irrigation in Nepal, for which purpose India also agreed to contribute such amount of money as India considered reasonable to meet the cost of construction. In the same context, the Nepalese Government allowed the Government of India to maintain such portion of the main Western Canal that falls in the territory of Nepal and to maintain the channels of communications for the purpose of the Project. The roads were to be essentially for Project use, and their use by commercial and non-commercial vehicles of Nepal were to be regulated through mutual agreement. The bridge over the Gandak Barrage was to remain open to public traffic but the Government of India reserved the right to close the traffic over the

---

[14] *See* the Letter, paragraph (a).

[15] Article 7 (ii).

[16] *See* the Letter, paragraph (d).

bridge for repair, or for any other valid reasons. India agreed to provide locking arrangements for facility for riverine traffic across the barrage free from payment of any tolls, provided that this traffic was regulated by the Project staff in accordance with the mutually agreed rules.[17]

Similarly, while Nepal agreed to permit installations of telegraph, telephone and radio communications as approximately indicated in the plan for the *bona fide* purpose of the construction, maintenance and operation of the Project, India permitted the use of such facilities to the authorized civil servants of Nepal in case of emergencies, provided such use did not interfere with the construction, maintenance and operation of the Project.[18]

The canal systems, including the service roads situated in the Nepalese territory (except the main western canal), were to be handed over to the Government of Nepal for operation and maintenance, according to the Agreement. Otherwise, all works connected with the Project in the territory of Nepal remained the property of, and were to be operated and maintained by, the Government of India. Also the Agreement provided that the Nepal Eastern Canal and the Nepal Western Canal would be completed, as far as possible, within one year of the completion of the barrage.[19]

Because the Kosi Project had raised the notion of sovereignty and aroused Nepalese nationalism to its extreme, the Gandak Agreement stipulated clearly that nothing in the Agreement was deemed to derogate from the sovereignty and territorial jurisdiction of the Nepalese Government in respect of lands it had acquired and made available to the Government of India for investigation, execution and maintenance of the Project.

3. Power Development and Reservation for Nepal

Under the Agreement, India agreed to construct one power house with an installed capacity of 15,000 kW in the territory of Nepal on the Main Western Canal. It also agreed to construct a transmission line from the power house in Nepal to the Bihar border near Bhaisalotan and from Sagauli to Raxaul in Bihar in order to facilitate the supply of power on any point in the Bihar Grid up to and including Raxaul. India agreed to supply power to Nepal at the power house and/or at any point in the grid up to and including Raxaul to an aggregate maximum of 10,000 kW up to 60 percent load factor at power factor not below 0.85. The charges for supply at the power

---

[17] Article 5 (iii).

[18] *See* Article 5 (v). Through another Exchange of Letters signed on April 30, 1964 (the 1964 Amendment), Article 7 (v) was amended and Nepal was permitted to operate the Don branch canal in such a manner as to ensure the flow of adequate water in Nepal Eastern Canal for irrigation requirements. The earlier Agreement did not provide for Nepal to operate the flow of water in the canal. Moreover, a supplemental Agreement executed between Nepal and India in October 1971 specifies that 24.1 m³/sec (850 cusecs) of water would be delivered through the Don branch canal to the Nepal border at all times, except when under necessary repair and maintenance.

[19] Article 7 (iv).

house were to be the actual cost of production, and on any point on the grid up to Raxaul it was to be the cost of production plus the cost of transmission on mutually agreed terms and conditions.[20]

The Government of Nepal, on the other hand, was made responsible for the construction and cost of the transmission and distribution system for supply of power within Nepal from the power house or from any point on the grid up to and including Raxaul.[21]

It was further agreed that the ownership and management of the power house shall be transferred to Nepal on one year's notice in writing given by Nepal to India after the full load of 10,000 kW at 60 percent load factor had been developed in Nepal from this power house. It is interesting to note in this context that the Letter exchanged recorded an understanding that for a period of 15 years after obtaining the ownership and management of the power house Nepal would continue to generate secondary power to the full extent possible and supply it to India on payment of its actual cost of production. The ownership of the transmission system built by India vested in the Government of India, but on transfer of the power house the Government of India was to continue the arrangements for transmission of power, if so desired by Nepal, on payment of the cost of transmission. However, the Agreement granted Nepal the right to purchase the transmission system from the power house to Bhaisalotan situated in the Nepalese territory on payment of the original cost minus depreciation. India was free to regulate the flow into or close the main western canal head regulator temporarily, if such works were found to be necessary in the interest of the efficient maintenance and operation of the Canal or the power house, provided that in such situations India agreed to supply the minimum essential power from the Bihar grid to the extent possible on mutually agreed terms and conditions.

4. Water Allocation for Irrigation in Nepal

In accordance with the Agreement, the Nepalese Government continues to have the right to withdraw for irrigation or any other purpose from the river or its tributaries in Nepal such supplies of water as may be required from time to time.[22] Nepal, on its part, agrees not to exercise this right in such manner as is likely to prejudicially affect the water requirements of the Project. Such requirements were set out in a Schedule to the Agreement (Table 4.1).

---

[20] Article 8 (iii).

[21] Article 8 (iv).

[22] In 1964, Article 9 of the Agreement was amended. The amendment provides for the exclusive right of Nepal to withdraw for irrigation or for any other purpose, from the river or its tributaries in Nepal, such supplies of water as may be required from time to time. The amendment, however, restricts the trans-valley use of Gandak water by Nepal during the months from February to April. Ironically, the first part of the amendment affirms Nepal's right to use any amount of water while the latter part restricts Nepal from utilizing the same for trans-valley uses during certain periods of the year. *See* for detail, Thapa and Pradhan, *supra* note 7, at 207.

Table 4.1
Water Allocation for Irrigation in Nepal Under the Gandak Agreement

Month	Western Canal System and Power House in Nepal	Eastern Canal System and Power House in Nepal	Total (in cusecs)
January	6,960	4,540	11,500
February	6,100	3,900	10,000
March	5,960	3,690	9,650
April	5,760	4,340	10,100
May	8,270	7,980	16,250
June	11,190	14,000	25,190
July	15,240	13,980	29,220
August	14,980	14,000	28,980
September	14,980	14,000	28,980
October	16,060	14,110	30,170
November	11,070	13,240	24,310
December	10,410	9,290	19,700

Source: Schedule to the Agreement.

The Letter exchanged recorded the understanding that if, at any time because of natural causes, the supplies in the river are insufficient, the Nepalese Government will be entitled to continue to withdraw water sufficient for the irrigation of such area.[23] Whenever the supply of water available for irrigation falls short of the requirements of the total area under the Project for which irrigation has to be provided the shortage shall be shared on pro rata basis between the two countries.[24]

As noted above, the Agreement has maintained an ominous silence as far as the Project's irrigation prospects for India were concerned. However, later developments revealed that India had actually been irrigating more than two million hectares as opposed to a few hundred in Nepal.[25] Not surprisingly, this kind of discrepancy was to be foreseen and will continue to grow, not only because of the size of India but also because the irrigation system on the Indian side operates at optimum level whereas the irrigation system on the Nepalese side is totally dependent on water controlled by India.[26]

5. Dispute Resolution Mechanism

Any dispute or difference arising out of or in any way touching or concerning the construction, effect or meaning of the Agreement, or of any matter pertaining to the

---

[23] Paragraph (f) of the Letter.
[24] Article 10. It should be noted that this article was later deleted in 1964.
[25] Aditya Man Shrestha, *supra* note 6, at 169.
[26] *Id.*

Project, or the respective rights and liabilities of the two parties, if not settled by discussion, shall be determined through arbitration. Any of the parties may by notice in writing inform the other party of its intention to refer to arbitration any such dispute or difference mentioned above, and within 90 days of the delivery of such notice each of the two parties shall nominate an arbitrator for jointly determining such dispute or difference and the award of the arbitrators shall be binding on the parties. In case the arbitrators are unable to agree, the parties may consult each other and appoint an umpire whose award shall be final and binding on them.

Like in the Kosi Agreement, despite the details provided by the Gandak Agreement, the arbitration mechanism may not give complete satisfaction because the provision is defective in two respects. First, there is no provision for the appointment of an arbitrator if one of the states concerned fails to nominate a member of the arbitration panel. Second, if the two arbitrators fail to agree on the disposition of the issue in dispute, the two parties then may "consult each other and appoint an umpire whose award shall be final and binding on them." In other words there is no obligation to appoint an umpire. Thus a desire to submit an issue to arbitration by one party to the agreement can easily be frustrated by the other.[27]

6. Coordination Committee

In the context of the Gandak Project, a coordination committee was also provided for in the Letter exchanged.[28] Both the governments agreed to set up a Coordination Committee consisting of three representatives of each government, including a minister. The Nepalese Government would be its Chairman and the Chief administrator would be its secretary. The Committee is to meet from time to time to consider such matters of common interest concerning the Project as referred to by either government with a view to expedite decisions for the early completion of the Project. The Government of India agreed to bear all expenditure in connection with the functioning of the Committee, such as salaries of special staff, travel allowance for members, and the like. This Committee, since the inception of the Project, is recorded to have had six meetings. The last meeting was held on December 22-23, 1980. Some of the main issues deliberated in the meetings included, *inter alia*, (a) royalty and collections of stones; (b) location of Nepal power house; (c) alignment of main western canal and western guide bund in Nepalese territory; (d) customs duty exemption on materials required for the project; (e) deposit of the royalty and land compensation; (f) river training works in Nepal; (g) irrigation of the additional 5,000 hectares of land near the main western canal; (h) navigation provisions in the river; (i) transmission line from the power house to feed Nepalese system; (j) follow up of Nepal power house construction; (k) compensation for land to be acquired for Nepal eastern canal; (l) cropping pattern in Nepal western canal; (m) proposed extension of Nepal western canal; (n) handing over of Surajpura power

---

[27] *See* Charles B. Bourne, "Nepal's International Water Resources and International Law," Report No. 6/4/280696/1/1 Seq.No.492, HMG, Water and Energy Commission Secretariat, at 35-36.

[28] Gandak Coordination Committee, *see* paragraph (g) of the Letter.

house; (o) water management in the Project area; (p) construction of channels below 20 cusecs capacity in Nepal western and eastern canals; (q) power tariff for electric supply to Tribeni bazaar and adjoining villages; and (r) augmenting water flow in Gandak River during the lean season.[29]

III. Conclusion

In order to appreciate the merits of the Gandak Agreement, it is important to compare it with the Kosi Agreement because there are numerous interesting differences between the two, and particularly because both were entered into with relatively similar objectives. Although not completely immune from shortcomings and criticisms, the provisions of the Gandak Agreement, from Nepal's perspective, certainly compare favorably with those of the Kosi Agreement. For instance, while Article 4 of the Kosi Agreement gave Nepal 50 percent share of the hydroelectric power that India generated as a result of the Project, it did not require India to produce any power. In fact, India has not generated any such power, thus depriving Nepal of the promised benefit. Again Article 10 of the Kosi Agreement stipulated that provision shall be made for free and unrestricted navigation at and around the barrage "if technically feasible," the qualifying conditional words providing a justification for India's doing nothing about navigation as required by the Article.

Article 8 of the Gandak Agreement, on the other hand, requires India to construct a power house in Nepal with a specified installed capacity, as well as a transmission line from the power house, and to supply a certain amount of power to Nepal at the actual cost of production. Similarly, in the case of navigation, by Article 5 (iii), India is required to provide locking arrangements for facility of riverine traffic across the barrage free from payment of any tolls whatever. India's obligations are not conditional; a failure to perform them would constitute a breach of the Agreement.

With regard to compensation for Nepal for the land that it transfers to India for Project purposes, Article 3 (i) and (ii) requires India to pay "reasonable compensation." With the exchange of Letter contemporaneous with the Agreement, the parties agreed to establish a committee of experts to set the rates. This would be a single payment in the nature of a purchase price. But unlike the Kosi Agreement, the Gandak Agreement, in Article 3 (iii), also provided that the lands vested in India as proprietor would be subject to payment of land revenue at the rates at which it is leviable on agricultural land in the neighborhood. This provision means that India is required to pay land taxes similar to those payable by any other proprietor of lands in the area. Based on this interpretation, Article 3 (iii) provides Nepal a measure of protection against inflation, for the land taxes payable by India will escalate along with the land values and tax rates applicable to the area.

In the matter of irrigation, the Gandak Agreement details India's obligations to build the canal works that will make possible extensive irrigation in Nepal. It also stipulates that the canal systems situated in Nepal (except the Main Western Canal)

---

[29] *See* for detail, Thapa and Pradhan, *supra* note 7, at 210-211.

shall be handed over to Nepal for operation and maintenance at cost. This contrasts sharply with the Kosi Agreement, which contains no provision on irrigation works for the benefit of Nepal.

On the issue of the barrage location, the Indian Ambassador to Nepal recently highlighted the rationale while emphasizing the obvious and direct benefits accruing to Nepal. At the outset one should note that the Bihar Government, because of the difficulty experienced with Kosi, was unwilling to have its Project in Nepal, to avoid any hassles. But ultimately a decision to build the barrage in Nepal was taken, and as a result Nepal also gained some irrigation potential, with India getting 3,400,000 hectares. If the Project was built in India, then instead of the 3,400,000 hectares that India gets by having the Project in Nepal, India would have received 2,900,000 hectares, but by having this Project inside India, there would have been no benefit to Nepal at all.[30]

It is a question of fact whether the benefits received by Nepal under the Gandak Agreement represent a reasonable and equitable share of the benefits to be derived from the project. The Agreement seems to confer substantial benefits on Nepal, but to judge their adequacy one would need the information that would allow balancing the costs and benefits of the Project for both the parties, an exercise that remains extremely difficult, if not impossible in the circumstances.

Another interesting element of the Gandak Agreement, particularly in comparison with the Kosi Agreement, is related to the ownership of land. In the Gandak Agreement, India owns the land acquired for the project, whereas under the Kosi Agreement it holds the land under a lease. For practical purposes, this is not significant because the term of the lease is 199 years. The terms of the Kosi Agreement are fixed at 199 years commencing on December 19, 1966, whereas there is no fixed term for the Gandak Agreement. In the Gandak case, thus, there is the possibility of the termination of the Agreement after the expiry of a reasonable time for the accomplishment of its purposes. What is reasonable time in the context of irrigation schemes would likely be a controversial question. A fixed term or at least some mechanism for review if not termination for this type of agreement would have been desirable.

There are also some other complaints, particularly from the Nepalese side.[31] The Gandak Agreement, like the Kosi Agreement, was wholly financed by India in the Nepalese territory. The benefits to Nepal have not been commensurate with the social costs it had to incur. It has been acknowledged that the social cost of submergence of the land behind the barrages and the rehabilitation of the displaced population, coupled with the economic costs of the natural resources involved in erecting the monumental structures, was quite significant.[32] Indeed, the Kosi and the

---

[30] Comment by H. E. Ambassador of India, Deb Mukharji, Face to Face Program, Reporter Club, 26 May, 2001.

[31] *See* Report prepared by Development Law Inc. Nepal, for WECS, "A Review of Existing Nepalese Laws, Policies and Practices on Land Acquisition, Compensation, Resettlement and Rehabilitation," Vol. 1, July 24, 1998, at 25-26.

[32] *See id.*

Gandak Projects both involved substantial submergence of scarce agricultural land, coupled with the problem of rehabilitation of displaced people, an issue that has neither been studied in depth to assess the full costs nor resolved fully to date. Some displaced people have still not been compensated even after four decades, and some resettled people seem to still suffer.[33]

Several obvious shortcomings notwithstanding, the conclusion of the Gandak Agreement, like the Kosi Agreement, should be considered in perspective. At a time when the international water rights were essentially based on customary law for which the importance of rivers related mainly to consumptive use, it was laudable to have attempted to tackle issues pertaining to non-consumptive use of water.

One final note: Although generally several problems have occurred in the course of the implementation of the Agreement, which had to be remedied on punctual bases, and not without tension, it is safe to mention that the Gandak Agreement seems appropriate for achieving the purposes envisaged by the two countries. In particular, from Nepal's viewpoint, it adequately safeguards its rights and interests in the water resources of this river in its territory. Certainly, many other items could have been captured, and confusion and incompleteness continue to exist, which are primarily due to the lack of experience on the Nepalese side in dealing with issues of water, as well as the unclear position of international law at the time of the negotiations of the Agreement. But the weaknesses resulting from the lack of experience, in the course of time, improved substantially, and during the period that followed, Nepal maintained a very cautious approach. This relatively grown maturity will be noticed in the context of negotiations of a Treaty in connection with the Mahakali River, which is discussed in the next chapter.

---

[33] *Id.*, at 26.

CHAPTER 5

The Mahakali River

I. Introduction and History

In February 1996, India and Nepal entered into the Mahakali River Treaty (the Mahakali Treaty).[1] This is a Treaty of significant importance because it sets forth the foundation for an integrated approach to water resources development and use between the two countries regarding the Mahakali River.

The Mahakali River begins where two rivers, the Kali River originating in the Taklakot area in the east, and the Kuthi-Yankti River originating in the Zanskar range of the Himalayas, meet at Kawa Malla in the Darchula District in Nepal. The merging of the Kali and Kuthi-Yankti Rivers is known as the Mahakali River. The Mahakali River flows southwest, where it makes numerous oxbow lakes and is joined by many tributaries, the largest of which are the Chamlia River and the Chavandigad River.[2] The Mahakali River drains an area of 188 sq. km. in Nepal. The average discharge of water recorded from the river is 7,288 cubic meters per second (cumec), while the maximum discharge amount is 121 cumec. The maximum annual discharge from the river is 1,066 cumec.[3]

The Mahakali River serves as a western boundary for long distances between Nepal and India along the border of the Indian State of Uttar Pradesh. It is called the Sarada River in India, and after it is joined by the Ghaghra River in the State of Uttar Pradesh, it is called the Ghaghra River. The Ghaghra River continues to flow eastward, and joins the Ganges River immediately after crossing the State of Uttar Pradesh in the State of Bihar.[4] The Mahakali River is an international river that flows from Nepal into India, and also serves as a boundary for large distances between these two countries. With respect to the Mahakali River, therefore, the problems of defining rights and obligations are further complicated and intensified.

---

[1] Treaty Between His Majesty's Government of Nepal and the Government of India Concerning the Integrated Development of the Mahakali River Including Sarada Barrage, Tanakpur Barrage and Pancheshwar Project. For the full text of the Treaty *see*, 36 I.L.M. 531 (1997). For a general discussion of the Treaty, *See* Salman M. A. Salman and Kishor Uprety, "Hydro-Politics in South Asia: A Comparative Analysis of the Mahakali and the Ganges Treaties," *Natural Resources Journal* 39 (1999), at 295-343.

[2] N. B. Thapa, *Geography of Nepal: Physical, Economic, Cultural and Regional* (Bombay: Orient Longmans, 1969), at 24.

[3] *See*, Chandra K. Sharma, *Geology of Nepal* (Kathmandu: Sangeeta Sharma, 1973), at 16.

[4] For detail *see*, A. R. Rao and T. Prasad, "Water Resources Development of the Indo-Nepal Region," *Water Resources Development* 10 (1994), at 160-161.

1. The Sarada Treaty

The efforts toward exploitation of the Mahakali River waters began before India's independence from Britain.[5] The British Government in India formalized with its Nepalese counterpart in 1920, the negotiations of the Sarada Treaty in the form of an Exchange of Letters.[6] The Treaty provided for the construction of a barrage on the Mahakali River (which is known as the Sarada River in India) at Banbassa bordering the present Mahendra Nagar in Nepal. The Treaty also provided for the construction of a power station at Khatima in connection with the Sarada Canal Project[7] in the State of Uttar Pradesh in India. Under the Sarada Treaty, the Government of Nepal agreed to exchange 4,000 acres of its territory for construction purposes with an equal amount of land from the British Indian Government.[8] Nepal also obtained the right to use a minimum of 400 cubic feet per second (cusecs) and a maximum of 1,000 cusecs of water from the Sarada Canal for irrigation purposes.[9] This land exchange placed the location of the left abutment of the weir and the left bank works within Indian territory. The headwork (the containing bank) of the Sarada Canal is situated a few miles below the point where the river emerges from the hills and forms part of the boundary between India and Nepal. The British Indian Government built the Banbassa Barrage across the Sarada River.

Despite the conclusion of the Sarada Treaty, Nepal was not entirely satisfied with the quantum of water of 400 cusecs it had obtained under this Treaty, and tried continuously to obtain an increase over the guaranteed flow of 400 cusecs. Its efforts constantly failed and because of shortage of water, it was hindered in developing one upstream project.[10] Amidst this tug of war between the two countries on the quantum of water allocated to Nepal, the regime established by the Sarada Treaty continued to exist for 76 years, from 1920 to 1996, when it was replaced by the Mahakali Treaty.[11]

2. The Tanakpur Agreement

In the spirit of furthering cooperation within the Mahakali River area, the Governments of India and Nepal entered into a Memorandum of Understanding (MOU), commonly referred to as the Tanakpur Agreement, on December 6, 1991.[12]

---

[5] B. C. Upreti, *Politics of Himalayan River Waters: An Analysis of the River Water Issues of Nepal, India and Bangladesh* (Delhi: Nirala Publication, 1993), at 94.

[6] The text of the Letter of Exchange dated August 23, 1920 and October 12, 1920 (the Sarada Treaty) is located in the Nepal National Archives (copy on file with authors).

[7] The Sarada Canal Project for the irrigation of about a million acres in Uttar Pradesh was started in 1915 and completed in 1926.

[8] Paragraph 2 of the Sarada Treaty, *supra* note 6.

[9] *Id.*, paragraph 1.

[10] The project is called the Mahakali Irrigation Project, a mega-project that was later also called the Pancheshwar Project. The Project was expected to generate 2,000 MW and provide irrigation benefits. *See infra.*

[11] For discussions, *see infra.*

[12] Memorandum of Understanding on Tanakpur Barrage Project, December 6, 1991, signed by

Map 4: The Mahakali River Basin

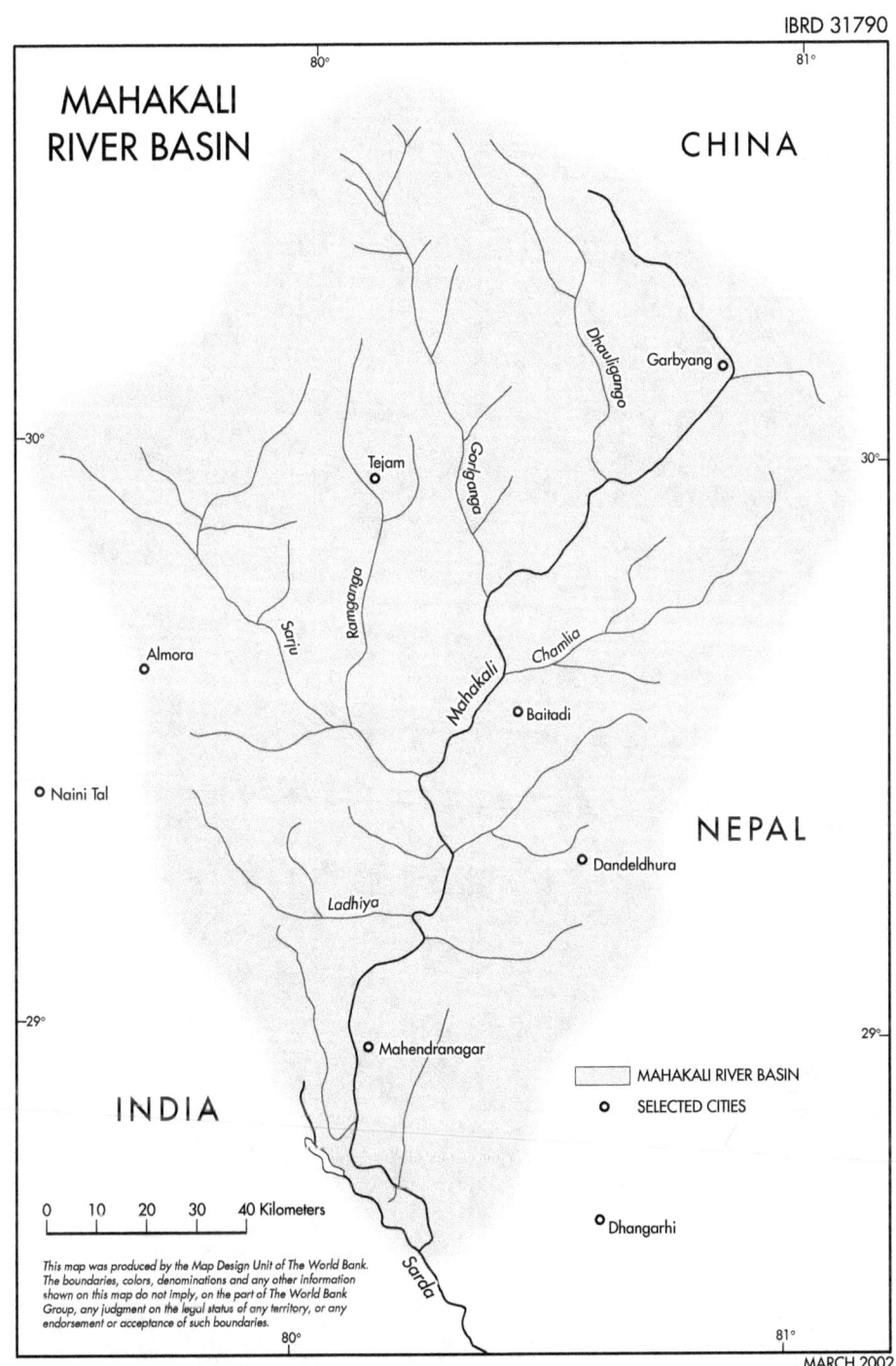

The Agreement provided for the construction of the left afflux bund (the retaining wall) on Nepalese territory for which the Nepalese provided 2.9 hectares of land. Unlike the Sarada Treaty, however, the Tanakpur Agreement did not provide for an even exchange of land from India. The Agreement, instead, provided for the installation of a head regulator (main part of the reservoir regulating the water flow) at the Tanakpur Barrage with a capacity of 1,000 cusecs, and required India to construct a canal so that 150 cusecs of water could be delivered to Nepal. India was further required to provide Nepal with 10 megawatts of electricity. The Tanakpur Agreement also stated that when there was an increase in the water supply at the Pancheshwar Reservoir, the supply of water to Nepal would also be increased. The provision of water and electricity by India to Nepal was seen as the *quid pro quo* to Nepal for providing India with 2.9 hectares of its land needed to construct the afflux bund.[13]

In hindsight, however, entering into the Tanakpur Agreement with India in December 1991 now seems like a hasty decision. The Nepalese Government, led by Prime Minister Girija Koirala, either did not appreciate the legal, socioeconomic, and political ramifications involved in the issue, or decided to overlook them to appease India.[14] The deal, which relinquished 2.9 hectares of Nepalese land to India to build a dam and a 120-megawatt power station in return for a share of the water and power, was immediately criticized by most of Nepal's opposing political parties.[15]

The issues raised in the objections dealt primarily with a concern for Nepalese territorial sovereignty and a belief that Nepal had not benefited from the Project as much as India had. Those opposing the agreement argued that because the agreement dealt with natural resources it fell under the articles of the Constitution and required ratification by a two-thirds majority of Parliament.[16] A writ petition was filed in the Supreme Court, with the Prime Minister as one of the respondents, chal-

---

Maheshwar Prasad Singh, Nepalese Minister of Law and Justice, and Madhav Singh Solonki, Indian Foreign Minister (hereinafter referred to as MOU or Tanakpur Agreement). The MOU has been published in Nepali in Nepal Gazette of January 1992. (Copy on file with authors.)

[13] A. T. S. Ahmed, "Challenges of Governance in Nepal: Politico-Economic and Ethno-Religious Dimensions," *Journal of Contemporary Asia* 24 (1994), at 360-362. see also generally, Stephen C. McCaffrey, "Water, Politics and International Law," in *Water in Crisis: A Guide to the World's Fresh Water Resources,* Peter H. Gleick, ed. (Oxford University Press, 1993), at 95; *see* also Ramjee P. Parajulee, *The Democratic Transition in Nepal* (Lanham, Maryland: Rowman and Littlefield, 2000) at 274-275.

[14] *Id.,* at 360.

[15] *Id., see* also Dipak Gyewali and Othmar Schwank, "Interstate Sharing of Water Rights: An Alps-Himalaya Comparison," in *Water Nepal,* Ajaya Dixit, ed. (1994), Vol. 4, No. 1, at 233-235; *see* also generally, Govind D. Shrestha, *"Himalayan Waters: Need for a Positive Indo-Nepal Cooperation,"* in *Water Nepal,* Ajaya Dixit, ed. (1994), Vol. 4, No. 1, at 268-269.

[16] According to Article 126 of the Constitution of Nepal, ratification of, accession to, acceptance of, or approval of treaties or agreements regarding natural resources and the distribution of their uses are to be approved by a two-thirds majority of the members present at a joint sitting of both houses of the Parliament. *See* Article 126 (2) (d) of the Constitution of Nepal (1990) (hereinafter the Constitution).

lenging the validity of the Tanakpur Agreement.[17] The petitioner maintained that the agreement should have been presented to Parliament for ratification prior to its enforcement in accordance with the provisions of the Constitution.[18]

The Prime Minister argued that the decision to give 2.9 hectares of land to India was merely part of a memorandum of understanding, signed by the Nepalese Minister of Law and Justice and the Indian Foreign Minister, and therefore was not a "Treaty" that was subject to the Constitutional provisions requiring ratification.[19] This argument, however, was rejected by most of the Nepalese who saw the Tanakpur Agreement as another concession to India regarding water resources issues.[20] Gradually the circumstances surrounding the Tanakpur Agreement became more complex and controversial. The Supreme Court issued its verdict in December 1992, and concluded that the Tanakpur Agreement was, indeed, a Treaty that required ratification by the Parliament, and was not a mere Memorandum of Understanding.[21]

It is worth noting that on water resources issues, the political parties in Nepal hold sharply contrasting views. This controversy has had a snowball effect on the political climate in Nepal and continues to polarize the political parties on the issue of nationalism. The Tanakpur controversy did not recede, especially because of division among political forces in the country and India's "no-negotiation" posture on the matter. Reportedly, Indian External Affairs Minister Dinesh Singh's cryptic statement that "Everything hinges on Tanakpur" loomed larger than was generally recognized.[22]

When the then Prime Minister of India, Narasimha Rao, visited Nepal in October 1992, he also made it clear that India would not change its stance on the Tanakpur issue. The water resources issues, and particularly the Tanakpur issue, became the most formidable challenge that has since rocked the succeeding Governments in Nepal.[23] The Tanakpur Agreement has never formally been ratified because the government has not presented it to the Parliament.[24] Ironically, however, by the time the Supreme Court verdict was rendered, the physical work at the Tanakpur area, par-

---

[17] B. K. Neupane vs Prime Minister of Nepal. Nepal Supreme Court Writ No. 1851 (1992).

[18] The petition invoked Article 126 (2) (d) of the Constitution. *See supra* note 16 and accompanying text.

[19] The Vienna Convention on the Law of Treaties, 1980, defines in Article 2.1 (a) the term *treaty* as "an international agreement concluded between States in written form and governed by international law, whether embodied in a single instrument or in two or more related instruments and whatever its particular designation." As such the Tanakpur Agreement would qualify as a treaty under international law.

[20] *See* generally, Ahmed *supra* note 13, at 361.

[21] *See* Ahmed, *supra* note 13, at 361.

[22] Ahmed, *supra* note 13, at 362.

[23] *Id.,* on Tanakpur issues from a political angle, *see* also generally, Rishikesh Shah, "Politics of Water in Nepal," in *Water Nepal,* Ajaya Dixit, ed. (1994), Vol. 4, No.1, at 282-290.

[24] *See* Krishna B. Bhattachan, "Nepal in 1993: Business as Usual," *Asian Survey* 34 (1994), at 177.

ticularly on the Nepalese side, was almost completed. Further discussion on the issue had, therefore, become moot.

II. The Mahakali Treaty Regime

It is important to point out at the outset of this section that the Mahakali Treaty emphasizes an integrated approach to the development of water resources and, more importantly, attempts to validate past activities taken to develop water resources on the Mahakali River.

1. Integrated Approach to Water Resources Development

Because of the contemporary political climate, the need to validate past activities carried out under the Tanakpur Agreement and the need to improve the Mahakali water sharing arrangements became pressing.[25] It is important for the purposes of this discussion to understand that the Mahakali water sharing arrangements were governed primarily by the Sarada Treaty, which was entered into when the political status of India and the needs of the two countries were different. Indeed, while India was under British rule at the time, the population of Nepal was small in size with a relatively low demand for water, and as such, water sharing did not get the same priority that it does today.

Considering the embedded views of both sides on the Tankapur controversy, it took five years of negotiations after the Tanakpur agreement was concluded before the foreign ministers of India and Nepal, Mr. Pranab Mukherjee and Mr. Prakash C. Lohani respectively, were able on January 29, 1996, to initial a Treaty between the two countries for the integrated development of water resources on the Mahakali River. Two weeks later, on February 12, 1996, the Mahakali Treaty was signed by the then Prime Minister of India Mr. P. V. Narasimha Rao, and the then Prime Minister of Nepal, Mr. Sher B. Deuba.[26]

The Mahakali Treaty deals with three projects related to water resources: the Sarada Barrage, the Tanakpur Barrage, and the Pancheshwar Multipurpose Project. Of these, it should be noted, the works at the Sarada Barrage and the Tanakpur Barrage were completed in 1920 and 1992 respectively. The Mahakali Treaty absorbed the regime established by the Sarada Treaty, validated the controversial Tanakpur Agreement,[27] and endorsed the idea of a new multipurpose project, the details of which, at the time of its conclusion, still needed to be worked out.[28]

---

[25] See *supra* notes 20-23, and accompanying text.

[26] The Mahakali Treaty was signed in two originals each in Hindi, Nepali and English languages, all the texts being equally authentic, and the English text prevailing, in case of doubt.

[27] As a consequence to the conclusion of the Mahakali Treaty, the earlier understandings reached between India and Nepal, in the context of the Sarada Treaty and the Tanakpur agreement, concerning the utilization of the waters of the Mahakali River from the Sarada Barrage and the Tanakpur Barrage have been replaced. The content of the previous agreements have been incorporated in the Mahakali Treaty. *See* Article 12.1 of the Mahakali Treaty.

[28] *See* the preamble and Article 3 of the Mahakali Treaty.

The Treaty is a first in many ways, primarily in laying down the principle that as a boundary river on large stretches,[29] the Mahakali River will be developed in an integrated way to maximize the total net benefit from such development. Both parties will, in theory, be entitled to equal benefits, and will thus share the costs in proportion to the share of benefits they actually receive. These principles, self-evident though they may be, were not observed in earlier agreements between India and Nepal, including the two existing projects on the Mahakali River itself, the Sarada and Tanakpur Barrages, located downstream from the site of the proposed Pancheshwar Dam.

The Mahakali Treaty, however, has also engendered a wide spectrum of debate within various segments of India's and Nepal's populations concerning the enchantments and disenchantments over the conclusion of the Treaty, the numerous hidden political agendas, environmental concerns, and strategic choices with respect to the location of the dam and the actual components of water sharing contained in the Treaty. Addressing all the aspects of the debate is beyond the scope of this chapter. Instead of dwelling on controversial political issues, this chapter will concentrate on the analysis of the content of the Mahakali Treaty.

A. Declaratory Provisions

The preamble of the Mahakali Treaty is quite comprehensive. It stresses the determination of India and Nepal to promote and strengthen their relations of friendship and close neighborliness for cooperation in the development of water resources. Most importantly, it recognizes that the Mahakali River is a boundary river on major stretches between the two countries, and focuses on the need of the two countries to enter into a Treaty on the basis of equal partnership to define their obligations and corresponding rights and duties thereto with regard to the utilization of the waters of the Mahakali River.[30]

Moreover, the preamble references several existing instruments, namely (i) the Exchange of Letters of 1920 through which both the parties had entered into an arrangement for the construction of the Sarada Barrage in the Mahakali River,[31] (ii) the decision taken by the Indo-Nepal Joint Commission[32] dated December 4-5, 1991

---

[29] As discussed earlier, international law, in terms of additional rights or duties, does not draw any legal distinction between boundary rivers and successive rivers. The same rules of international law apply to both types of rivers. This has been concluded by the Permanent Court of International Justice in the *River Oder* case. *See* for detail, *The International Commission of the River Oder*, P.C.I.J., ser A, No. 23, at 5, 27 (1929).

[30] *See* preamble of the Mahakali Treaty.

[31] *Supra* note 6 and accompanying text.

[32] The reference to the Indo-Nepal Joint Commission is found in the preamble of the Mahakali Treaty and concerns the Joint-Commission established pursuant to an agreement (Agreement Between His Majesty's Government of Nepal and the Government of the Republic of India on the Setting Up of a Joint Commission), dated June 20,1987 (on file with authors), for the purpose of strengthening mutual understanding and reinforcing bilateral relations and cooperation in various fields. It aims at covering a series of issues (economic, transit, trade, industry as well as water). This observation becomes relevant to the extent that the India-Bangladesh Joint Rivers

and the Joint Communiqué issued during the visit of the Prime Minister of India to Nepal on October 21, 1992 regarding the Tanakpur Barrage,[33] and finally (iii) a detailed Project report regarding the Pancheshwar Multipurpose Project (PMP) that India and Nepal intended to prepare and that was to be implemented on the Mahakali River.[34] In this context, it is worth noting that the Mahakali Treaty does not mention the controversial MOU of December 1991. The critical decision of the Nepalese Supreme Court on this MOU could have been the main reason why this MOU was not specifically mentioned in the preamble to the Treaty.[35]

The Mahakali Treaty provides a false impression that the two governments have taken a "basin approach" to water resource management.[36] However, given the fact that the considerations used to negotiate the Treaty were limited to the tributaries covered by the future Pancheshwar Multipurpose Project (PMP), and that this initial investigation was limited in its examination of other water resource management options, it is clear that the Treaty only seeks to develop water resources at the Pancheshwar Barrage.[37] From a structural viewpoint, the Mahakali Treaty, in fact, combines three distinct agreements, the Sarada Treaty, the Tanakpur Agreement and the PMP, insofar as the principle for sharing water and electricity between India and Nepal is concerned.

B. Status of Sarada and Tanakpur Barrages

The first part of the Mahakali Treaty deals with the Sarada Barrage. Accordingly, Nepal shall have the right to a supply of 1,000 cusecs of water from the Sarada Barrage in the wet season, that is from May 15 to October 15, and 150 cusecs in the dry season, that is from October 16 to May 14.[38] Moreover, India is required to maintain a flow of not less than 350 cusecs downstream of the Sarada Barrage in the Mahakali River to maintain and preserve the river ecosystem.[39]

Section 1.03 of the Mahakali Treaty provides assurances to Nepal that in case the Sarada Barrage becomes nonfunctional due to any cause, Nepal shall continue to have the right to a supply of 1,000 cusecs of water by using the head regulator(s) constructed by India near the left undersluice (an artificial passage of water fitted with a gate for stopping or regulating flow) of the Tanakpur Barrage. This supply of water shall be over and above the amount of water agreed upon by the Treaty to be supplied to Nepal. Moreover, in this case, India is also required to maintain the river

---

Commission (*see infra*) has a completely different legal status and specific mandate.

[33] *Supra* note 12, and accompanying text.

[34] *See* the preamble of the Mahakali Treaty.

[35] *See supra* note 21 and accompanying text.

[36] A basin approach is where the basin is looked upon as having no international boundaries, and planning concepts are applied to the basin as a whole.

[37] Deepak Gyewali, "Ke Ke Chan Dosh Mahakali Sandhi Ma" (The Mistakes of the Mahakali Treaty) in Mulyankan, Vol. 41, 1997, at 39.

[38] Mahakali Treaty, Section 1.1.

[39] *Id.*, Section 1.2.

flow from the tailrace (the race for conveying water away from the turbine after use) of the Tanakpur Power Station downstream of the Sarada Barrage.[40]

The second part of the Mahakali Treaty deals with the Tanakpur Barrage. According to Article 2, in continuation of the decisions taken in the Joint Commission dated December 4-5, 1991, and the Joint Communique issued during the visit of the Prime Minister of India to Nepal on October 21, 1992, India and Nepal agreed to carry out some work in the area. This work includes the construction of the eastern afflux bund of the Tanakpur Barrage at Jimuwa and tying it up to the high ground in the Nepalese territory at an elevation level of 250 meters. For this purpose, Nepal agreed to let India use a portion of its land consisting of about 577 meters in length (an area of about 2.9 hectares) in its territory at the Jimuwa Village in Mahendranagar Municipal Area and a certain portion of the "no-man's land" on either side of the border. The Mahakali Treaty explicitly states that this land, and a tract of about nine hectares of land to the West up to the Indo-Nepalese border, continue to remain under the sovereignty and control of Nepal, and that Nepal would continue to be free to exercise all attendant rights thereto.[41]

In lieu of construction of the eastern afflux bund of the Tanakpur Barrage at Jimuwa, Nepal obtained the right to a supply of 1000 cusecs of water during the wet season[42] and 300 cusecs of water during the dry season.[43] For this purpose, as well as for the purpose of supplying water from the Sarada Barrage, India agreed to construct the head regulator(s) near the left undersluice of the Tanakpur Barrage and to build waterways with appropriate water capacity all the way to the Indo-Nepalese border. Such head regulator(s) and waterways are to be operated jointly by India and Nepal.[44]

In this context, it is worth adding that, pursuant to the Letter exchanged between the Prime Ministers of India and Nepal on the day the Treaty was signed, India also agreed to complete an all-weather road connecting the Tanakpur Barrage to the east-west highway at Mahendranagar in Nepal within one year of the effective date of the Mahakali Treaty.[45]

Regarding electricity, Nepal is entitled to an annual supply of 70 million kilowatt-hours on a continuous basis free of cost, from the effective date of the Mahakali Treaty. For this purpose, India agreed to construct a 132 kV transmission line all the

---

[40] *Id.,* Section 1.03.

[41] *Id.,* Section 2.1.

[42] The wet season is the period starting May 15 and ending October 15.

[43] The dry season is the period starting October 16 and ending May 14.

[44] Section 2.2 (a) of the Mahakali Treaty.

[45] Paragraph 1 of the Letter of Exchange dated February 12, 1996, between the Prime Minster of Nepal and the Prime Minister of India (hereinafter the Letter). For the full text of the Letter, *see,* 36 I.L.M. 544 (1997). The Letter was originally sent by the Prime Minister of Nepal, and on the same date the Prime Minister of India acknowledged and confirmed that the Letter correctly set out the agreement made between the two governments.

way to the Indo-Nepalese border from the Tanakpur Power Station.[46] The Letter further clarified that the annual supply of 20 million kilowatt-hours of electricity, free of cost, to Nepal from the Tanakpur Power Station, as provided for in the Mahakali Treaty, shall be reconciled with the energy procured or to be procured by Nepal from India under the existing power exchange arrangements. This supply of electricity was previously authorized by the Joint Communique beginning when the Tanakpur Power Station was commissioned in July 7, 1992, and was to remain in effect until the power station was able to meet its expected annual supply of 70 million kilowatt-hours of electricity.[47]

The Mahakali Treaty also described the arrangements that would be made at the Tanakpur Barrage at the time of development of any storage project(s) including the Pancheshwar Multipurpose Project upstream of the Tanakpur Barrage.[48] Accordingly, additional head regulators and necessary waterways, as required by the Treaty, up to the Indo-Nepalese border would be constructed to supply additional water to Nepal. Such head regulators and waterways would be operated jointly by both Nepal and India.[49] Moreover, Nepal would have additional energy equal to half of the incremental energy generated from the Tanakpur Power Station on a continuous basis from the date of augmentation of the flow of the Mahakali River. Under the Treaty, Nepal was obligated to bear half of the additional operational costs and, if required, half of the additional capital costs at the Tanakpur Power Station for the generation of this incremental energy.[50]

The possibility of augmentation of the flow of the Mahakali River is mentioned both in the Treaty and the Letter. Because there are no details as to how such augmentation is to take place, one can only assume that the augmentation will be part of the Detailed Project Report.

C. Pancheshwar Multipurpose Project

Although the newly conceived Pancheshwar Multipurpose Project is a very important part of the Mahakali Treaty, it remains a controversial aspect of the Treaty. The

---

[46] Section 2.2 (b) of the Mahakali Treaty. The Tanakpur Barrage has, at the time of its completion, an installed capacity of 120,000 kilowatt generating 448.4 millions kilowatt-hour of energy annually on 90 percent dependable year flow.

[47] Paragraph 2 of the Letter. In this context, it is also useful to note that India and Nepal on June 5, 1997, signed an agreement (The Agreement between HMG of Nepal and the Government of India Concerning the Electric Power Trade) to promote private sector participation in the hydropower projects. The Agreement was signed on the day when the two sides also exchanged instruments of ratification pertaining to the Mahakali Treaty. The Power Trade Agreement was signed by Minister of State for Power, S. Venugopalachari, and Nepal's Minister of State for Water Resources Rajiv Parajuli. The Agreement, which was initialed earlier at Bombay at the Secretaries' level in February 1996, aims particularly at facilitating the entry of the private sectors of both countries in the sale and purchase of power (copy of the Agreement on file with authors).

[48] Mahakali Treaty, Section 2.3.

[49] *Id.*, Section 2.3 (a).

[50] *Id.*, Article 2 (3) (b).

PMP[51] is to be constructed on a stretch of the Mahakali River that forms the boundary between the two countries. The Mahakali Treaty specifies that both India and Nepal have equal entitlement to utilize the waters of the Mahakali River without prejudice to their respective existing consumptive uses.[52] The Mahakali Treaty further specifies that both countries agree to implement the PMP on the Mahakali River in accordance with the Detailed Project Report (DPR) being jointly prepared by the countries.[53]

The Mahakali Treaty also added, in this context, that India would supply 350 cusecs of water for the irrigation of Dodhara-Chandani area in Nepal. The technical and other details regarding this supply need to be agreed upon mutually.[54]

(i) General Principles: Along with the issues of water distribution, power generation, and energy sharing, the Mahakali Treaty established some other general principles. While the water requirements of Nepal are to be given prime consideration,[55] both India and Nepal are entitled to draw their share of waters from the Mahakali River at the Tanakpur Barrage and/or other mutually agreed upon points as provided for by the Mahakali Treaty or any subsequent agreement between the two countries.[56] Moreover, any project, other than the Sarada, the Tanakpur, and the PMP, to be developed on the international boundary area of the Mahakali River in the future will need to be designed and implemented by agreement between the two countries using the principles established by the Mahakali Treaty.[57]

Maintaining the flow and level of water in the Mahakali River is another general principle established by the Mahakali Treaty. According to Article 7, India and Nepal each agreed, except by an agreement between them, not to use, obstruct, or divert the waters of the Mahakali River, so as to adversely affect the natural flow and level of the river. While the notion of adverse effect is not defined in the Treaty, and thus leaves room for controversy, this requirement does not preclude the use of the waters of the Mahakali River by the local communities living along both sides of the Mahakali River as long as such use does not exceed five percent of the average annual flow at Pancheshwar.[58] Furthermore, the Mahakali Treaty does not preclude either country from planning, surveying, developing and using any of the tributaries originating from the Mahakali River, as long as such activities take place

---

[51] The Treaty includes, *inter alia*, the construction of a 315-meter high dam (Pancheshwar Dam) with a capacity for generating 3,480 MW of electricity. *See* Rishikesh Shah, "Whither Mahakali Treaty?" in *The Kathmandu Post,* September 4, 1997.

[52] Mahakali Treaty, Article 3.

[53] *Id.*

[54] *Id.*, Article 4.

[55] *Id.*, Article 5.1.

[56] *Id.*, Article 5.2.

[57] *Id.*, Article 6.

[58] *Id.*, Articles 7 and 8.

in each country's own territory and do not adversely affect the flow of the Mahakali River.[59]

(ii) Specific Principles: The Mahakali Treaty establishes four main principles for the design and implementation of the PMP. The first principle is that the PMP will be designed to produce the maximum total net benefit for both countries in the forms of power generation, irrigation use and flood control.[60] These benefits will be assessed on a continual basis to ensure maximum performance. The second principle regarding the construction of the PMP is that both countries are working together in an integrated manner to develop and share their water resources. Indeed, the PMP will be implemented as a joint effort including the erection of power stations of equal capacity on each side of the Mahakali River. The two power stations will be operated together, and the total energy generated will be shared equally between India and Nepal.[61]

The third principle is that both countries will share the cost of the project. As specified in the Treaty, India and Nepal will share the cost of the PMP in proportion to the benefits accruing to each, and will jointly endeavor to mobilize the financing required to implement the PMP.[62] The fourth principle is that a portion of Nepal's share of energy will be sold to India. The quantum of such energy and its price shall be mutually agreed upon between the parties.[63]

In addition, the Letters exchanged between the Prime Ministers of Nepal and India regarding the Mahakali Treaty also establishes principles to be applied and arrangements to be made in finalizing the Detailed Project Report (DPR), completing negotiations, and implementing the PMP. Accordingly, the Letter mandates that the DPR must be finalized by both countries within six months from the effective date of the Mahakali Treaty,[64] and provides that the exchange of necessary data and reports must be expeditious. The Letter clarifies further that, during the preparation of the DPR and the accompanying assessment of the benefits to each country as a result of the construction of the PMP, an assessment of irrigation benefits would also

---

[59] *Id.*, Article 8.

[60] *Id.*, Article 3.1.

[61] *Id.*, Article 3 (2).

[62] *Id.*, Article 3 (3).

[63] Article 3 (4). In order to maximize its revenues from the Project, Nepal has been keen to maximize the power component and to design the Project as a peaking station to run for about four and a half hours a day. India's own preference initially was for a project with a lower capacity of about 2,000 MW, operating over a longer number of hours. However it has agreed to go along with Nepal, given an expected deficit in peaking power of about 20,000 MW in the northern grid by the time the project comes on stream in about 2010. *See*, "Pancheshwar: Challenges Ahead," in *The Economic Times,* (Nepal) Wednesday, July 2, 1997.

[64] The Mahakali Treaty was ratified on June 5, 1997, by both parties and has entered into force and effect. However, as yet, the DPR has not been finalized. Water resources officials, the technical team, from India and Nepal meeting for the finalization of the DPR, requested their respective governments to give them another two years for its preparation. *See*, "Two Years Extension Sought to Prepare Pancheshwar DPR," in *The Kathmandu Post,* December 11, 1998.

be conducted. The Letter directed that the assessment of irrigation benefits for both countries should focus on incremental and additional benefits due to augmentation of river flow, and on the value of works saved and damage avoided due to increased flood control resulting from construction of the PMP. Likewise, the Letter instructs that the net power benefits will be assessed on the basis of savings in costs to the two countries as compared with the relevant alternatives available.[65] This comparison of cost with available alternatives is likely to emerge and remain as another contentious issue.[66] The Letter further precludes claims, in any form and by either country, on the unutilized portion of its share of the waters of the Mahakali River.[67]

The Letter also specifies that an agreement for the financing and implementation of the PMP, including the proposal for the establishment of the Pancheshwar Development Authority, must be negotiated and finalized by both countries within one year from the finalization of the DPR.[68] It should also be noted that pursuant to the Mahakali Treaty, a Mahakali River Commission will oversee the Authority. The Commission comprises an equal number of members from both parties and, in the event of disputes, both parties must submit to resolution of the dispute by independent arbitration.[69] This is indeed a major breakthrough. Rarely are such projects between countries financed, implemented and operated jointly by a bi-national authority.

The target date for completion of construction of the PMP is eight years from the date of the Treaty, subject to the completion of the DPR. To expedite the implementation of the PMP, the Letter further provides that field investigation and detailed design, including tender document preparation, should start immediately after the finalization of the DPR and should parallel the negotiations necessary to implement the PMP. For this purpose, the Letter also specifies that both countries need to agree on a separate financing agreement to carry out these activities.[70]

Thus, despite the detailed principles established by the Treaty and the Letter, this appears to be an agreement to agree, and the implementation of the PMP, which is

---

[65] Paragraph 3 (a) of the Letter.

[66] Indeed, a unanimous resolution of the Nepalese Parliament stated that the principle of "avoided cost" should be the only criterion. Even if it is decided that the price should be somewhere between avoided cost and the actual cost of generation, the question remains, what is the relevant alternative, especially for peaking power. See, "Pancheshwar: Challenges Ahead," *supra,* note 63. It should also be added that absence of clear principle of pricing of power is even more serious because of the situation of a *de facto* single buyer monopoly. See Gyewali, "Ke Ke Chan Dosh Mahakali Sandhi Ma," *supra* note 37, at 39.

[67] Paragraph 3 (b) of the Letter.

[68] Paragraph 3 (c) of the Letter.

[69] See Article 1 and Article 11 of the Mahakali Treaty; While there are bi-national hydroelectric projects in other parts of the world, the largest being the 12,600 MW Itaipu Dam shared by Brazil and Paraguay, Pancheshwar will be the first truly bi-national project in the Ganges Basin, and could serve as a model for cooperative development of its vast hydro-power resources. See "Pancheshwar: Challenges Ahead," *supra,* note 63.

[70] Paragraph 3 (d) of the Letter.

the *raison d'être* of the Mahakali Treaty, relies heavily on a financing package that the two governments will have to obtain.[71]

D. Water Sharing Issues

The provisions regarding Nepal's share of the waters of the Mahakali River under the Mahakali Treaty are scattered throughout the Treaty. Read together, Nepal's share of water stipulated by the Treaty can be consolidated as reflected in Table 5.1:

TABLE 5.1
Nepal's Share of the Waters of the Mahakali River Under the Mahakali Treaty

Source	Wet season	Dry season
Sarada Barrage	1000 cusecs	150 cusecs
Tanakpur	1000 cusecs	300 cusecs
Dodhara-Chandani	350 cusecs	350 cusecs
Total	2350 cusecs	800 cusecs

Source: Articles 1, 2 and 3 of the Mahakali Treaty.

The Mahakali Treaty appears to have attempted to follow a model based on the principles of "equitable utilization" and "no harm."[72] However, in spite of the attempt to follow these models, the treatment of these two notions is not completely clear. The provisions regarding the sharing of water of the Mahakali River thus raise some issues. Articles 3 and 5.1 of the Treaty, as well as paragraph 3 (b) of the Letter, when read together, result in some ambiguity. For instance, according to Article 3 of the Treaty, both India and Nepal agreed that they have equal entitlement to use the waters of the Mahakali River without prejudice to their respective existing consumptive uses of the waters of the Mahakali River. Thus the Treaty protects the "respective consumptive use of the waters of the Mahakali River" without actually specifying the nature of the use.[73]

The Letter, moreover, in paragraph 3(b) contains some restrictions as to the notion of equal entitlement. It states:

---

[71] Indeed, to mitigate risk in a proposed cooperative arrangement, negotiators often take this kind of approach. By doing so, they enter only into some preliminary type of general understanding which, while legally and theoretically appearing binding, is in practical effect devoid of specific substantive commitments. Such techniques, in essence, only involve a commitment to future negotiation. *See* for detailed discussion, Richard B. Bilder, *Managing the Risks of International Agreements* (Madison: Univ. Wisconsin Press, 1981), at 34. Nevertheless, it should also be noted that the principle that nations may commit themselves to good-faith negotiations of a common problem, without necessarily committing themselves to reaching a final agreement, is an acceptable practice. This was suggested in the 1957 *Lac Lanoux Arbitration* between France and Spain, involving French diversion of waters of a river system shared by the two countries. *See id.,* at 35.

[72] For discussion of the principle of equitable utilization and the no-harm rule, *see supra*, Chapter 1, Introduction, note 38 and accompanying text.

[73] For discussions, *see* K. L. Shrestha, "Mahakali Sandhi Ra Rastriya Hitko Sawal" (The Mahakali Treaty and the Question of National Benefit) (Kathmandu: Sumitra Shrestha, 1997), at 32-33.

It is understood that Section 3 of Article 3 of the Mahakali Treaty precludes the claim, in any form, by either party on the unutilized portion of the shares of the waters of the Mahakali River of that Party without affecting the provision of the withdrawal of the respective shares of the water of the Mahakali River by each Party under this Treaty.

These provisions do not guarantee that equal entitlement of water, from a Nepalese standpoint, should be half of the total use for each country.[74] The term "existing consumptive use" is a key phrase adding to the confusion. Its full and meaningful implementation requires that the countries first identify the "existing consumptive use" of both India and Nepal.[75] Only then can the phrase "without prejudice to their respective existing consumptive uses" be objectively applied. Unfortunately, the Mahakali Treaty defines Nepal's existing consumptive use,[76] but does not do so for India and therefore leaves open an opportunity for India to unilaterally define the scope of its consumptive use.

The resulting ambiguity caused by this provision contradicts the spirit of Article 5.1 of the Mahakali Treaty, which states that the water requirements of Nepal are to be given prime consideration. Furthermore, although Nepal's prospective water requirements are to be given priority, its existing and prospective water requirements are small in proportion to India's water requirements, and may impact Nepal's plans to forgo part of its water entitlement for a proportionately lower share of the costs of the non-hydroelectric component.[77]

The negotiators, however, have had difficulty ascertaining what share of costs each country must pay. Even if the power component is assumed to cost about 80 percent of the total cost of the project,[78] small differences in the apportionment of the remaining 20 percent can translate into hundreds of crores.[79] Nepal believes that India is overstating its existing utilization of water flows in order to minimize its share of incremental irrigation and flood control benefits from the project.[80] Along

---

[74] As discussed in the first chapter, equality of right, in international law, does not give a co-riparian the right to an equal division of the waters. Rather, equality of right is the equal right of each co-riparian state to a division of the waters on the basis of its economic and social needs, consistent with the corresponding rights of its co-riparian states, and excluding from consideration factors unrelated to such needs. This formula will, of course, often result in a compromise that will permit each co-riparian state to satisfy its needs to the greatest extent possible, with a minimum of detriment to each. *See* Garretson et al., eds., *The Law of International Drainage Basins* (Dobbs Ferry: Oceana Publications, 1967), at 63; *see* also Chapter 1, Introduction, *supra* at note 21.

[75] Ajay Dixit, "Mahakali Nadi Sajha Ho, Paani Adha Ko Adha Ho" (Mahakali River is common, water secured is one half of the half), in Mulyankan Vol. 42, 1997, at 8-9.

[76] *Id.*, *see* also, for detailed discussions, Gyewali, *supra* note 37, at 39; *see* also K. L. Shrestha, *supra* note 73, at 23, 32-33.

[77] "Pancheshwar: Challenges Ahead," *supra* note 63. Non-hydroelelectric component in this context includes all components related to the water use except hydropower.

[78] Such cost may be as much as Rs 15,000 crore, or Rs 2.5 crore per megawatt.

[79] "Pancheshwar: Challenges Ahead," *supra* note 63.

[80] *See* Gyewali, *supra* note 37, at 74; *see* also, K. L. Shrestha, *supra* note 73.

these lines, India in the past has claimed that it uses up to three times the amount of water that it is now claiming.[81]

The not-so-unfamiliar dispute on the issue of downstream use and benefits manifests itself in this case as difference in interpretation of the Treaty provision regarding existing uses. The dispute is entirely unnecessary. All that India may gain in the end, even if it wins the argument, is some savings by reducing its share of the investment cost for the regulated water it uses for irrigation.[82] Similarly, all that Nepal may gain is the theoretical right over a modest quantity of water, for which the demand is yet not quantifiable anyway. Indeed, both countries, to cater to their domestic political audience, have a tendency to continue their rhetoric of equitableness, thus losing time and resources on trivial matters.

Additionally, these claims by India are higher in some months than either the amount of water observed in the river at specified times, or the water capacity of the Sarada Canal into which the bulk of the flows are diverted by the Sarada Barrage in India. This has partly to do with the link canal India has built between the Ghaghra and the Sarada canal system to supplement the Sarada River.[83] India, however, argues that the canal is used only for part of the year because the Ghaghra River carries a heavy load of silt during and after the rains, which would build up in the canal and cause blockage. For the rest of the year, India claims that the flows it utilizes come from the Mahakali River itself.[84]

India estimates that augmentation of flows of water by the PMP, unassisted by the waters of the Ghaghra River, will enable it to raise the intensity of spring irrigation from 26 to 50 percent in about two million hectares command area in the State of Uttar Pradesh.[85] This would correspond to utilization of only half the augmented waters and a cost share of eight percent. Although its share of flows would remain largely unutilized, Nepal's cost share would also remain at eight percent. The remaining four percent would be apportioned to flood control benefits.[86]

2. The Mahakali Commission and Dispute Resolution

An interesting feature of the Mahakali Treaty is the establishment of a joint Indo-Nepalese commission,[87] called the Mahakali River Commission. This Commission is guided by the principles of equality, mutual benefit and no harm to either of the

---

[81] *Id.*, supra note 37. See Devendra Raj Panday, *Nepal's Failed Development: Reflections on the Mission and the Maladies* (Nepal South Asia Center, 1999), at 336.

[82] *See* Panday, *Nepal's Failed Development, supra* note 81.

[83] *Id.*

[84] *Id.*

[85] *Id.*

[86] *Id.*

[87] Mahakali Treaty, Article 9.1.

countries.[88] The joint nature, both from an organizational as well as financial standpoint, is well reflected because the Commission will be composed of an equal number of representatives from both countries[89] and its expenses also are to be borne equally by both India and Nepal.[90]

The Commission has been given a relatively broad mandate. Among other things, the Commission has been directed to: (i) seek information on and, if necessary, inspect all structures included in the Mahakali Treaty and make recommendations to both India and Nepal for necessary steps to implement its provisions; (ii) make recommendations to both India and Nepal for the conservation and utilization of the Mahakali River as envisioned by and provided for in the Mahakali Treaty; (iii) provide expert evaluation of projects and make recommendations thereto; (iv) coordinate and monitor plans of action arising out of the implementation of the Mahakali Treaty; and (v) examine any differences arising between the two countries concerning the Treaty's interpretation and application.[91]

Nevertheless, both India and Nepal continue to reserve their rights to deal directly with each other on all matters, notwithstanding the competence of the Mahakali River Commission.[92] In addition, both the parties can form, if they wish, specific joint entities for the development, execution and operation of new projects including the PMP in the Mahakali River for their mutual benefit.[93] The Commission is also directed to draft its rules of procedure that shall be submitted to both India and Nepal for their concurrence.[94]

The dispute resolution mechanism envisaged by the Mahakali Treaty is relatively elaborate and advanced. In case the Mahakali River Commission fails to come up with a recommendation after examining any disparities between the countries within three months, or if either party disagrees with the Commission's recommendation, then a dispute shall be deemed to have arisen and shall then be submitted for arbitration. In so doing, either country is required to give three months' prior notice to the other country.[95]

A tribunal composed of three arbitrators conducts all arbitration. One arbitrator is to be nominated by Nepal, one by India, and neither country is allowed to nominate its own national representative. The third arbitrator is to be appointed jointly by the two arbitrators, who shall preside over the tribunal. In the event that the two countries are unable to agree upon the third arbitrator within 90 days after receipt of a proposal, either country may request the Secretary-General of the Permanent Court

---

[88] *Id.*, Article 9.1.

[89] *Id.*, Article 9.2.

[90] *Id.*, Article 9.4.

[91] On functions of the Commission, *see id.*, at Article 9.3.

[92] *Id.*, Article 9.6.

[93] *Id.*, Article 10.

[94] *Id.*, Article 9 (5).

[95] *Id.*, Article 11.1.

of Arbitration at The Hague to appoint an arbitrator. The arbitrator so chosen, however, cannot be a national of either country.[96]

Regarding the modus operandi of arbitration, the Mahakali Treaty states that it shall be determined by the arbitration tribunal and that the decision of a majority of the arbitrators shall be considered to be the decision of the tribunal. The proceedings of the tribunal shall be conducted in English and the decision of the tribunal shall be in writing. Both countries are obligated to accept the decision as final, definitive and binding.[97] The Mahakali Treaty, however, is silent regarding the venue of arbitration, the administrative support of the arbitration tribunal, and the remuneration and expenses of its arbitrators. The Treaty simply states that these aspects would be dealt with by an exchange of notes between the parties. Moreover, through an exchange of notes, the parties can also agree on alternative procedures for settling differences arising under the Mahakali Treaty.[98]

III. Conclusion

The Mahakali Treaty entered into force on June 5, 1997, the date the instruments of ratification were exchanged by both parties, pursuant to its Article 12.[99] It will remain valid for a period of 75 years.[100] The provisions of the Treaty must be reviewed by both countries at 10-year intervals or earlier if requested by either country and amendments thereto will be made, if necessary.[101] In order to give effect to its provisions, the two countries shall enter into additional agreements[102] as required.

Although there are still several unclear provisions and incomplete arrangements, the Mahakali Treaty has provided a mechanism for a reinforced legal collaboration between India and Nepal on the Mahakali River. Undeniably, there are problems on both sides of the border. However, if both countries cooperate in good faith to carry

---

[96] *Id.*, Article 11.2.

[97] *Id.*, Article 11.3.

[98] *Id.;* Article 11.4.

[99] The Nepalese Parliament ratified the Mahakali Treaty with a two-thirds majority. *See* "The Rising Nepal," June 6, 1997; *see* also, "India Nepal Sign 5 Pacts, Ratify Mahakali Treaty," in *The Hindustan Times,* June 5, 1997. Prior to ratification, the Joint Session of the Nepalese Parliament had raised certain issues and the resolution related thereto recommended that such issues be addressed during the preparation of the DPR. The Prime Minister of India, while exchanging the instruments of ratification, agreed that the issues would receive attention. *See* Paragraph 14 of the Nepal India Joint Statement issued in June 7, 1997, in People's Review, June 19, 1997; *see* also, "Time Frame Fixed To Resolve Bilateral Issues. Chand, Gujral Hold Talks," in *The Rising Nepal,* June 6, 1997. Chand and Gujral were Prime Ministers of Nepal and India, respectively, at that time.

[100] *The Rising Nepal,* June 6, 1997. For an extensively elaborate comment on the pros and cons of the Treaty, *see*, Dipak Gyewali and Ajaya Dixit, "Mahakali Impasse and Indo-Nepal Water Conflict," *Economic and Political Weekly,* Vol XXXIV, No. 9, February 27, 1999.

[101] Mahakali Treaty, Article 12.3.

[102] *Id.*, Article 12.4.

out the provisions of the Treaty many economic, political and social advantages will materialize. In order to reap these benefits, however, each country may need to temper its nationalistic ego, which has remained a predominant feature in the water resource relations between the two countries.

With regard to the Pancheshwar Multipurpose Project, the flagship Project under the Mahakali Integrated Development scheme, there is currently a great deal of concern over the growing wave of public indifference toward it. This is especially troublesome because differences have erupted between Nepal and India over the interpretation of certain provisions of the Mahakali Treaty that relate to how the waters of the Mahakali River should be shared. Notwithstanding these differences, the Mahakali Treaty, as noted by some, "remains a milestone because it is more than a project."[103] The Treaty "has informed the world of a conducive environment in the region for development of water resources."[104] Projects as big as Pancheshwar take time to materialize. "What is necessary for the success of the PMP and other projects of equal magnitude is durable consensus and consistency in the working of the parties."[105]

The first two parts of the Treaty, dealing with Sarada and Tanakpur, only codify in one text the improved version of the existing regime. The part of the Treaty that deals with the PMP from a theoretical standpoint, on the other hand, definitely asserts some positive attributes. For instance the following principles established by the Treaty are extremely valuable: utilizing the water of the Mahakali River so that each country enjoys equal entitlement to the water (Article 3); designing the Project so that the total net benefit to each country is maximized (Article 3.1); basing the price of the energy produced on a cost avoided principle (paragraph 3[a] of the Letter); requiring each country to invest in the Project in proportion to the benefits they each receive (Article 3.3); and accounting for incremental and additional irrigation benefits and flood control benefits (paragraph 3[a] of the Letter).

However, a great deal remains to be done. The progress made in establishing the DPR has been relatively slow.[106] Still, the very fact that the Mahakali Treaty has brought so much attention to hydro-development is noteworthy.[107] The mode of financing mega-projects in the days to come will be very different from the common practices until now. The vast quantum of capital required for these projects and the fact that such funds are only available in the private sector of most developed countries implies that these big projects will have to be developed through foreign direct investments. In this context, one may also argue that the signing of the Mahakali Treaty has also provided an advantage of limiting the political risk. The

---

[103] Statement of H. E. Rajan, Indian Ambassador. *See* "Sub-regional Water Conference Begins," in *Kathmandu Post,* February 10, 1998.

[104] *Id.*

[105] *Id.*

[106] The technical teams from the governments have requested an extension. *See supra* note 64.

[107] Statement of the Nepalese Minister of Water Resources. *See,* "Sub-Regional Water Conference Begins," in *Kathmandu Post,* February 10, 1998.

Treaty provides a framework for not only sharing the Mahakali's waters, but for all hydroelectric projects. It thus surmounts the old political uncertainties and provides more confidence to multinational corporations or foreign companies to invest in hydropower for the country.

So far, talks between Nepal and India on the DPR have not been conclusive and the DPR has not been completed within the six months mandated by the Treaty. The technical teams working on the DPR asked for two more years.[108] This did not come as a surprise to many. Most concerns raised earlier by the two sides have resurfaced, including the conditions attached to the ratification by the Nepalese parliament.[109] For instance, the provision regarding the equal sharing of water in the Mahakali Treaty is applicable only to that water not already in use by India. This was established by the "prior use" clause in the Mahakali Treaty. India has recently been asking under the "prior use" clause not only for water for the Sarada Barrage but also for water from the lower Sarada Canal.[110] This will mean that India will have to be assured of 449 cusecs of water. It is only after India receives its quota of "prior use" of Mahakali waters that the remaining flow will be divided equally between the two countries.

The technical level talks, however, have not been entirely unfruitful. India has agreed to construct a larger 6,000-plus megawatt power station at Pancheshwar. The final DPR, however, is yet to be prepared.[111] Moreover, because of the political strictures of the Nepalese Parliament, the technicians by themselves will hardly be in a position to resolve all the issues.[112] Hence, political level talks between leaders of the two countries are of prime importance if the DPR talks are to bear any fruit. Already, skeptics are predicting that nothing will come of the Mahakali Treaty for the next two decades or so.[113]

---

[108] It should be noted that the two governments approved the opening of a Joint Projects Office for Pancheshwar Investigations (JPO-PI) in Kathmandu on November 1, 1999. This office will facilitate the carrying out of additional investigations and studies required for preparing the Joint DPR. *See,* "Kathmandu Joint Project Office Opened," in *The Independent,* November 17-November 22, 1999, Vol. IX, No. 37, Kathmandu.

[109] *See Kathmandu Post, supra* note 108 and accompanying text.

[110] *See Kathmandu Post,* November 12, 1997.

[111] On the eventual possibility of preparing and finalizing the DPR, as per the restrictions imposed by the Nepalese Parliament, Dipak Gyewali and Ajaya Dixit, in "Mahakali Impasse and Indo-Nepal Water Conflict," *Economic and Political Weekly,* Vol. XXXIV, No. 9 (February 27, 1999), at 562, conclude emphatically that the Pancheshwar DPR is a technical engineering document regarding the construction of a very high dam, and thus it cannot negotiate rights on water nor can it negotiate the modality for fixing the price of electricity. The Prime Minister of Nepal, Girija Koirala, during an official visit to India, stated that the DPR would be completed by 2001. However, it has not yet materialized. *See,* Kalyan Chaudhuri, "The neighbours indeed," in *Frontline* (August 19-September 1, 2000), at 52. For generic problems faced by the Mahakali Treaty, *see* also, Rajendra K. Chhetri, "Mahakali Treaty: Progress and Problems," *Kathmandu Post,* January 19, 2000.

[112] *Id.*

[113] *Id.* For the impact of the Treaty from the political parties' perspective, *see* Parajulee, *supra* note 13, at 288-299.

Despite its shortcomings, the Mahakali Treaty has made attempts to reconcile the conflicting interests between the two countries as much as possible. When compared with the previous agreements relating to the Mahakali River, the Sarada Treaty and the Tanakpur Agreement, the Mahakali Treaty has made significant progress in broadening the scope of water resource development as well as defining the rights and obligations of the two countries. Possibilities for improvement exist. The Mahakali Treaty envisions extensive bilateral cooperation. Regular reviews may take place. The Joint Commission may also provide a continuing point of contact and appropriate exchange of information that may help the two governments along in their decision-making. If the finalization of the DPR never materializes, the Mahakali Treaty would still continue to exist, but would be reduced in scope and limited only to regulating the Sarada and Tanakpur Barrages. In conclusion, the signing of the Mahakali Treaty has indeed provided India and Nepal with an opportunity for meaningful cooperation to benefit the millions of people in the two countries whose livelihood depends on the waters of the Mahakali River.

CHAPTER 6

The Kosi, Gandaki and Mahakali: An Overview

The previous three chapters noted the commonalities of objectives and the closeness and similarities between India and Nepal. However, despite such commonalities, water resources development has faced many setbacks due to technical, economic and political factors that acted against the interests of the two countries. In fact, coordinated actions between the two countries have not been forthcoming and trust and understanding have been eroded, creating major impediments to cooperative development.[1] A significant factor fueling problems between the two countries is that the provisions contained in the existing water sharing agreements lack specificity, leaving room for ambiguity and controversy in the interpretation and enforcement of their provisions. In addition, the subject matter of the agreements varies depending on what the pressing issue was at the time they were negotiated. For example, they deal with such topics as catchment area ratios, land area development ratios, investment ratios, riparian rights, and the value of water, in varying degrees.

The history of negotiations regarding water projects on the Nepalese rivers has been dominated by controversies due primarily to a perceptional difference and lack of trust between the citizens and governments of the two countries. Most Nepalese are convinced that they have not been dealt with fairly by the treaties.[2] These Nepalese believe further that India is draining Nepal's watershed for its own benefit.[3] Many Nepalese maintain that Nepal's kindness and generosity in sharing its water with India in the existing agreements has been taken advantage of by India because the people of Nepal have received far fewer benefits than the people of India from the projects carried out under these treaties.[4] Similar conclusions could be possibly made in the case of the Mahakali, which will need to be evaluated again once the DPR is completed and the Project implemented, if at all.

In response to the Nepalese contentions, the Indian stance has been to defend, as a lower riparian country, its equitable use of these international rivers according to

---

[1] For detail, *see* Santosh Kumar, A. K. Sinha and Nigam Prakash, "Culture and Water Bonds," in *Water Nepal* Vol. 4, No.1, Ajaya Dixit, ed., (September 1994).

[2] *See* A. R. Rao and T. Prasad, "Water Resources Development of the Indo-Nepal Region," *Water Resources Development* 10 (1994), at 166; *see* also generally, Ben Crow and Nirvikar Singh, *Impediments and Innovations in International Rivers: The Waters of South Asia* (August 1999), at 12-13, 20-21.

[3] *Id.,* at 166.

[4] *Id.*, at 167; *see* also *supra,* Chapters 3, 4 and 5.

international law and practice. India has contended that it has the right to use the water in accordance with its needs, with the term "need" embracing its unlimited socioeconomic requirements dependent on the waters of the rivers flowing from Nepal into India. The Indo-Nepal efforts to cooperate in the management of water resources have, thus, continuously revolved around this dichotomy of perception, and have involved continual controversy and tension, resulting in a slow development of water resources projects that may have proven to be beneficial to both India and Nepal.

The influence of politics is curiously disproportionate in the relations between these two countries. The Nepalese have long viewed India as a hegemonic power that arm-twists tiny neighbors. They feel they got an unfair deal in the Kosi and the Gandak Projects, and are determined not to be taken advantage of again. All political parties in Nepal accuse one another of selling the country down the river to India. That is, perhaps, why the new Nepalese constitution requires that any agreement for sharing the country's natural resources be approved by a two-thirds majority of parliament.[5]

India, in turn, has long regarded Nepal as suffering from a small-country syndrome, imagining conspiracies that do not exist, and so being incapable of striking common sense deals.[6] The Indian apprehensions may be exaggerated, but not baseless. Because of the age-old nature of relations between the two counties, India has often had to be the pioneer in most development works, in the field of water or other fields. Being a pioneer, it also had to take a bigger risk because of the untested terrain and population, leading, in some cases, to unpredicted outcomes that were below public expectations. As a result, the Projects suffered from unnecessary delays. Consequently, although positive, the disenchantment of the public prevented the Indian side of the story from being disseminated in an unbiased manner.

Moreover, the internal political uncertainties prevalent in a fragile Nepal, particularly the extreme ideological differences among the parties, coupled with the side effects of the Cold War, have created an unfavorable situation to highlighting the Indian role in a just and positive fashion. The political organizations, in some cases maneuvered by alien forces, have not hesitated fomenting anti-Indian feelings aimed at dislodging India from the dominant position it held in Nepal, and to redirect Nepal from one sphere of influence to another, again at the detriment of Indian sentiments. The real cause of anti-Indian sentiment in Nepal, as noted by Girija Shankar Bajpai, a renowned Indian scholar, "is the frustrations of the ambitions of the political parties who could not secure for themselves the reigns of government in Nepal."[7] India was, in Mr. Bajpai's view, "made a scapegoat of their disappointment and malice," a view seconded by the then Prime Minister of Nepal, B. P.

---

[5] *See*, "Multinational Oil Troubled Indo-Nepalese Waters," *Times of India,* January 19, 1997.

[6] *Id.*

[7] Girija Shankar Bajpai, Indian Yearbook of International Affairs, Madras (1994), at 213.

Koirala, who considered the criticisms against India "as borne out of ignorance and politically motivated and unrealistic and baseless."[8]

With this perceptional differences in the background, it can be concluded that the water resources cooperation between India and Nepal has not always emphasized equitable sharing of the benefits from the concerned international rivers. Nepal, as a result, has remained dormant for long (almost until the early 1990s) and also evasive about starting new projects, at a huge cost to its own development needs. Also internally, for the same reasons, the exploitation of water resources in Nepal has been influenced by independent development rather than joint development philosophy. The caution and patent discomfort of the Nepalese are understandable. Lopsided views and vested interests on the part of political parties have spread an atmosphere of distrust, suspicion and misunderstanding, leaving the successive governments in Nepal hesitant to make bold decisions for the positive use of the country's water resources. The negotiations and execution of the Mahakali Treaty in the mid-1990s showed an improved trend in favor of Nepal, but a lot needs to be done for the situation to be considered a major progress in this area.

While the 1990s have shown that the Nepalese technicians and bureaucrats have grown more mature in their understanding of the water issues as well as in the negotiations of legal instruments, credit should also go to the positive rules of international law that have taken firm shape. For instance, the UN Convention on the Law of the Non-Navigational Uses of International Watercourse, adopted by the United Nations Generally Assembly in May 1997, provides a comprehensive framework for negotiations on matters of water rights, allocation, management, planned measures, and dispute resolution. It is hoped that the framework will trigger balanced deals in the future.

Another dimension in the Indo-Nepalese relations has been added by the fact that studies indicate that almost all sites in India (in the states of Uttar Pradesh and Bihar) for developing irrigation have now been exhausted. But the growing demand for irrigation water in India continues to necessitate a solution in large-scale inter-basin transfers and particularly developing storage in Nepal.[9] Therein lies the key to taking the downstream benefits into account. It should be noted that storage in Nepal gives significant downstream benefits to India, whether small or big projects, including not only irrigation but also flood control, power as well as navigation and fishing. Hence, justifications for appropriate compensation for Nepal abound. Clearly, India cannot take advantage of Nepalese hydropower resources that could be the least expensive energy source for Northern India without appropriate agreement with Nepal. Nepal, on the other hand, cannot take advantage of its huge water

---

[8] *See*, P. C. Rawat, *Indo Nepal Economic Relations* (New Delhi: National Publishing House, 1974), at 216.

[9] It should also be noted that questions have been raised regarding the feasibility of building enough storage-reservoirs to regulate the immense volume of water flowing down the Himalayan rivers. *See*, news item by Mahesh Uniyal, "Development South Asia: Solving a Himalayan Water Problem," IPS/MU/an/99. For discussions on the issue of storage reservoirs in Nepal, *see* Part III, *infra*.

resources potential for hydropower development in the absence of agreements with India. In order for both countries to reap the potential benefits from these resources, carefully orchestrated, constructive and probably protracted negotiations would be required.[10] Indeed, all riparian negotiations are conditioned by the recognition that fresh-water diplomacy is a symbol and the test for friendly relations between the two countries. A balance must be made between the various national interests, including the competitive domestic demands that go with the availability of water, the emotions that go with territorial sovereignty on one hand, and the uncontrollable imperatives of international interdependence on the other. Ignoring the logic of integral unity of river basins and common stakes in the optimal progress of upper riparian and lower riparian partners is self-destructive. Indeed, the management of international watercourses should be determined less by the traditional notion of "restricted sovereignty" than by a positive spirit of cooperation and effective interdependence.[11]

As has been noted by two eminent scholars, "[W]ater sharing agreements that flow from a good scientific understanding by both the riparians of the river system, of its behavior and capabilities, will lead to peace and understanding that last, while those with scientific uncertainties will always provide opportunities for strife and dispute."[12] If a successful and healthy partnership is to develop between India and Nepal, an environment of trust that facilitates unfettered exchange of information is a prerequisite that can only lead to purposeful dialogue between the two countries. Thus a sense of pragmatism preceded by good faith between the two countries seems warranted, if both intend to avoid "mutual self-impoverishment." Therefore it is imperative that both countries encourage a culture of behavior and thinking in which water related issues are not used as sensational tools for internal demagogic propaganda, but as economic and development realities manifested in well-balanced and well-drafted comprehensive legal instruments.

---

[10] *See,* A. H. Shibusawa, "Cooperation in Water Resources Development In South Asia," in *Commerce*, Vol. 154, No. 3959 (April 4-10, 1987), at 14.

[11] *See* Green Cross International, *National Sovereignty and International Watercourses*, Report of the Sovereignty Panel (2000), at 18.

[12] *See* Dipak Gyewali and Othmar Schwank, "Interstate Sharing of Water Rights: An Alps-Himalaya Comparison," in *Water Nepal* Ajaya Dixit, ed. (1994), Vol. 4, No.1, at 235.

PART FOUR

India-Bangladesh Relations

Chapter 7
The Ganges River

I. Introduction and History

1. The Formative Era

On April 10, 1971, the proclamation of independence of the People's Republic of Bangladesh (which was until then East Pakistan) was issued under the authority of the Constituent Assembly that was elected four months earlier. The turn of events that followed the elections resulted in wide scale violence within Bangladesh, and the eruption of a full-scale war between India and Pakistan. This was the third war they fought since the partitioning of the Sub-continent in 1947; the second one was fought only six years earlier, in 1965. The geopolitics of the South Asian Sub-continent at that time forced the newly emerging nation of Bangladesh into close ties with its mighty neighbor, India. One of the first acts of the newly constituted *de facto* government in Bangladesh was to seek recognition by India, and a request to this effect was sent to India on April 24, 1971, two weeks after the issuance of the proclamation of independence. The request was repeated again in early December 1971. A positive response to this request was granted when it became clear that the war was coming to an end, with India emerging as the clear winner, and with Bangladesh poised to finally emerge as an independent nation. On December 6, 1971, India became the first country to announce its recognition of Bangladesh as an independent and sovereign nation. On December 16, the Pakistan army surrendered to the Joint Command of the Indian and Bangladesh forces, and the following day India declared a unilateral cease-fire. Thus, the People's Republic of Bangladesh emerged as an independent nation, exacerbating further the partitioning of the Indian Sub-continent.[1] The idea of one state consisting of two wings tied together only by religion but divided by many other elements, including thousands of miles and an unfriendly country in-between, did not seem as viable to many people. The results of the elections and the events that followed, particularly the widespread violence, indicated clearly the rift between the people of the two wings of Pakistan. Those circumstances certainly facilitated the role played by India, the main regional power, and presented India as a liberator of the people of Bangladesh. Moreover, the emergence of Bangladesh was not followed by an immediate rush of recognition by other nations. After all, many countries have their own "East Pakistans" in one form or another, and they needed to watch carefully the development of events there.

---

[1] *See supra,* Chapter 2, on partition of the Indian Sub-continent into India and Pakistan.

Hence, Bangladesh continued to rely on the support of India, and India continued to provide support. About a month after recognition of Bangladesh by India, the Minister of Foreign Affairs of Bangladesh visited India on January 5, 1972, the first visit by an official of the new nation of Bangladesh to another country. One purpose for the visit was "to thank again the Government and people of India for their contribution to the liberation struggle and for their efforts for the release and restoration of Bangabandhu Sheikh Mujibur Rahman."[2] During this visit, India assured Bangladesh of all cooperation in the task of reconstruction of Bangladesh, and committed to meet the shortages of essential commodities and supplies caused by the devastation of war and the disruption of the communication system. Furthermore, India assured Bangladesh of its support for the latter to secure its rightful place in the international and regional economic and financial organizations. The return, resettlement and rehabilitation of the refugees who fled Bangladesh to India during the war was also discussed, and India assured Bangladesh of their full cooperation on this matter. India also agreed, at the request of Bangladesh, to look after the welfare of Bangladeshi nationals who may have been in pilgrimage in Saudi Arabia during that time.

Sheikh Mujib, who was released from detention in Pakistan during the Bangladeshi Foreign Minister's visit to India, was allowed to fly to Bangladesh on January 10, 1972. On his way to Bangladesh, he stopped at Delhi airport where he was met by both the President and the Prime Minister of India. This gesture had even stronger significance than that of his Foreign Minister. Indeed, Sheikh Mujib went to Delhi before he even touched the soil of Bangladesh. The purpose of his stopover was "...to pay personal tribute to the best friends of my [Bangladesh] people...." Less than a month later, on February 6, 1972, he would pay another visit to India as the first Prime Minister of Bangladesh. The joint communique issued at the end of the visit on February 8, addressed a number of issues. It was agreed that the withdrawal of the Indian army from Bangladesh would be completed by March 25, 1972. Bangladesh resolved to ensure, by every means, the return of all the refugees who had taken shelter in India since March 25, 1971, and to strive by all means to protect their safety, human dignity and means of livelihood. In the fields of development and trade, the two Prime Ministers agreed that regular talks, consultations and visits of delegations would take place between the two countries, and appropriate machinery would be set up, where necessary. They also discussed the problem of flood control, Farakka Barrage and other problems of development of water and power resources, and further desired that the two governments would engage in exchanging ideas, in identifying areas of cooperation, and in setting up suitable machinery for the formulation of appropriate programs.[3]

---

[2] *See* Joint Communique issued at the end of the visit of the Bangladesh Foreign Minister Mohamed Abdus Samad Azad to New Delhi, January 9, 1972, in Avtar Singh Bhasin, *India – Bangladesh Relations, 1971–1994, Documents,* Volume 1 (Delhi: Siba Exim Pvt. Ltd., 1996), at 12. Sheikh Mujibur Rahman was the leader of the Awami League that won the elections, and the leader of the struggle for independence.

[3] *See* Joint Communique issued at the end of the visit of the Prime Minister of Bangladesh Sheikh Mujibur Rahman to India, Calcutta, February 8, 1972, in Bhasin, *supra* note 2, at 18. The issue of the Farakka Barrage is discussed in Section 4 of this Part.

2. Formalization of the Close Ties

This process of strengthening the ties between the two countries continued. On March 17, the Prime Minister of India, Mrs. Indira Gandhi, visited Dacca[4] a few days after the first ambassador of Bangladesh to India presented his credentials to the President of India. During that visit, Mrs. Gandhi gave a passionate speech in support of Bangladesh and the two Prime Ministers signed the Treaty of Friendship, Cooperation and Peace between the Republic of India and the People's Republic of Bangladesh.[5]

The Treaty is the culmination of the efforts of the two countries to strengthen and formalize their relationship. Bangladesh, a still newly born nation not yet recognized by any country, needed the help of India in a number of areas. It needed immediate economic assistance following the devastating war that had just ended. Although India is itself a poor country, it could still assist in the reconstruction of Bangladesh through its own technology, human resources and through trade. Bangladesh also needed India's assistance to become a member of the world community at a time when breakaway provinces were frowned upon. India was, at that time, a leading member of the non-aligned movement and could muster such help there. At the time, India was also a close friend of the Soviet bloc, and could assist in influencing the decision of the Eastern European countries vis-a-vis the new nation. To dispel any perception that the new nation was an Indian satellite, India started pulling its troops out of Bangladesh and agreed to March 25, 1972 as the date for completion of such withdrawal.

Bangladesh also needed the cooperation of its neighbor in resolving a number of problems that had cropped up during the quarter of a century since the partitioning of the Sub-continent. Some of those problems, such as the sharing of water resources common to the two countries and flood control, were pressing at the time of Bangladesh's emergence. On the other hand, India was certainly happy to see its archenemy, Pakistan, split into two nations, with one of them closely aligning itself with India. With East Pakistan gone, India now had a close ally not far from its borders with China, its large and strong rival, rather than an enemy who had close ties to China, and who was situated almost in the midst of its northeastern part. In her speech at a public rally in Dacca on March 17, 1972, Mrs. Gandhi alluded to some of the reasons why India helped Bangladesh. She said:

> If India has helped you, it is because we could not sit idle after hearing your voice and after knowing of the sorrow and suffering that you have undergone. If we have helped you, it is in order to be true to ourselves, and to the principles to which we have adhered for years. I trust that, in the coming years, friendship between our two countries will be built not on the basis of the assistance that we might have given to you now, but on the basis of the full equali-

---

[4] The spelling of Dacca was changed later to Dhaka. Hence, both forms are used in this study, depending on the period.

[5] For the full text of the Treaty, *see* Bhasin, *supra* note 2, at 25. The Treaty was signed on March 9, 1972, in Dacca.

ty and mutual benefit of two free and sovereign nations....If we offer you cooperation, it is not out of any desire to wield influence over you. We want you to stand on your own legs.[6]

In view of the geopolitical situation in the Sub-continent, and with the Cold War dominating the world, it would be simplistic to accept the above as the only reasons for the Indian intervention in the war and for the help India gave Bangladesh in securing its independence. Given the military and financial help, and the goodwill provided to the new nation, India can expect a *quid pro quo* in terms of close collaboration in dealing with the regional problems, particularly with Pakistan and China, and also with resolving some of the pressing bilateral problems. The Joint Communique issued at the end of the visit of Sheikh Mujib to India had already identified two pressing bilateral issues. The first problem concerned the 10 million refugees who crossed into India during the war and whose return to Bangladesh was eagerly awaited by India. The second issue was the Farakka Barrage that India had built to divert some of the waters of the Ganges River away from Bangladesh, to the Hooghly River that flows toward Calcutta. The barrage added to the many problems that India and Pakistan had to deal with in the 1950s and 1960s, and was a thorny issue in their relationship. Ironically, the Farakka Barrage was completed in the very same year that Bangladesh emerged as an independent nation with the help of India. Work in the feeder canal had already started and would continue at the time India and Bangladesh were trying to strengthen and formalize their relationship. The barrage would continue to be the single most important and difficult issue in the relationship of the two nations for the next quarter of a century, and, indeed, the axis around which the relationship between the two countries would revolve.

The Treaty of Friendship, Cooperation and Peace was signed by the two Prime Ministers in Dacca on March 19, 1972. The Treaty consisted of a preamble and 12 articles. The preamble specified peace, secularism, democracy, socialism and nationalism as the common ideals that inspired the two nations. The preamble also stressed their determination to maintain fraternal and good neighborly relations and to transform their border into a border of eternal peace and friendship. The first article of the Treaty reiterated the declaration that there would be lasting peace and friendship between the two countries and their peoples. The Treaty condemned colonialism, reaffirmed faith in the policy of non-alignment and peaceful co-existence and confirmed the need to maintain regular contacts on major international problems affecting the interests of both states. It contained a solemn declaration that they would not enter into or participate in any military alliance directed against the other party. The Treaty stated that the parties would continue to strengthen and widen their mutually advantageous and all-round cooperation in the economic, scientific and technical fields, and would develop mutual cooperation in the fields of trade, transport and communications. They would also promote relations in the fields of literature, education, culture, sports and education. In the area of water resources, the parties agreed "to make joint studies and take joint action in the fields

---

[6] Speech of the Prime Minister of India, Mrs. Indira Gandhi, at a public rally in Dacca, March 17, 1972, in Bhasin, *supra* note 2, at 22.

of flood control, river basin development and the fields of hydroelectric power and irrigation."[7] The Treaty would come into force with immediate effect and would remain in force for 25 years.

The Treaty was a strong political statement that called for cooperation and strengthened relations between the two countries. Its signature was followed by the conclusion of other agreements, including the trade agreement signed on March 28, 1972.[8] However, this goodwill and determination to maintain and strengthen the friendly relationship would soon meet problems and difficulties, some of which pre-dated the birth of Bangladesh, whereas others started cropping up from the start of Bangladesh's independence. The problem of the Farakka Barrage, the most difficult of all, was raised by Bangladesh during the visit of Sheikh Mujib two months after Bangladesh was recognized by India, and reference to it was already included in the joint communique issued at the end of the visit.

3. Shared Water Resources

As appears from the above, shared water resources and the problems associated therewith figured out quite prominently in the relationship of India and Bangladesh from the very start. Fifty-four rivers, including the three large ones, the Ganges, Brahmaputra and Meghna, are shared between India and Bangladesh, with Bangladesh being the lowest riparian for all of them. Utilization of those rivers, particularly the Ganges, has been a hotly contended issue. It is worth mentioning that no agreement was reached between India and Pakistan, prior to the emergence of Bangladesh, on any of those rivers.

Of the three large river basins that are shared, the Ganges River has been the most contentious and difficult. The Ganges Basin, known in India as the Ganga and in Bangladesh as the Padma, is an international river to which India, Bangladesh, Nepal and China are the riparian states. It rises in the slopes of the Himalayas at the border between Nepal and China, and India and China. The tributaries that originate in Nepal and China, including the Kosi, Gandaki, Kamala, Bagmati, Karnali and

---

[7] *Supra* note 3 and accompanying text. It should be also noted in this context that the 1950 Treaty of Peace and Friendship between India and Nepal does not contain any provision regarding waters shared between India and Nepal. *See supra* Chapter 3, note 2. The clear statement regarding cooperation in the area of water resources included in the India-Bangladesh Treaty of Friendship, Cooperation and Peace, confirms the prominence given to water in the India-Bangladesh relations.

[8] Trade Agreement between the Government of India and the Government of Bangladesh, signed in New Delhi on March 28, 1972, *see* Bhasin, *supra* note 2, at 1208. According to Article V of the Agreement, "The two governments agree to make mutually beneficial arrangements for the use of their waterways, railways and roadways for commerce between the two countries and for passage of goods between places in one country through the territory of the other." India actually needs those arrangements more than Bangladesh because the northeast states of India are almost separated from the rest of India by Bangladesh. Based on Article V of the Trade Agreement, the two countries signed the Protocol between the Government of India and the Government of Bangladesh on Inland Water Transit and Trade in Dacca on November 1, 1972. *See* Bhasin, *supra* note 2, at 1233. The Protocol defined certain routes in both countries, and laid down certain obligation with regard to the use of those inland water routes. The Protocol was to remain in force for five years.

Mahakali, account for about 45 percent of the Ganges flow.[9] The river is joined by a number of other tributaries originating inside India such as the Yamuna, the Tons and the Gomti. The total length of the Ganges from the slopes of the Himalayas to the Bay of Bengal is about 1,600 miles (about 2,600 kilometers). Of the total drainage area of 1,117,000 km^2, 188,220 km^2 are in Nepal and China, 861,390 km^2 are in India and 67,390 km^2 are in Bangladesh.[10] As such, the largest portion of the Ganges falls within India. Indeed, the Ganges is the largest basin in India. Within India the river is an inter-state river shared by the states of Uttar Pradesh, Himachal Pradesh, Rajasthan, Haryana, Madhya Pradesh, Bihar, West Bengal, and the National Capital Territory of Delhi.

The delta of the Ganges River starts at Farakka, in the state of West Bengal. Downstream from Farakka the river splits into two: the Padma, which flows eastward forming the boundary between India and Bangladesh for about 80 miles before entering Bangladesh, and the Bhagirathi which continues to flow southward into West Bengal. After the Bhagirathi is joined by the Jalangi River it is known as the Hooghly River. Calcutta city, the capital of West Bengal and one of India's most important ports, is situated on the Hooghly River. South of Calcutta, the Hooghly is joined by the Damodar River and flows into the Bay of Bengal. In Bangladesh, the Ganges, which is known as the Padma, is joined by both the Brahmaputra River, which is known in Bangladesh as the Jamuna River, and also by the Meghna River. The combination of the three rivers, which continues to be called the Padma, splits downstream into a number of channels, all flowing into the Bay of Bengal.[11]

The Brahmaputra rises in the eastern slopes of the Himalayas and flows for about 1,800 miles (about 2,900 kilometers) through China, India and Bangladesh. It is joined by a major tributary, the Manas, which originates in China and flows across Bhutan, thus adding Bhutan as a riparian to the Brahmaputra River. The Meghna, the smallest of the three rivers, is shared by India and Bangladesh. It originates in the Indian State of Mizoram where it is known as the Barak, and enters Bangladesh to join the Padma River.

No agreement was concluded between any of the riparian states on the Brahmaputra or the Meghna Basins. India and Bangladesh entered, as we shall see, into a series of short-term successive agreements on the Ganges, starting in 1975, the last of which expired in 1988. Finally, India and Bangladesh concluded a Treaty

---

[9] Arun P. Elhance, *Hydropolitics in the Third World: Conflict and Cooperation in International River Basins,* (Washington, DC: World Bank, 1999), at 157.

[10] Nahid Islam, "The Regime of International Watercourses: The Case of The Ganges from an Asian Perspective," in *International Boundaries and Environmental Security – Framework for Regional Cooperation*, Gerald Blake et al., eds. (London: Kluwer Law International, 1997), at 323.

[11] For a detailed description of the Ganges Basin, *see* B. R. Chauhan, *Settlement of International and Inter-State Water Disputes in India* (New Delhi: Indian Law Institute, 1992); *see also,* Tauhidul Anwar Khan, "Management and Sharing of the Ganges," *Natural Resources Journal* 36, (1996), at 455; *see also* generally B. C. Upreti, *Politics of Himalayan River Waters: An Analysis of the River Water Issues of Nepal, India and Bangladesh* (Delhi: Nirala Publication, 1993).

Map 5: The Ganges River Basin

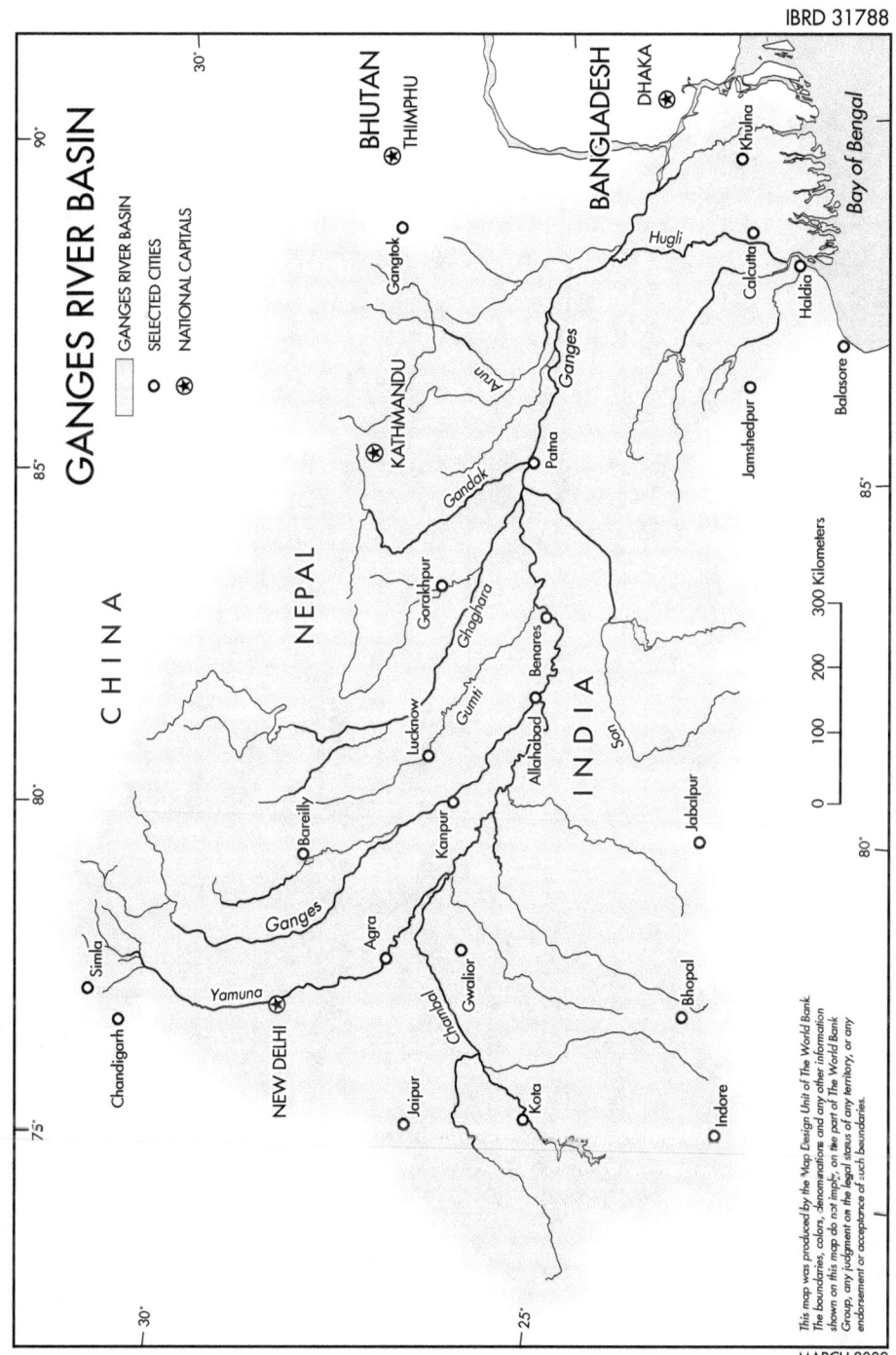

on December 12, 1996, on the sharing of the Ganges. The other two riparians, Nepal and China, however, are not party to the Treaty.

The Ganges-Brahmaputra-Meghna Basins are three of the most densely populated basins in the world, with a total population of about 600 million,[12] almost one-tenth of the world population. They also have the largest concentration of poor people in the world. Of the three basins, the Ganges is the most densely populated. According to 1993 figures, the estimated population of the Ganges was then "about 405 million people, including 346 million in India, 19 million in Nepal and about 40 million in Bangladesh."[13] The population density of the Ganges is estimated at 375 persons per square kilometer, one of the highest in the world.[14] This heavy population density has resulted in significant pressure on the Ganges Basin and has caused it to be one of the most polluted rivers in the world.

The seasonal variations in the flow of the Ganges is so acute that it can result in both drought and floods. During the dry season from January to May every year, drought could prevail, particularly in Bangladesh after the diversion of some of the waters of the Ganges through the Farakka Barrage and its feeder canal. On the other hand, Bangladesh suffers from severe floods during the monsoon which lasts from June to September when the melting snow of the Himalayas and the heavy rain in the region reach Bangladesh through the three mighty rivers and the smaller rivers, on their way to drain at the Bay of the Bengal. This situation is made worse by the monsoon rain in Bangladesh. "About 2.6 to 3 million hectares (in Bangladesh) are flooded annually. In an abnormal year, when there is a synchronization of very heavy rainfall with peak discharges simultaneously in the Ganga and Brahmaputra, this figure may reach 6.5 million hectares or some 45 percent of the total area as happened in 1955 and 1974."[15] These floods usually result in deaths and destruction of property, crops and livestock, and soil erosion. Water-borne diseases spread rapidly during this season and contribute to the deaths and economic problems of the country.

It is not surprising, under those circumstances, that Bangladesh felt the pressing need to raise the issue of water resources with India from the start of its emergence, and even before the new state had fully taken off. As we have noted, the Joint Communique at the end of Sheikh Mujib's visit to India in February 1972, about a month after his return to Bangladesh, raised the issue of the Farakka Barrage and the other problems of development of water and power resources. Although no agreement was reached on how to deal with the Farakka Barrage, the two Prime Ministers agreed that the countries would engage in exchanging ideas and in setting up suit-

---

[12] B. G. Verghese, *Waters of Hope – From Vision to Reality in the Himalaya-Ganga Development Cooperation* (New Delhi: Oxford & IBH Publishing, 1999) at 335; *see* also Elhance, *supra* note 9, at 161.

[13] *See* Khan *supra* note 11, at 456.

[14] *See* The World Commission on Dams, *Dams and Development – A New Framework for Decision-Making* (2000), at 17. According to the report, and by way of comparison, the population density of the Yangtze River in China is 224 persons per square kilometer; *id.*, at 17.

[15] *See* Verghese, *supra* note 12, at 121.

able machinery for formulating appropriate programs. The Treaty of Friendship, Cooperation and Peace included one article on flood control, river basin development and the development of hydroelectric power and irrigation. The Joint Declaration issued at the end of the visit of the Prime Minister of India, Mrs. Indira Gandhi, to Bangladesh on March 19, 1972 included the decision "To establish a Joint Rivers Commission comprising the experts of both countries on a permanent basis to carry out a comprehensive survey of the river systems shared by the two countries, formulate projects concerning both the countries in the fields of flood control and to implement them."[16] The Joint Declaration went on to state: "Experts of the two countries are directed to formulate detailed proposals on advance flood warnings, flood forecasting, study of flood control and irrigation projects on the major river systems and examine the feasibility of linking the power grids of Bangladesh with the adjoining areas of India, so that the water resources of the region can be utilized on an equitable basis for the mutual benefit of the people of the two countries."

The Joint Rivers Commission was subsequently established, and held its first meeting in New Delhi in June 26, 1972. That meeting was devoted to the issue of the flood situation in the eastern region of Bangladesh and adjacent areas in India. The Commission decided to set up a joint study group to assess the situation and formulate possible short-term and long-term measures for reducing the flood damage in this area. The Commission prepared in that meeting rules of business and other procedural matters for its work. However, it was decided to formalize the status of the Commission through the issuance of a legal instrument that described the functions and structure of the Commission. Hence, on November 24, 1972, the two countries signed the Statute of the Indo-Bangladesh Joint Rivers Commission in Dacca.[17] The Statute consists of nine articles divided into five chapters. According to the Statute, each country would appoint four members, including a chairman, who would hold office for a period of three years. Two of the four members shall be engineers. The chairmanship of the Commission is to be held annually in turn between the two countries. The functions of the Commission, according to Article 4 (i) are: "(a) to maintain liaison between the participating countries in order to ensure the most effective joint efforts in maximizing the benefits from the Common River System to both countries; (b) to formulate flood control works and to recommend implementation of joint projects; (c) to formulate detailed proposals on advance flood warnings, flood forecasting and cyclone warnings; (d) to study flood control and irrigation projects so that the water resources of the region can be utilized on an equitable basis for the mutual benefit of the two countries; (e) to formulate proposals for carrying out coordinated research on problems of flood control affecting both the countries." In addition, according to Article 4 (ii), "The Commission shall also

---

[16] *See* Joint Declaration issued at the end of the visit of the Prime Minister of India, Mrs. Indira Gandhi, to Bangladesh; Dacca, March 19, 1972, in Bhasin, *supra* note 2, at 33.

[17] *See* Statute of the Indo-Bangladesh Joint Rivers Commission, in Bhasin, *supra* note 2, at 370–372; *see* B. M. Abbas, *The Ganges Water Dispute* (Dhaka: Univ. Press, 1984) at 138–141.

perform such other functions as the two governments may, by mutual agreement, direct it to do."

Ordinary sessions of the Commission would be held as often as necessary, generally four times a year, and the decisions of the Commission shall be unanimous. Differences in the interpretation of the Statute would be referred to the two governments to be dealt with on a bilateral basis.

Thus, the spirit of cooperation was carried further by the establishment and functioning of the Joint Rivers Commission. With regard to the common river system, the role of the Commission is no more than maintaining the liaison between the two countries, formulating proposals and carrying out studies, and no powers have been granted to the Commission to take a proactive role and make decisions with regard to such rivers. The Commission is clearly not a river basin management organization, nor is it intended to be so. The emphasis on its functions is basically on flood control, and the authority the Commission has is largely of making recommendations, formulating proposals and studying projects, rather than taking decisions and implementing them. As we shall see, the issues of Farakka Barrage and floods dominated the meetings of the Joint Rivers Commission for the next 20 years, with no agreement on what could be done. The meetings have not been as regular as the Statute prescribes, basically as a result of the dispute over the Ganges that shaped, to a large extent, the work of the Commission.

4. The Farakka Barrage

The dispute over the Ganges erupted as a result of India's decision to construct a barrage in West Bengal, known as the Farakka Barrage, about 10 miles from the borders with Bangladesh that was then East Pakistan.[18] The Farakka Barrage, India contended, was needed to divert enough waters from the Ganges to the Hooghly River to maintain the flow of the Hooghly River and make it navigable, and thus make the Calcutta Port accessible, by flushing down the silt that gradually deposits in the Calcutta Port. Other incidental reasons for the barrage were to overcome the problem of salinity, and to provide water to Calcutta for irrigation, domestic and municipal purposes.

The decision to construct the Farakka Barrage was made in 1951. Actual work on the barrage started in 1961 and was completed in 1971. The barrage is about 2,240 meters long. The feeder canal from the barrage, which is about 25 miles long, was

---

[18] According to the World Commission on Dams, a barrage is "A structure built across a river consisting of a series of gates that when fully open allow the flood to pass without appreciably increasing the water level upstream of the barrage, and that when closed raise water levels upstream to facilitate diversion of water to a canal for irrigation or to powerhouse for the generation of electricity." *See* Dams and Development, *supra* note 14, at 344. The difference between a dam and a barrage is worth noting. "A dam is built with the purpose of storing water and it is built in the upper, deep valleyed reaches of a river, thereby raising the level of water by hundreds of feet. On the other hand, a barrage is built with the aim of diverting water and it is built in the plains, across wide meandering rivers. Since it is a long and wide structure, the water level is only raised by a few feet." *See* Bharat Desai, "Sharing of International Water Resources," *Asia Pacific Journal of Environmental Law* 3 (1998), at 172-173.

completed in 1975 and the barrage came into operation on April 21, 1975. The purpose of the barrage was to ensure that the Hooghly River would receive, however low the flow of the Ganges may be, up to 40,000 cubic feet per second (cusecs) of water diverted from the Ganges. With the assumption that the availability of water in the Ganges at Farakka in the worst lean season would be around 50,000 to 55,000 cusecs, the remaining 10,000 to 15,000 cusecs would be released to East Pakistan.

During the 1950s and 1960s, Pakistan strongly opposed the construction of the barrage, and tried different diplomatic channels to stop its construction. In opposing the barrage, Pakistan insisted that the lean flow of the Ganges of 50,000 to 55,000 cusecs constituted its normal and basic requirements for irrigation, domestic, municipal and other uses, and any decrease in the flow of the Ganges would negatively affect irrigation, water supply, fishery production, groundwater tables, and river navigation which is the most common mode of transportation in East Pakistan, and would worsen the problem of salinity. Occasionally, talks between India and Pakistan over the Farakka Barrage took place, but no serious discussion or negotiations at a high level were conducted. "India has maintained for much of the dispute that the Ganges is not an 'international river.' To have entered into negotiations with Pakistan would have been a denial of this line of argument."[19] This claim was based, as we have noted, on the fact that about 80 percent of the Ganges Basin area lies in India.

However, despite the contention that the Ganges is not an international river, and as such is not subject to international negotiations, India denounced on March 26, 1956 the "International Convention and Statute Concerning the Regime of Navigable Waterways of International Concern, 1921,"[20] commonly known as the Barcelona Convention. According to Article 1 of the Convention a waterway that separates or traverses different states is declared to be a navigable waterway of international concern. Paragraph 1 of Article 10 states:

> 1. Each riparian State is bound, on the one hand, to refrain from all measures likely to prejudice the navigability of the waterway, or to reduce the facilities for navigation, and on the other hand, to take as rapidly as possible all necessary steps for removing any obstacles and dangers which may occur to navigation.

Pakistan protested the denunciation of the Barcelona Convention by India, concluding that the action was meant to enable India to go ahead with the construction of the Farakka Barrage without being accused of breaching its international obligations. India replied that "the Barcelona Convention and Statute dealt with only some aspects of inland navigation and its purpose had been superseded by GATT."[21] The

---

[19] Ben Crow et al., *Sharing the Ganges – The Politics and Technology of River Development*, (New Delhi: Sage Publications, 1995), at 84.

[20] *See* M. J. Bowman and D. J. Harris, *Multilateral Treaties – Index and Current Status*, (London;:Butterworth, 1984), at 46; *see* also Introduction, *supra*.

[21] *See* Abbas, *supra* note 17, at 19.

Indian contention was difficult to accept and the linkage of the denunciation of the Barcelona Convention to the Farakka Barrage cannot be escaped.

It should be recalled that during those years, negotiations between India and Pakistan over the Indus River, which were mediated by the World Bank, were progressing well.[22] Those negotiations culminated in the signing of the Indus Treaty on September 19, 1960. With this in mind, Pakistan proposed to India the intervention of an agreed United Nations body to assist in the cooperative development of the Eastern Rivers. But India was not persuaded.[23] The meetings between India and Pakistan were infrequent and continued to be held at a low level. India continued to demand more information and data on the utilization of the Ganges in East Pakistan, but the supply of this data was not used for any meaningful purpose. In 1962 Pakistan proposed the construction of the Ganges Barrage, which would be built on the Ganges River at the Hardinge bridge area in East Pakistan close to the borders with India. Ostensibly, the barrage would be used for restoring the wet season flow of the Ganges for use during the dry season. It would also be used for irrigating large areas in the Southwestern parts of East Pakistan. In 1969, Pakistan presented the feasibility report to India. However, India viewed the idea of the Ganges Barrage as a retaliatory measure against the Farakka Barrage. India also claimed that because of backwater effect some areas in the Indian State of West Bengal would be submerged.[24] The idea of the Ganges Barrage kept emerging during the different eras of the dispute but has not yet materialized.

As the Pakistani era in the dispute over the Ganges was coming to an end by 1970, it became clear that the expert level meetings between India and Pakistan yielded no results, and the Farakka Barrage, the construction of which started in 1961, was about to be completed. Indeed, by the time Bangladesh emerged as an independent nation, the Farakka Barrage was completed and work on the feeder canal had started. Despite the close ties between India and Bangladesh, the Farakka Barrage remained a thorny issue. As we have seen, the issue was included in the Joint Communique issued at the end of the visit of Sheikh Mujib to India in February 1971. The third meeting of the Joint Rivers Commission held in Delhi on December 11–13, 1972, "…recommended a program of joint survey of the river Ganges from Farakka up to Gorai off-take to enable the planning of development works of mutual interest."[25]

The Bangladesh authorities were clearly in a difficult position. They had been assisted militarily and economically by India during and after the struggle for independence. India had also provided strong support for Bangladesh to gain diplomatic recognition and to join the international community. The conclusion of the Treaty of Friendship, Cooperation and Peace was indicative of the extent to which

---

[22] *See supra* Chapter 2.

[23] *See* Verghese, *supra* note 12, at 359.

[24] *See* Abbas, *supra* note 17, at 25. *See* also Ben Crow, *supra* note 19, at 92–93.

[25] *See* Joint Press Note Issued on the Conclusion of the three-day meeting of the Indo-Bangladesh Joint Rivers Commission, New Delhi, December 13, 1972, in Bhasin, *supra* note 2, at 373.

Bangladesh was relying militarily and politically on India for its protection. At the same time Bangladesh was watching as India was completing the Farakka Barrage and starting the work on the feeder canal that would divert most of the lean season flow of the Ganges away from Bangladesh to the Hooghly River. There was not much that Bangladesh could do other than to keep raising the issue at high level meetings and hope that a solution could be found. On July 16, 1973 the Minister of Flood Control, Water Resources and Power of Bangladesh visited India and met with the Minister of External Affairs. The purpose of the meeting was to discuss the 54 rivers shared between India and Bangladesh. The meeting reiterated that matters concerning the development of those rivers common to both countries would be settled through mutual discussion with a view to ensuring benefits to the peoples of both countries, and in accordance with Article 6 of the Treaty of Friendship, Cooperation and Peace, and the Statute of the Indo-Bangladesh Joint Rivers Commission. The meeting also discussed "the commissioning of the Farakka Feeder Canal and its impact on Bangladesh. A point of view was expressed in the discussion that the Farakka Project might increase the flood intensity of Padma in Bangladesh by reducing the natural spill discharges into the Bhagirathi. The Indian side assured the Bangladesh side that the feeder canal and the Jangipur Barrage will be so operated that the Bhagirathi will continue to receive during the monsoon period so much water as before, or more if possible."[26] It was agreed further that the two sides would meet again and continue the discussion with a view to arriving at a solution of the problem of the Farakka Barrage. "The two sides further agreed that a mutually acceptable solution will be arrived at before operating the Farakka Barrage Project."[27]

The Farakka Barrage had gradually sunk in the minds of the Bangladesh authorities as a *fait accompli*. It had been completed and there was no way that India would demolish the barrage or cancel its commissioning. The issues that the Bangladeshi authorities kept raising related mainly to the modus operandi of the barrage, not whether there would be a barrage. And the answers to the questions they kept raising were more studies and investigations, and an agreement to agree on a mutually acceptable solution. Bangladesh's options were clearly limited as appeared in Sheikh Mujib's visit to India May 12–16, 1974. That was his third visit to India. The Joint Declaration issued at the end of his visit addressed in detail the issue of the Farakka Barrage, and stated that:

17. The two Prime Ministers took note of the fact that the Farakka Barrage Project would be commissioned before the end of 1974. They recognized that during the periods of minimum flow in the Ganga, there might not be enough water to meet the needs of the Calcutta Port and the full requirements of Bangladesh and therefore, the fair weather flow of the Ganga in the lean months would have to be augmented to meet the requirements of the two coun-

---

[26] Joint Press Note Issued at the Conclusion of the Talks between the Delegations of India and Bangladesh on the Eastern Rivers, New Delhi, July 18, 1973, in Bhasin, *supra* note 2, at 375-376.

[27] *Id.*, at 376.

tries. It was agreed that the problems should be approached with understanding so that the interests of both countries are reconciled and the difficulties removed in the spirit of friendship and cooperation. It was accordingly, decided that the best means of such augmentation through optimum utilization of the water resources of the region available to the two countries should be studied by the Joint Rivers Commission. The Commission should make suitable recommendations to meet the requirements of both countries.

18. It was recognized that it would take some years to give effect to the recommendations of the Commission as accepted by the two governments. In the meantime, the two sides expressed their determination that before the Farakka Project is commissioned, they would arrive at a mutually acceptable allocation of the water available during the periods of minimum flow in the Ganga.[28]

The above two paragraphs of the Joint Declaration provided substantive concessions to India. The Farakka Barrage was now a reality that Bangladesh formally accepted, and whose timing and commissioning it endorsed. Consequently, Bangladesh also accepted the fact that the dispute had moved from the existence of the barrage to water allocation during the lean season, and augmentation of the flow of the Ganges during such season. Furthermore, Bangladesh agreed that the augmentation would be through "optimum utilization of the water resources of the region available to the two countries." This last statement would come to haunt Bangladesh when the discussion on augmenting the flow of the Ganges started. The statement clearly adopted the position of India on augmentation when it referred to the "water resources of the region" because India's proposal for augmentation rested, as we shall see, on using the waters of the Brahmaputra to augment the flow of the Ganges. Bangladesh had consistently and vehemently opposed this proposal.

5. The Early Agreements and Interventions
A. The 1975 Partial Accord

During the rest of 1974, more visits of high level delegations continued between the two countries. Each of the two Presidents visited the capital of the other country, and so did the Ministers of Foreign Affairs. The joint declarations kept expressing confidence that a mutually satisfactory solution to the issue of the Farakka Barrage would be arrived at soon. The tide was clearly flowing in favor of the commissioning of the Farakka Barrage. Sheikh Mujib, who in January 1975 introduced a presidential system in Bangladesh and assumed the presidency, had clearly succumbed to the pressures of India. On April 18, 1975, Bangladesh agreed to the test running of the feeder canal through diversion of waters from the Ganges. The agreement to commission the barrage, the Partial Accord between India and Bangladesh on

---

[28] Joint Declaration Issued at the End of the Visit of the Bangladesh Prime Minister Sheikh Mujibur Rahman to India, May 16, 1974, in Bhasin, *supra* note 2, at 88-93. The issue of commercial relations and economic and trade cooperation between the two countries were also discussed. It was noted in Paragraph 15 of the Declaration that during the financial year 1974-75, Rs. 38 crores would be available from India to Bangladesh.

Farakka, was announced in a joint press release in Dacca, and as such, was not signed by the parties.

The Accord referred to the talks held between the Indian delegation led by the Minister of Agriculture and Irrigation and the delegation from Bangladesh led by the Minister of Flood Control, Water Resources and Power from April 16–18, 1975. The Accord stated that "while discussions regarding allocation of fair weather flow of the Ganga during lean months in terms of the Prime Ministers declaration of May 1974 are continuing, it is essential to run the feeder canal of the Farakka Barrage during the current lean period."[29] The Accord showed the amounts diverted through the feeder canal, as reflected in Table 7.1:

Table 7.1
Amounts of the Waters of the Ganges Diverted to the Feeder Canal Under the 1975 Partial Accord

Month	Ten-day period	Withdrawal
April, 1975	21–30	11,000 Cusecs
May, 1975	1–10	12,000 Cusecs
	11–20	15,000 Cusecs
	21–31	16,000 Cusecs

Source: Partial Accord between India and Bangladesh on Farakka.

The Accord established joint teams to observe at appropriate places in both countries the effects of the agreed withdrawals at Farakka, in Bangladesh, and on the Hooghly River for the benefit of Calcutta Port. A joint team would also be stationed at Farakka to record the discharges into the feeder canal and the remaining flows for Bangladesh. Those teams would submit their reports to the two governments for consideration.

Thus the Farakka Barrage came into operation, taking the Indo-Bangladesh relationship into another controversial chapter. India had finally fulfilled its quarter-of-a century-old plan of diverting the waters of the Ganges to the Calcutta Port, and did so through an agreement rather than unilaterally, thus giving legitimacy to its initial controversial and contested action. Bangladesh culminated its acceptance of the barrage, not only through an accord, but it also sent a delegation to attend the inauguration of the Farakka Barrage.[30]

Taking into account the dependable supplies at Farakka as established in the later agreements between India and Bangladesh, the remaining flow for Bangladesh during those 41 days was fairly high. Table 7.2 shows the amounts of water that each country would be getting during the 41-day period of the Accord:

---

[29] Partial Accord Between India and Bangladesh on Farakka, in Bhasin, *supra* note 2, at 386; *see also* Abbas, *supra* note 17, at 41–42.

[30] *See* Abbas, *supra* note 17, at 42.

TABLE 7.2
Share of India and Bangladesh of the Waters of the Ganges at Farakka Under the 1975 Partial Accord

Ten-day Period	Dependable supplies at Farakka (in Cusecs)	Amount agreed upon for Hooghly (in Cusecs)	Remaining flow for Bangladesh (in Cusecs)
April 21–30, 1975	55,000	11,000	44,000
May 1–10, 1975	56,500	12,000	44,500
May 11–20, 1975	59,250	15,000	44,250
May 21–31, 1975	65,500	16,000	49,500

Source: The 1975 Partial Accord, and Column 2 of Table 7.3 (infra).

Under this Accord, India's share during each of the four 10-day periods was far less than the 40,000 cusecs it initially demanded, and varied between 20–25 percent of the available water. On the other hand, the share of Bangladesh ranged between 75–80 percent of the available water. The share of Bangladesh during those 41 days represented about 77 percent of the total amount of water for that period, while the share of India for the same period was about 23 percent.

The Accord lasted only for the remaining period of 41 days of the lean season of 1975. It expired on May 31, 1975, and was not renewed or replaced by another agreement. India started withdrawals to the full capacity of the feeder canal of 40,000 cusecs after expiry of the Accord. However, because such withdrawal was begun during the monsoon season, its effects were not immediately felt in Bangladesh.

The Joint Rivers Commission held six meetings between June 1974 and June 1975, and one of the main issues discussed in those meetings was the augmentation of the flow of the Ganges River.[31] India proposed augmenting the flow of the Ganges through diversions from the Brahmaputra by a link canal connecting the two rivers. Bangladesh proposed storage reservoirs in the upper reaches of the Ganges in India and Nepal.[32] The impasse over their contrasting proposals would last for the next 21 years.

Relations between the two countries started to deteriorate. On August 15, 1975, Sheikh Mujib and some members of his family were assassinated, and the army took over power in Bangladesh. Anti-India propaganda started appearing in the Bangladesh press. The honeymoon was clearly coming to an end. An attempt on the life of the Indian High Commissioner in Bangladesh in November 1975 indicated the level of deterioration of the relationship between the two countries.

The Accord of 1975 appears in retrospect to have been a miscalculation on the part of Bangladesh. It gave India the right to commission the barrage without a real

---

[31] *Id.*, at 43.

[32] For discussion of the proposal of each country, *see infra*, Part D 2.

quid pro quo in terms of fixed amounts of releases to Bangladesh for a reasonable number of years until the issue of augmentation was agreed upon. Now that the feeder canal was working to its full capacity, Bangladesh's argument that the 1975 Accord was just for test running the feeder canal did not seem to carry much weight. It was not reasonable for Bangladesh to expect India to close the gates to the feeder canal, after test running it for six weeks of the dry season and seven months of the monsoon season. Perhaps Sheikh Mujib was optimistic of working out some kind of an agreement with Mrs. Indira Gandhi during the wet season of 1975. That might have been the basis of his agreement to the test-running of the feeder canal, and perhaps that might have been the reason why the agreement was termed "Partial Accord," meaning that it was not a complete agreement. Now that Sheikh Mujib was gone, there was not much Bangladesh could do. India continued diversion of the water of the Ganges to the full capacity of the feeder canal after the end of the monsoon season and during the lean season of 1976. The bilateral talks were showing no progress, and the relations between the two countries continued to deteriorate.

B. Role of the United Nations

On August 21, 1976, Bangladesh decided to take its dispute with India over the Farakka Barrage to the United Nations. Justifying the decision to take the issue to the United Nations, Bangladesh explained, "It is not that we do not believe in bilateral discussions, but because we can not wait indefinitely, we want an expeditious solution to Farakka before the next dry season."[33]

India indicated its regret that Bangladesh had interrupted the process of bilateral negotiations and had sought to internationalize the issue. In preparation for the discussion of the issue at the United Nations, Bangladesh prepared in September 1976, a White Paper on Farakka, describing the disastrous effects the withdrawal had on Bangladesh. India responded by issuing its own paper on India's Case of the Farakka Barrage, which addressed the points raised by Bangladesh and tried to negate them.

(i) *The White Paper on Farakka:* After describing the importance of the Ganges to the 37 percent of the total area of the country served by the Ganges, and the one-third of the population dependent on the river, the paper went on to describe the adverse impact of India's withdrawals on Bangladesh. The most devastating effect of the diversion, the paper claimed, was the marked increase in salinity reflected in both, intrusion upstream, and soil moisture depletion caused by the lowering of groundwater tables. The saline intrusion from the tides of the Bay of Bengal was counteracted by upland flows of the Ganges. With the decrease in the upland flows, salinity has increased and advanced far distances inland. The major direct adverse impact of salinity was felt on agricultural production, fishery, forestry, power generation and industry. Health and expected mortality were also affected. As soil

---

[33] Press Conference of Deputy Chief Martial Law Administrator Rear Admiral Mosharraf Hossain Khan on Bangladesh's decision to raise the Farakka issue at the United Nations, Dacca August 25, 1975, in Bhasin, *supra* note 2, at 407.

becomes saline, productivity is reduced, and eventually the soil becomes barren. Water itself becomes less suitable for irrigation. The paper claimed that more than 400,000 acres of land were affected as a result of increased salinity and soil moisture deficiency, and more than 400 low lift pumps suffered because of water scarcity and salinity. All the shallow tubewells were adversely affected, and a large number of deep tubewells were also affected because of the fall in the sub-soil water level. The level of water at the Gorai Bridge on the river Gorai fell to 11 feet compared to an average of 15 feet in the previous four years. Delayed planting reduced high-yielding variety yields by 30 percent, and the inability to provide supplemental irrigation reduced the crop yield by roughly 10 percent. Moreover, the paper stated, the reduced water availability significantly reduced the landing of fish probably because of the disturbance of the historic food chain and the inability of the fish to tolerate shallow depths and high levels of salinity. The reduced water flow and increased salinity also had deleterious effects on the Sunderbans forests, an area of unique ecological status. The forest itself is graded on a three-tier quality standard, with the quality and yield directly correlated to the soil salinity. The yield difference over a 20-year growing cycle between quality I, the bulk of the Sundri, and quality III was 640 cubic feet per acre. Such a reduction in yields, the paper claimed, would naturally affect the 45,000 people directly employed in clearing the forest. The paper also addressed the issue of navigation and claimed that the reduced flow of water seriously impeded inland water navigation that is critical in Bangladesh because of the poorly developed transport infrastructure. The reduced flow forced the major ferry terminals to shift their operations, and 90 miles of navigation on the Ganges, 45 miles on the Gorai and 15 miles on the Padma went out of commission. The salinity level of the river water was too high for the tolerance of the Goalpara thermal power station and the power station had to close for some time. The station was operated intermittently by fresh water brought long distances by barges. The impact of the loss of power to the industries dependent on the power station was significant. The paper mill and the newsprint mills suffered from loss of power and the unusable saline water for processing end products. Increased salinity in drinking water affected health too. The results were a number of diseases, including dysentery and hypertension. The paper also highlighted the effects of the reduced flow of the Ganges on ecocycle and ecology, and contended that the wildlife of the Sunderbans were already endangered species.

The paper chronicled the events from 1951 until 1976 and concluded by stating that "India's repeated assurances of safeguarding the legitimate rights of both countries will be demonstrated by her restoring the normal flow of the Ganges to Bangladesh and agreeing to a permanent solution to the problem by the cooperative efforts of the co-riparian countries through construction of storages in the Ganges Basin. Another dry season will be on very soon. The present situation cannot persist further."[34]

---

[34] For the full text of the "White Paper on Farakka Issue," published by the Government of Bangladesh, Dacca, September 1976, *see* Bhasin, *supra* note 2, at 415.

(ii) *India's Case on Farakka:* Similarly, India published its own paper too, entitled "India's Case on the Farakka Barrage" in September 1976. The paper started by highlighting the importance of Calcutta Port, stating that it was the largest Indian city, with a population of eight million, was the commercial nerve center and one of the principal ports, serving seven states as well as the neighboring countries of Nepal and Bhutan, with half the Indian trade passing through the port. The entire trade was carried by the Hooghly River as the port is about 200 kilometers from the coast. The Hooghly is known as the Bhagirathi after the Ganges splits into two arms, the other one is the Padma that flows to Bangladesh. The paper claimed that for 200 years the Bhagirathi carried the bulk of the Ganges flow, but gradually the Ganges changed its course and the Padma became the principal carrier of the waters of the Ganges, "thus marking the deterioration of the Bhagirathi-Hooghly waterway and the threat to the survival of the Calcutta Port and its great metropolis."[35] Furthermore, the paper added, sea tides from the south and lack of adequate flow from the Ganges contributed to the progressive silting of the Hooghly, causing a decline in the use of the Calcutta Port and posing a threat to its survival. In turn, silting led to an increase in the intensity and frequency of tidal bores in the Hooghly, exposing ships to the danger of capsizing and twists. Moreover, salinity has intruded up the river, endangering the water supply of the metropolis and the ecology there, and the deterioration of the Ganges flow in the Bhagirathi resulted in an almost total loss of its navigability. For more than a century it was recognized by various commissions that the only means of saving the port of Calcutta from choking with silt was construction of a barrage across the Ganges near Farakka. The paper stated that the barrage and the feeder canal were commissioned following agreement with Bangladesh on April 18, 1975, and went on to detail the bilateral consultation with Pakistan before 1971, and with Bangladesh after that, and recounted the different joint declarations between the two countries. It noted that Bangladesh was politicizing and internationalizing the issue, and stated that by insisting that the "normal" or "historical" flow be restored, Bangladesh was implying that the Farakka Barrage be closed and the Calcutta Port should continue to languish and suffer. The paper discussed briefly the two proposals to augment the flow of the Ganges during the lean season and stated that India agreed to consider Bangladesh's proposal despite its belief that such proposal was not feasible. The paper stated that the available technical and economic data, studies and observations showed that the operation of the Farakka Barrage would not affect Bangladesh adversely, though some minor problems may arise that could be remedied without impeding the diversion of the Ganges into the Hooghly. The paper went on to address the adverse effects of the barrage raised by Bangladesh, stating that they were gross exaggerations, and to respond to each of them.[36]

---

[35] *See* "India's Case of the Farakka Barrage," Ministry of External Affairs, Government of India, New Delhi, September 1976, in Bhasin, *supra* note 2, at 437.

[36] For further discussion of the arguments presented by each of the papers, and the effects of Farakka, *see* Ben Crow, *supra* note 19, at 124.

On irrigation, the paper claimed that the maximum requirements of Bangladesh would be 9,000 cusecs, and would continue to be for the next 10 to 15 years, thus the release to Bangladesh after diversion of 40,000 cusecs should be more than adequate. Soil moisture, the paper alleged, depends entirely on the soil characteristics and local rainfall and has nothing to do with groundwater tables. The Padma reach was totally unaffected by salinity, and in the Gorai reach salinity effects could not be significant. The paper claimed that navigation was possible only in the months of high flow from June to November and practically ceased in the lean months, and as such it should not be affected by the diversion. The paper alleged that the problem of salinity was exaggerated out of all proportions because over 1,000 million acre-feet of water from the river system of Bangladesh drain into the Bay of Bengal and create a freshwater reservoir in the coastal areas that helps check penetration of seawater inland. As such, the reduction in flows in the Padma reach would not have any significant adverse consequences. On the issue of fisheries, the paper stated that the barrage could not have harmful results on fisheries because it did not alter the flow pattern in the monsoon months, and at any rate, Bangladesh had been experiencing over the years a decline in fish production that could be due to a variety of factors. Such factors could include indiscriminate netting because of the existing system of leasing fishing ponds, conversion of ponds into agricultural lands and uncontrolled use of pesticide and insecticide. The paper alleged that lean season flows of the Padma could not reach any part of the Sunderbans forest in Bangladesh, and thus the Farakka withdrawals could not have harmful effects on forestry in Bangladesh. On the issue of the effects of the diversion on industries, the paper claimed that India had been asking Bangladesh for data to enable it to study the results of salinity jointly, but no data had been furnished. On the issue of ecology, the paper stated that as the affected region is close to the sea, the problem of salinity with its adverse environmental implications has always been there. Floods that devastate the region every year and withdrawal of water for beneficial reasons would also have impact.

The paper went on to explain the relative dependence of India on the Ganges, stating that for 90 percent of its 1,925 km, the river flows through India. With its principal tributaries, it flows through 8,000 km of Indian territory with a catchment area of 777,000 sq. km, and with more than 40 percent of the population dependent on the Ganges. On the other hand, the length of the main channel of the Ganga in Bangladesh, the paper claimed, is only 141 km, excluding the common boundary of 112 km the catchment area of 5,600 sq. km hardly 0.7 percent of the catchment area in India. The paper concluded, "Thus as between India and Bangladesh, India is by far the major riparian country for the Ganga waters in terms of catchment area (99 percent), ultimate irrigation potential (94.5 percent), and population of the Ganga Basin (94 percent)".[37]

(iii) *Analysis of Bangladesh's and India's positions Under International Water Law:* Both papers discussed the principles of international water law and both

---

[37] *See* Bhasin, *supra* note 2, at 449.

claimed that those principles favored their position in the dispute over the Ganges. Both countries referred to the Helsinki Rules and cited Article IV that "each basin state is entitled within its territory to a reasonable and equitable share in the beneficial use of the waters of an international drainage basin." The factors listed in Article V of the Rules were also referred to by both states.[38] However, Bangladesh enumerated its uses of the water of the Ganges River and claimed that those were existing uses that have been made of the Ganges for centuries, resulting in a pattern of interdependence between land, water and human life, whereas the use of the Ganges by India for the Calcutta Port was totally new and a wasteful use as the silt could be removed by dredging the channel. In this regard, Bangladesh quoted Article VIII of the Helsinki Rules which states: "An existing reasonable use may continue in operation unless the factors justifying its continuance are outweighed by other factors leading to the conclusion that it be modified or terminated so as to accommodate a competing incompatible use." Bangladesh also invoked the theory of injury claiming that the injury caused to Bangladesh through the diversion of the waters to the Hooghly River was clear and substantial, quoting Principle 21 of the Declaration on the Human Environment.[39]

India's reply was that the Helsinki Rules do not oblige the upper riparian to leave intact the existing quantum of flow, and that insistence on the historical or natural flow was a total denial of the principle of equitable sharing enshrined in the Helsinki Rules, and amounted to an exercise of a veto on the rights of the upper riparian's right to a reasonable and equitable share.

Clearly, each country presented and interpreted the facts concerning the Ganges and the effects of diversion differently, and this was extended to the principles of international water law as well. India's position seemed initially to lean toward the principle of "absolute territorial sovereignty," according to which a riparian state has an unrestricted right to regulate and use within its territory the waters of an international river basin. However, its paper presented its case on the principle of equitable apportionment, claiming that on the basis of the factors laid down in Article V of the Helsinki Rules, it was entitled to that amount, but parrying the question of the diversion itself. On the other hand, Bangladesh seemed to rely on three principles: the principle of prior appropriation, which it referred to in terms of "existing uses" and "natural flow," equitable apportionment and the obligation not to cause appreciable harm. The reliance of each party on the principle of "equitable and reasonable utilization," and interpreting the principle to favor its position, is worth noting. Because India has viewed the Ganges as largely an Indian river, the invocation of the principle of equitable and reasonable utilization seemed logical. On the other

---

[38] For those factors, *see supra* Introduction, note 60.

[39] Principle 21 reads: "States have, in accordance with the Charter of the United Nations and the principles of international law, the sovereign right to exploit their own resources pursuant to their own environmental policies, and the responsibility to ensure that activities within their jurisdiction or control do not cause damage to the environment of other States or of other areas beyond the limits of national jurisdiction." *See* Principle 21, Declaration of the UN Conference on the Human Environment (Stockholm June 5, 1972), in *Basic Documents of International Environmental Law*, Vol.1 (Harald Hohmann, ed.), at 25-26.

hand, for Bangladesh as a lower riparian, invoking, *inter alia*, the obligation not to cause appreciable harm which Bangladesh linked to the notion of "existing rights" was natural and to be expected. Those positions underscore the problems associated with interpretation and application of some of the basic principles of international water law.[40] If this dispute was referred to an arbitral tribunal or to the International Court of Justice, the outcome would have most likely been a major contribution to the field of international water law.

The decision of Bangladesh to take the dispute over the Ganges River to the United Nations represented a major escalation in the dispute and indicated the extent of deterioration of the relationship between the two countries. Bangladesh was able to muster enough support to get the issue included in the agenda of the thirty-first session of the General Assembly, and to have it discussed in the political committee.[41] Bangladesh presented a resolution that included five elements: (i) calling on the parties concerned in the interests of peace and prosperity to arrive at immediate resolution of the dispute, (ii) recommending that in the meantime no unilateral action be taken that would affect the historical and traditional usages of the Ganges River, (iii) requesting the Secretary General of the United Nations to assist the parties in the immediate resolution of the dispute, (iv) requesting the Secretary General to follow up on the implementation of the resolution, and (v) including the item in the provisional agenda of the thirty-second session of the General Assembly of the United Nations.

However, Bangladesh was not able to muster enough support for this resolution. Instead, a Consensus Statement was adopted on November 26, 1976, which included six points: (i) affirmation by the parties of their adherence to the Declaration on Principles of International Law concerning Friendly Relations and Cooperation among States in accordance with the Charter of the United Nations, (ii) recognition by the parties of the urgency of the situation, particularly with the onset of another dry season, (iii) agreement by the parties that the situation called for an urgent solution, and to that end, the parties agreed to meet at Dacca at the Ministerial level for negotiations with a view to arriving at a fair and expeditious settlement, (iv) agreement to facilitate the establishment of an atmosphere conducive to the successful outcome of the negotiations, (v) undertaking to give due consideration to the most appropriate ways of utilizing the capacity of the United Nations system, and (vi) either party could report to the General Assembly at its thirty-second session on the progress achieved in the settlement of the problem.[42]

Although Bangladesh was not able to get its resolution adopted, the Consensus Statement should still be seen as a partial triumph for Bangladesh. Bangladesh was able to get wider publicity for the issue, which the Statement referred to as "a prob-

---

[40] *See* the discussion on "International Water Law," *supra* Chapter 1.

[41] For further details on the issue *see* Abbas, *supra* note 17 at 53, and Ben Crow, *supra* note 19, at 110. Bangladesh had earlier raised the issue at the Seventh Islamic Foreign Ministers Conference that was held in Istanbul, Turkey in May 1976, *see* Abbas, *supra* note 17, at 59.

[42] For the text of the Consensus Statement, *see* UNGA, A/SPC/31/7, dated 24 November 1976. *See* also Bhasin, *supra* note 2, at 488, and Abbas, *supra* note 17, at 65.

lem" and to the situation as "urgent" in light of the onset of another dry season. The undertaking to give due consideration of utilizing the capacity of the United Nations, as the Statement stated, should be viewed as another success to Bangladesh, as India had always resisted involvement of a third party. The Consensus Statement also gave the parties the right to report to the General Assembly in its thirty-second session, and this should also been seen as a concession to Bangladesh, as Bangladesh was the one likely to report back to the United Nations. Verghese saw the Statement as a definite embarrassment to India.[43] As we will see later, the Consensus Statement was one of the factors that facilitated the agreement that was reached by India and Bangladesh in 1977 over the Ganges River.

C. Role of the World Bank

One question that keeps being raised by scholars interested in the Ganges is why the World Bank did not play any role in the Ganges dispute. This question is legitimate because the Bank had successfully mediated the dispute between India and Pakistan over the Indus Basin, and is a signatory to the Indus Waters Treaty for the purposes of certain Articles and Annexures.[44] It is also a legitimate question in light of the expectation that the Bank could have used its leverage with both countries to try to assist in resolving one of the most difficult contemporary water disputes. It is noteworthy that while India and Pakistan were negotiating their dispute over the Indus in the mid- to late-fifties, they were already deadlocked over the Ganges and the meetings on that dispute were leading nowhere.

The Bank's involvement in the Ganges actually started in 1958 with the financing of a port project in Calcutta. The Project consisted of a program of rehabilitation and improvement of the port of Calcutta, including one component dealing with improvement of the river Hooghly.[45] Despite very extensive maintenance dredging in the Fulta Point reach of the river, navigable depths over the bars during much of each year were decreasing. It was apparent that dredging alone would not ensure access throughout the year to the port of Calcutta to vessels drawing 26 feet, nor was it cost feasible.[46] The Project thus aimed at improving the navigability of the Fulta Point-Hooghly Point reach of the river Hooghly by cutting back Fulta Point to a maximum of about 1,200 feet, constructing dikes above and below the mouth of the Damodar River for the purpose of extending the river Hooghly bank river-ward, and carrying out the related works. The wrapping jetty at the entrance to King George's Dock was also to be reconstructed and the bull nose at the upstream side of the

---

[43] *See* Verghese, *supra* note 12, at 361.

[44] *See supra*, Chapter 2.

[45] For the details of the Project *see* World Bank Report No. TO-164b, "Appraisal of the Port of Calcutta Rehabilitation Project," dated April 7, 1958. *See* also Loan Agreement for Calcutta Port Project between International Bank for Reconstruction and Development and the Commissioners for the Port of Calcutta, Loan No. 198 IN, dated June 25, 1958. The Bank extended a $29 million loan to the Commissioners for the Port of Calcutta, with a guarantee from India.

[46] *See id.*, Appraisal Report, at 9.

entrance was to be removed. In addition, the Project included three other components that dealt with improving the harbor and railway facilities, providing floating equipment and facilities, and miscellaneous works including construction of a new tea warehouse and installation of improved fire protection devises. The total cost of the Project was estimated at $59 million, of which the Bank provided $29 million as a Loan.[47] The Project was expected to be completed in five years, by 1963.

As a sequel to the above, three years later, in 1961, the Bank extended another loan for the Second Calcutta Port Project, again with the objective of improving the port of Calcutta.[48] Indeed, in 1958, rapid and unexpected siltation had given rise to serious deterioration of several of the bars of the river Hooghly and gravely limited the draught of ocean-going vessels using the port. The Commissioners for the Port of Calcutta, with its dredging fleet, were unable to deal adequately with the worsened riverine conditions, and the Bank, when approached, agreed to make funds available to provide increased dredging capacity to deal with the new situation.[49] The Project consisted of provision of floating and other port equipment, construction of roads, bridges, a dock water recirculation scheme, extension of docks and berths, and hydraulic studies of the Hooghly River. The hydraulic studies aimed at providing additional information that would lead to improvements of dredging techniques, indicate beneficial river training works and determine the feasibility of maintaining deep water along side the satellite port site, and improving deep water access thereto and to the existing Port of Calcutta.[50]

In parallel to the above activities, it is worth recalling that in 1961 India had started to construct, with its own funds, the Farakka Barrage, which aimed at diverting waters from the Ganges River to the Hooghly River. The decision regarding construction of the barrage was protested, as noted earlier, by Pakistan following which a dispute had gradually erupted between India and Pakistan. The eruption of the dispute between the two countries over the Ganges, apparently, prompted the Bank to stop financing new projects for the port of Calcutta, and the second port Project was the last Project that the Bank financed there. It should also be emphasized that, contrary to some perceptions in Bangladesh, the Bank was not involved in any way in the financing of the Farakka Barrage.[51]

---

[47] *See id.*, Loan Agreement, Description of the Project, at 14.

[48] For the details of the Project see, World Bank Report No. TO-280b, "Appraisal of the Port of Calcutta River Maintenance and Port Improvement Project," dated June 27, 1961. *See* also Loan Agreement for Second Calcutta Port Project between International Bank for Reconstruction and Development and the Commissioners for the Port Calcutta, Loan No. 294 IN, dated August 17, 1961. The Bank extended a Loan of $21 million to the Commissioners for the Port of Calcutta, with a guarantee from India.

[49] *See id.*, Appraisal Report, at 1.

[50] *See id.*, Loan Agreement, Description of the Project, at 15.

[51] Although the Bank was not involved in any way in the Farakka Barrage, more than 20 years after the barrage became operational, a civil suit was instituted against the World Bank in Bangladesh in 1997. *See* Memorandum of Appeal From Original Decree, the Supreme Court of Bangladesh, High Court Division (Civil Appellate Jurisdiction) F.A.T. No. 268 of 1997, F.A.T. 99

Although the dispute continued during the 1960s and escalated as the work on the barrage progressed, the Bank did not get directly involved in the dispute until early 1976. In that year, Mr. Robert McNamara, the then President of the World Bank "...indicated that he was interested in a long-term solution of the problem and that he would do whatever he could in the matter even though India was not going to approach the Bank."[52] Later on, Mr. McNamara decided to visit the region. He arrived in Bangladesh on November 3, 1976, where he was presented with Bangladesh's formulation for resolving the dispute. The short-term part of that formulation included an extension of the 1975 Partial Accord. "On the long term, Bangladesh...desired that the World Bank undertook a comprehensive study of the water resources of the Ganges Basin for the development of additional water supplies in the dry season as well as for multi-purpose benefits."[53] Mr. McNamara visited India after that, but no progress was reported. The Bank believed in an integrated approach to the entire Ganges Basin, as it initially had proposed for the Indus Basin. This was in line with the proposal of Bangladesh, which India had turned down repeatedly.

In January 1977, the International Development Association (IDA), the soft-financing arm of the World Bank, agreed to finance a study on the environmental assessment of decreased Ganges flow in Bangladesh under one of the projects financed by IDA.[54] Bangladesh selected International Engineering Company to carry out the study, and the Report was published jointly by the Bangladesh Water Development Board and International Engineering Company in 1977.[55] The Report confirmed some of the claims made by Bangladesh,[56] concluding that water-borne diseases would intensify with any decrease in fresh water in the Ganges-dependent area, including malaria and schistosomiasis. It also concluded that the Sunderbans

---

of 1997). The suit was summarily dismissed in the same year by the First Sub-Judge Court in Dhaka. However, that decision was appealed to the High Court Division of the Supreme Court of Bangladesh which served notice to the Bank office in Dhaka on May 2, 1999. The appeal listed as the principal defendants/respondents the World Bank represented by its Chairman, the World Bank Resident Mission in Dhaka and the High Commissioner of India to Bangladesh.

[52] *See* Mikiyasu Nakayama, "Successes and Failures of International Organizations in Dealing with International Waters," in *International Journal of Water Resources Development* 13 (1997), at 378.

[53] *See* Abbas, *supra* note 17, at 67.

[54] The study was financed as one of the sub-projects under Second Technical Assistance Project, Credit No. 622-BD, Development Credit Agreement between People's Republic of Bangladesh and International Development Association dated April 8, 1976. The title of the sub-project was Southwest Region Study. For further discussion on the study *see* Ben Crow, *supra note* 19 at 128, and also note 3, at 258.

[55] *See* R. Goodland, *Environmental Assessment of Decreased Ganges Flow in Bangladesh*, International Engineering Company and Bangladesh Waters Development Board Special Studies Directorate (April 1977).

[56] *See* Bangladesh White Paper, summarized in section B. (i) of the present chapter.

forest would be adversely affected, and severely endangered fauna would be increasingly threatened by any degradation of the Sunderbans.[57]

Despite several openings for intervention, the Bank was not able to play any role in the Ganges dispute. Although India accepted a role for the World Bank in the Indus Basin, that was not the case for the Ganges where India insisted on a bilateral approach with no role for a third party. It should also be pointed that the Indus Basin could be divided, but that was not true of the Ganges and it had to be shared. The formula for sharing proved difficult because not enough water was available, and the deadlock over the augmentation proposals was, as we shall see, absolute. As observed by an author, "...unlike the situation in the 1950s, when the Indus Waters Treaty was under discussion, lending to India had become a routine business of the Bank by the 1970s. The funding capability of the Bank thus did not work as a powerful 'stick and carrot' to let India have talks with Bangladesh."[58]

With little or no role for the good offices of a third party, Bangladesh and India were virtually left alone to reach an agreement on how to share the waters of the Ganges. There was certainly a need for a change either in the attitude of the parties, or in the political leaders that dominated the scene, to achieve any agreement on the sharing of the waters of the Ganges.

D. The 1977 Agreement

The Consensus Statement adopted by the United Nations General Assembly on November 26, 1976, proved to be a jump starter to the Indo-Bangladesh negotiations over the Ganges. The first ministerial level meeting between the two countries was held, pursuant to the Consensus Statement, in December 1976, in Dacca, and the meetings were continued in January 1977 in Delhi. However, the political change that resulted from the elections in India in March 1977 proved more important to the Ganges dispute. The Congress Party was voted out of office for the first time since India's independence, and the Janata party came to power, with Mr. Morarji Desai as Prime Minister. The Janata party was not shackled by previous positions and did not have any close ties with Sheikh Mujib. They wanted to open a new chapter in the relations with Bangladesh, and bearing in mind the perceived embarrassment emanating from the United Nations Consensus Statement, the Janata Party moved quickly in the direction of reaching an agreement with Bangladesh over the Ganges River. After a series of ministerial level meetings and lengthy negotiations, the two parties were finally able to define the issues for an agreement: a temporary arrangement for sharing the waters of the Ganges while a long-term solution for augmenting its flow during the dry season was being sought.

An Agreement incorporating those two principles and specifying the share of each country was initialed on September 30, 1977, and was signed on November 7, 1977, in Dacca, by the Minister of Agriculture and Irrigation on behalf of India, and

---

[57] *See* Goodland, *supra* note 55, Summary, at 1.

[58] *See* Nakayama, *supra* note 52, at 378. *See* also Ben Crow, *supra* note 19, at 92.

by a member of the President's Council of Advisers in charge of the Ministry of Communications, Flood Control, Water Resources and Power on behalf of Bangladesh. The Agreement was signed almost a year after the Consensus Statement was adopted, and about seven weeks before the start of the 1978 lean season. The Consensus Statement, no doubt, put pressure on both parties to reach an agreement. The political change in Delhi had certainly made the agreement easier for India, and the dawning of the lean season must have also put pressure on Bangladesh because they had witnessed the adverse effects the diversion had during the previous lean season, and should have been keen on coming to agreement on the Ganges.

The Agreement consisted of 15 articles, a schedule and a Side Letter. It was divided into three parts, Part A: Arrangements for Sharing the Waters of the Ganga at Farakka; Part B: Long-term Arrangements; and Part C: "Review and Duration."[59] The preamble dealt with the determination of the parties to promote and strengthen their friendship and good neighborliness, and the desire of promoting the well being of their people. It also referred to the desire of sharing by mutual agreement the waters of the international rivers flowing through the territories of the two countries, and making the optimum utilization of the water resources of the region through joint efforts. The preamble summarized the approach adopted by the provisions of the Agreement by mentioning both the need for an interim arrangement for sharing the waters of the Ganges, as well as the need for a long-term solution of the problem of augmenting the flow of the Ganges. The preamble emphasized the desire for finding a fair solution of the question before the parties "without affecting the rights and entitlements of either country other than those covered by this Agreement, or establishing any general principles of law or precedent." Clearly, India did not want the Ganges Agreement to tie its hands in any future negotiations over any of the more than 50 rivers that it shares with Bangladesh as an upper riparian.

(i.) Arrangements for Sharing the Waters of the Ganges at Farakka: Two principles established by the 1975 Partial Accord were followed again in this Agreement: the quantum of water to be released by India to Bangladesh would be at Farakka, and the waters to be withdrawn by India and those to be released to Bangladesh would be in 10-day periods (with 11-day periods in the case of 31-day months). The lean season would start on January 1 and end on May 31 every year. The flow reaching Farakka was based on 75 percent availability of the average flow from observed data for the period 1948 to 1973. The share of each country between January 1 and May 31, for the years 1978 to 1982, was included in the Schedule to the Agreement as produced in Table 7.3:

---

[59] Agreement between the Government of the Republic of India and the Government of the People's Republic of Bangladesh on Sharing of the Ganga Waters at Farakka and on Augmenting its Flows, 17 I.L.M. 103 (1978). For a general discussion of this Agreement *see*, Salman M. A. Salman and Kishor Uprety, "Hydro-Politics in South Asia: A Comparative Analysis of the Mahakali and the Ganges Treaties," *Natural Resources Journal* 39 (1999), at 295-343.

Table 7.3
Share of India and Bangladesh of the Waters of the Ganges at Farakka Under the 1977 Agreement

Period	Flows reaching Farakka (based on 75 percent availability from observed data; (1948-73)	Withdrawal by India at Farakka	Release to Bangladesh
January	Cusecs	Cusecs	Cusecs
1-10	98,500	40,000	58,500
11-20	89,750	38,500	51,250
21-31	82,500	35,000	47,500
February			
1-10	79,250	33,000	46,250
11-20	74,000	31,500	42,500
21-28/29	70,000	30,750	39,250
March			
1-10	65,250	26,750	38,500
11-20	63,500	25,500	38,000
21-31	61,000	25,000	36,000
April			
1-10	59,000	24,000	35,000
11-20	55,500	20,750	34,750
21-30	55,000	20,500	34,500
May			
1-10	56,500	21,500	35,000
11-20	59,250	24,000	35,250
21-31	65,500	26,750	38,750

Source: Schedule to the 1977 Agreement.

A comparison of the share of each country under the 1975 Partial Accord and the 1977 Agreement shows that the share of Bangladesh under the 1977 Agreement decreased in comparison with its share under the 1975 Accord as follows:

(i) The total amount agreed for release to Bangladesh under the 1975 Accord from April 21 to May 31, 1975, represented about 77 percent of the total amount of the available water for that period, whereas the release for the same period to Bangladesh under the 1977 Agreement decreased to about 61 percent. On the other hand, withdrawal by India at Farakka for the same period under the 1975 Accord was about 23 percent, but increased under the 1977 Agreement to about 39 percent for the same period.

(ii) The total amount agreed for release to Bangladesh under the 1977 Agreement for each dry season represented about 59 percent of the total availability, whereas withdrawals by India during the same period were about 41 percent of the total availability.

Two observations are noteworthy. First, the Agreement used the term "Ganga" which is the name used in India for the Ganges River, and not the term "Ganges," the name by which the river is known internationally. This was perhaps an assertion by India that the river is an overwhelmingly Indian river and as such the name given to it by India should be the name to be used in the Agreement. Second, column 4 of the Schedule to the Agreement (Table 7.3) is entitled "Release to Bangladesh" which implies something less than a right. Perhaps those were concessions that Bangladesh had to make to get the Agreement. It is also equally likely that Bangladesh, with another dry season dawning, was eager to obtain an agreement and as such did not pay attention to the possible implications of those details.

(a) Excess and Deficit Flows

The 1977 Agreement, like most treaties on sharing the waters of an international river, included a mechanism for sharing excess or deficit flows of the Ganges. The Agreement stated that if the actual availability of water at Farakka during a 10-day period were higher or lower than the quantum shown in column 2 of the Schedule to the Agreement, it would be shared in the proportion applicable at that period. In addition, the Agreement included a clause dealing with the case of exceptionally low flow of the Ganges. The clause guaranteed Bangladesh a minimum of 80 percent of its share during each such 10-day period, however low the flow of the Ganges may be during that period. Describing how the guarantee clause was supposed to work, the Agreement stated that, "if during a particular 10-day period the Ganga flows at Farakka come down to such a level that the share of Bangladesh is lower than 80 percent of the value shown in column 4, the release of waters to Bangladesh during that 10-day period shall not fall below 80 percent of the value shown in column 4."[60]

(b) Implementation of the Sharing Arrangements

Under the Agreement, a committee consisting of an equal number of representatives nominated by the two governments, called the "Joint Committee," was established.[61] It was authorized to set up suitable teams at both Farakka in West Bengal, and Hardinge Bridge in Bangladesh, to observe and record at Farakka the daily flows below Farakka Barrage, in the Feeder Canal, and the Hardinge Bridge. The Committee was also authorized to decide on its own procedures and method of functioning, and was required to submit to the two governments all the data collected, in addition to an annual report. The main responsibility of the Committee was implementation of the arrangements contained therein, "…and examining any

---

[60] *Id.*, Article II (ii).
[61] *Id.*, Article VII.

difficulty arising out of the implementation of those arrangements, and of the operation of the Farakka Barrage."[62]

The mandate of the Joint Committee was specific and limited to the implementation of the sharing arrangements under the Agreement. The Committee could also attempt to resolve any difference or dispute arising in the implementation of the sharing arrangements. If the Committee failed to resolve such difference or dispute, then the difference or dispute would be referred to a panel of equal number of experts, and if this panel also failed to resolve such dispute, then it would be referred to the two governments, which would meet urgently at the appropriate level to resolve it by mutual discussion. Failing that, the dispute would be resolved by such other arrangements as the two governments may mutually agree upon. As such, the parties opted for political means as the method for resolving any difference or dispute arising out of the implementation of the Agreement, with no role for a third party in such a dispute. It should be clarified, however, that this dispute settlement procedure, laid down in Part A of the Agreement, was limited only to the sharing arrangements of the waters of the Ganges.

The Agreement was subject to a review at the expiry of three years from the day of its coming into force, with further reviews taking place six months before the expiry of the Agreement or as may be agreed upon by the two parties. Such reviews would entail consideration of the working impact; implementation and progress of the arrangements contained in Part A, sharing arrangements, and Part B, long-term arrangements. Article XV of the Agreement stated that the Agreement would come into force upon signature, thus indicating that it did not require ratification by either of the two governments.[63] The Agreement would remain in force for five years that would cover the lean season of the years 1978 to 1982. It could be extended for a specified period by mutual agreement in light of the reviews to be carried out three years after coming into force and six months before the expiry of the Agreement.

(ii.) Long-term Arrangements: Part B of the Agreement laid down the long-term arrangements for dealing with the problem of the low flow of the Ganges during the lean season. The Agreement stated that the two governments recognized the need to cooperate with each other in finding a solution to the long-term problem of augmenting the flows of the Ganges during the dry season. Article IX of the Agreement

---

[62] *Id.*

[63] The Constitution of India, as a general rule, does not require ratification of treaties by parliament. The Seventh Schedule of the Constitution of India divides responsibilities over matters into three lists: the Union List, the State List and the Concurrent List. The Union List includes, as per Entry 14 of List 1 of the Seventh Schedule "entering into treaties and agreements and conventions with foreign countries and implementing of treaties, agreements and conventions with foreign countries." On the other hand, the Constitution of Bangladesh states in Article 145A that "All treaties with foreign countries shall be submitted to the President who shall cause them to be laid before Parliament," which again does not specify the need for ratification of treaties. It should be added, however, that all treaties that result in financial obligations are presented to the Indian Parliament for ratification. This explains why the Indus Waters Treaty between India and Pakistan (*supra* Chapter 2), and the Mahakali Treaty between India and Nepal (*supra* Chapter 5), both of which obliged India to make certain financial contributions toward implementation of works specified in either Treaty, required ratification by the Indian Parliament.

entrusted the Joint Rivers Commission with the responsibilities of carrying out investigation and study of schemes relating to the augmentation of the dry season flow of the Ganges, proposed or to be proposed, by either government with a view of finding an economical and feasible solution. The Commission was given three years to submit its recommendations to the two governments, a date that coincided with the date of review of the Agreement. The Agreement obliged the two governments to consider and agree upon the scheme or schemes for augmentation, taking into account the recommendations of the Commission, and to take the necessary measures to implement such scheme or schemes as speedily as possible. As the Agreement would remain in force for five years, this would leave two years for the governments to consider the proposals and agree on the augmentation scheme or schemes. Any difficulty, difference or dispute with regard to this Part of the Agreement, if not resolved by the Commission, would be referred to the two governments for resolution. Although the dispute settlement mechanism for this Part was slightly different from that for Part A, the Parties opted for political means for resolving disputes for both parts of the Agreement.

The Side Letter to the Agreement was signed the same day as the Agreement and by the same officials who signed the Agreement. The Letter referred to Article IX of the Agreement on the schemes for augmentation of the flows of the Ganges proposed or to be proposed by either government, and stated that the two governments have:

> reached an understanding to the effect that the words "proposed or to be proposed by either Government occurring in Article IX in Part B of the Agreement," relate to any schemes which may have been proposed or may be proposed by Bangladesh or India and do not exclude any scheme or schemes for building storages in the upper reaches of the Ganges in Nepal.[64]

The Letter went on to add that the proposals designed to find a long-term solution to the problem would be treated on equal footing and accorded equal priority.

There are two noteworthy points about this Letter. First, it is quite surprising that India agreed to Bangladesh spelling out its proposal without India doing the same in the Letter. The proposal of each of the two countries for augmentation of the flows of the Ganges during the dry season had been known almost since 1972. India had proposed the canal linking the Brahmaputra and the Ganges and running through both India and Bangladesh, and Bangladesh had proposed the storage reservoirs in the upper reaches of the Ganges in India and Nepal. Bangladesh had asserted its proposal in this Letter, but had also agreed that other proposals would be treated on equal footing and accorded equal priority. Secondly, the reference to Nepal in the Letter was quite unusual because, as a matter of international law, the

---

[64] It is worth noting that the Side Letter is not attached to the Agreement as published in 17 I.L.M. 103 (1978), *supra* note 59. For the text of the Letter, *see* Abbas, *supra* note 17, at 101–102; *see* also Bhasin, *supra* note 2, at 503-504. It is also worth noting that the Side Letter used the name "the Ganges" and not "the Ganga." This could probably be attributed to the fact that the Letter was signed by Bangladesh first.

contracting parties do not have the right to oblige a third party without its consent.[65] Moreover, India had always insisted on bilateral approaches and solutions to its water problems, so it is surprising that they agreed to a specific reference to Nepal in the Letter.

The Joint Rivers Commission held its fourteenth meeting in January 1978 in Dacca. The Agreement had, indeed, reactivated the Commission as the last meeting was held in June 1975, immediately after the expiry of the Partial Accord. Moreover, the two countries agreed to upgrade the chairmanship of the Commission to the ministerial level during the visit of the President of Bangladesh to India in December 1977, a few weeks after the signature of the 1977 Agreement, thus giving the Commission more political prominence.[66] The issue of augmentation of the lean season flow of the Ganges was on the top of the agenda, and the Commission asked the two countries to submit their proposals by mid-March 1978. However, the meetings of the Commission continued throughout 1979 and 1980 with no agreement on any scheme for augmentation of the Ganges during the low season.

The Indian proposal for augmentation consisted of construction of a barrage across the Brahmaputra River in the Indian state of Assam, and a link canal about 200 miles long from the barrage to the Ganges at a point above Farakka. About two-thirds of the link canal would be in India and the remaining third would be in Bangladesh. The proposal also included the construction of two storage dams on the Brahmaputra River and a third one on the Barak (Megha) River to feed the barrage. Thus the waters of the Brahmaputra would be used to augment the dry season flow of the Ganges. India further stated that the Ganga-Brahmaputra-Meghna should be considered as one large international drainage basin, of which the Ganges is just one part. The link canal connecting the Brahmaputra and the Ganges would not only augment the Ganges, but would also provide the much needed communication line through navigation.

On the other hand, the Bangladeshi proposal consisted of construction of storage reservoirs in the upper reaches of the Ganges River in India and Nepal. Three river basins in Nepal, Karnali, Kosi and Gandaki were identified as the sites for the storage reservoirs in Nepal. Bangladesh contended that in addition to augmenting the dry season flow of the Ganges, those reservoirs would be a good source for generation of hydropower, and the groundwater in that area would provide an additional source of water.

---

[65] Article 34 of The Vienna Convention on the Law of Treaties states "A treaty does not create either obligations or rights for a Third State without its consent." Article 35 states "An obligation arises for a Third State from a provision of treaty if the parties intend the provisions to be the means of establishing the obligation and the Third State expressly accepts that obligation in writing." For the Vienna Convention *see*, 8 I.L.M. 679 (1969).

[66] The upgrading of the chairmanship of the Joint Rivers Commission to the ministerial level did not require amending the Statute of the Commission, as the Statute does not specify the level of representation of each country.

Each party stuck to its proposal and emphasized what it saw as problems with the proposal of the other party. Bangladesh was critical of the Indian proposal for a number of reasons. It alleged that this inter-basin transfer did not have sound basis because the dry season flow of the Brahmaputra was not adequate to meet all the requirements of the basin itself, let alone have part of it transferred to another basin. Bangladesh was also concerned about the negative environmental impact, such as water logging, and the social impact as a result of land acquisition and displacement of hundreds of thousands of people. There was also the concern that the link canal could exacerbate the flood problems in Bangladesh. Bangladesh was also concerned that the barrage and link canal would give India control of the Brahmaputra, just as the Farakka Barrage has given India control of the Ganges. India, on the other hand, also rejected the Bangladesh proposal claiming that the storage reservoirs in the upper reaches of the Ganges would not store enough water to solve the problem of the low flow of the Ganges during the dry season. India also pointed out that those waters are needed for its future development. Moreover, India preferred bilateral negotiations with its neighbors, and did not want Nepal to be a party to the negotiations on the augmentation of the Ganges. This is notwithstanding the Side Letter to the Agreement.[67]

As per Article XIII of the Agreement which specified that the Agreement would be reviewed by the two governments at the expiry of three years from the date of its coming into force, the review of the Agreement took place in November 1980 and was continued in January 1981. The November meeting was held in Dacca and the January meeting took place in New Delhi. On the discussion of Part A of the Agreement, India reiterated its position that it is the major riparian of the Ganges in terms of the catchment area, population and area dependent on the Ganges waters, and as such India's interests suffered as the result of the operation of Part A, and there was an urgent need for a larger share of the flows of the Ganges for Calcutta. On the other hand, Bangladesh emphasized its historic rights and rights to the natural flow of the Ganges, and claimed that the decreased flow of the Ganges had adversely affected Bangladesh, and also demanded a larger share of the waters of the Ganges. However, the discussion centered on the proposals for augmenting the flow of the Ganges. Each side reiterated its proposal and rejected the other proposal, criticizing what it saw as its weak points. Each side accused the other of rejecting their proposal without actually studying it and each side held the other responsibile for the failure of the Joint Rivers Commission to arrive at an acceptable proposal.[68]

The mandate of the Commission with regard to the augmentation proposal had come to an end without the Commission being able to present a recommendation,

---

[67] For detailed discussion of the proposal of each party *see*, Ben Crow et al., *supra* note 18, at 159; Abbas, *supra* note 17, at 123; Verghese, *supra* note 12, at 362; *see* also *Water Resources Cooperation in the Ganges-Brahmaputra River Basin* (Lyndon Johnson School of Public Affairs, Policy Research Project Report Number 101, 1993).

[68] For the speeches of each of the two ministers at the review meeting *see*, Bhasin, *supra* note 2, at 623.

as Article IX stated that such recommendation would be submitted within a period of three years. The two delegations did not agree on the next step. While Bangladesh wanted the Commission to continue its study and investigation of augmentation schemes, India felt that the Commission had failed its mandate under the Agreement and there was no point in continuing the discussion of the augmentation proposal. At the end, the two parties concluded that the question of augmentation would have to be decided upon by the two governments at a high political level.

Although the Agreement was to remain in force for a period of five years from the date of coming into force, which meant until November 5, 1982, the Agreement for all practical purposes expired on May 31, 1982, at the end of the dry season for that year. This is because the sharing arrangements under the Agreement ended on May 31 and the mandate for the Commission with regard to the augmentation proposal ended in 1980 and was not renewed. Although Article XV of the Agreement stated that the Agreement might be extended for a specified period by mutual agreement, it did not happen. The Janata party was voted out of office in January 1980 and the Congress Party was back in power. In response to a question on the meetings of the Joint Rivers Commission and the sharing of the Ganges waters, the new Minister of Energy and Irrigation and Coal had stated in Parliament that "I have said that the requisite water (for Calcutta) is 40,000 cusecs. The Janata Government, very unfortunately, overlooked the national interest."[69]

Bangladesh witnessed another military takeover in March 1982 led by H. M. Ershad, adding more uncertainty to the situation. The review of the 1977 Agreement carried out on June 26, 1982, six months before the expiry of the Agreement, as per Article XIII, was clearly indicative of the demise of the Agreement. In respect of Part A, both noted that the arrangements for sharing the Ganges waters at Farakka had been fully implemented. "The two sides however, differed as to the impact of the sharing of their respective countries."[70] On the issue of augmentation of the flow of the Ganges during the dry season "the two sides recalled that the subject was no longer before the Indo-Bangladesh Joint Rivers Commission. It is now a matter for decision between the two governments at a high political level and the process has started."[71]

E. The 1982 Memorandum of Understanding

General Ershad, who had then become President of the Council of Ministers of Bangladesh, visited India in October 1982, less than a month before the expiry of the 1977 Agreement. The purpose of his visit was to discuss the issue of sharing the waters of the Ganges before the expiry of the 1977 Agreement and the start of another dry season. Rather than agreeing to extend the 1977 Agreement as provided under Article XV of that Agreement, the two countries concluded a new agreement. The

---

[69] *See*, Question in the Rajya Sabha: "Indo-Bangladesh Joint Rivers Commission meeting on sharing of Ganga waters," New Delhi, March 1980, in Bhasin, *supra* note 2, at 606.

[70] *See* Agreed minutes of the Second Review of the Indo-Bangladesh Agreement on Farakka signed on November 5, 1977, New Delhi, June 26, 1982, in Bhasin, *supra* note 2, at 656.

[71] *Id.*

Memorandum of Understanding on the sharing of the Ganges was signed in New Delhi on October 7, 1982, by the two Ministers of Foreign Affairs.[72]

The 1982 MOU stated that the two leaders discussed the working of the 1977 Agreement and agreed that it had not proved suitable for finding a satisfactory and durable solution, and that with its termination fresh efforts were necessary to arrive at such a solution. The two leaders recognized that the basic problem was one of inadequate flow of the Ganges during the dry season and agreed on the need for a long-term solution for augmenting such a flow. They also agreed on sharing the waters of the Ganges while the long-term solution was being pursued. The Joint Rivers Commission was entrusted with the responsibility of completing the pre-feasibility study and deciding upon the optimum solution within 18 months of signing the 1982 MOU. At the end of that period the two governments would immediately implement the augmentation proposal agreed upon by the Joint Rivers Commission. The two leaders agreed on sharing arrangements for the Ganges for the next two dry seasons of 1983 and 1984, as shown in Table 7.4:

---

[72] Indo-Bangladesh Memorandum of Understanding, New Delhi, October 7, 1982 (hereinafter 1982 MOU; on file with the authors). It is noteworthy that the 1982 MOU was signed by the two Ministers of Foreign Affairs, and not the Ministers of Irrigation, as was done under the 1977 Agreement.

Table 7.4
Share of India and Bangladesh of the Waters of the Ganges at Farakka Under the 1982 Memorandum of Understanding

Period	Flows reaching Farakka (based on 75 percent availability from observed data; 1948-73) Cusecs	Withdrawal by India at Farakka Cusecs	Release to Bangladesh Cusecs
January			
1-10	98,500	40,000	58,500
11-20	89,750	38,000	51,750
21-31	82,500	35,500	47,000
February			
1-10	79,250	33,000	46,250
11-20	74,000	31,250	42,750
21-28/29	70,000	31,000	39,000
March			
1-10	65,250	26,500	38,750
11-20	63,500	25,500	38,000
21-31	61,000	25,250	35,750
April			
1-10	59,000	24,000	35,000
11-20	55,500	20,750	34,750
21-30	55,000	20,500	34,500
May			
1-10	56,500	21,500	35,000
11-20	59,250	24,250	35,000
21-31	65,500	26,500	39,000

Source: Annexure A to the 1982 MOU.

Except for deleting the guarantee clause and replacing it with a formula less favorable to Bangladesh, the 1982 MOU was, by and large, similar to the 1977 Agreement. Both identified two issues to be dealt with: the long-term problem of finding a solution to the lean season flow of the Ganges, and the short-term problem of sharing the waters of the Ganges during the interim period of the search for the long-term solution. Both instruments entrusted the Joint Rivers Commission with the responsibility of finding a solution to the augmentation problem. The Commission was given 18 months under the 1982 MOU, as opposed to three years under the 1977 Agreement, but this should be viewed in the overall length of the two agreements—five years for the 1977 Agreement and two years for the 1982 MOU. The amounts allocated to each country under the 1982 MOU were similar to the allocation under the 1977 Agreement, except for slight changes not affecting the overall allocation. A Joint Committee was established with similar composition and responsibilities to the one under the 1977 Agreement, and with similar procedures for dispute settlement. With those similarities in mind, one wonders why the leaders of India and Bangladesh agreed that the 1977 Agreement "...had not proved suitable for finding a satisfactory and durable solution and that with its termination fresh efforts were necessary to arrive at such a solution."[73]

It is quite surprising that Bangladesh agreed to the deletion of the guarantee clause. The 1982 MOU stated that excess or deficit flow would be shared in the proportion applicable to the period. In case of exceptionally low flow during the two years of the duration of the 1982 MOU, the two governments would hold immediate consultation and decide on how to minimize the burden to either country. This is completely different from the manner in which the 1977 Agreement dealt with the situation. As we have seen, Bangladesh was guaranteed that its share would not be less than 80 percent of the amount it was supposed to receive. The effects of the deletion of the guarantee clause were felt in the 1983 dry season. "The Ganges at Farakka recorded an all time low flow on April 5, 1983, of 39,000 cusecs against an expected availability at 75 percent, of 59,000 cusecs. Out of its scheduled share on this day of 35,000 cusecs, Bangladesh received only 24,425 cusecs."[74] Consultations were held between the two countries and resulted in an agreement on July 20, 1983, which was added as Annexure B to the 1982 MOU.[75] The agreement reached would be applicable only to the remaining dry season of 1984 because the MOU would expire at the end of that dry season.

The agreement reached provided for two situations. If the flow at Farakka was 75 percent or more of the standard flow[76] for the corresponding 10-day period, the release to Bangladesh would be in the proportion agreed for that period. If the flow is below 75 percent of the standard flow, the agreement reached provided that release to Bangladesh would be calculated as follows:

"(a) Calculate the pro-rata release for Bangladesh at 75% of the standard flow.

(b) Calculate the pro-rata release for Bangladesh at the actual flow.

(c) "(a)" minus "(b)" would be termed as the burden.

(d) The burden would be shared between India and Bangladesh on a 50:50 basis, i.e. 50% of (c) would be added to (b)."

This complex arrangement was certainly far less favorable to Bangladesh than the guarantee clause under which Bangladesh's share would not go below 80 percent of

---

[73] *Id.*

[74] *See* Abbas, *supra* note 17, at 115.

[75] *See* Agreement on Sharing of Exceptionally Low Flow at Farakka for 1983-1984 (on file with authors), added as Annexure B to the 1982 MOU. The Agreement was signed at Dacca on July 20th, 1983 by the Additional Secretary In-Charge of Irrigation, Water Development and Flood Control on behalf of Bangladesh, and Secretary, Ministry of Irrigation on behalf of India.

[76] Annexure B to the 1982 MOU defined the term "standard flow" as the flow reaching Farakka for the various 10-day periods as specified in Annexure A of the MOU.

what was specified under the 1977 Agreement. However, under the circumstances it was negotiated, it was perhaps the best deal Bangladesh could obtain.

The Joint Rivers Commission continued its deliberations on the proposals for augmentation of the flow of the Ganges during the dry season, but no progress was made. Each side stuck to its position and no new ideas were brought to the discussion. Bangladesh kept pressing the issue of bringing Nepal in the discussions, but India rejected that proposal.

F. Interim Agreement on the Teesta River

While the Joint Rivers Commission was deadlocked over the augmentation proposals for the Ganges, it held discussions over another shared river, the Teesta. The river (known in India as the Tista and in Bangladesh as the Teesta) originates in the southern slopes of the Himalayan mountains in the Indian State of Sikkim. After flowing through the Indian State of West Bengal, it enters Bangladesh and joins the Brahmaputra. As such the Teesta is also an international river shared by India and Bangladesh only.[77] The issue of sharing this river was raised in a number of meetings of the Commission before, but no action was taken. The Commission decided that it needed more scientific studies and data. In its twenty-fifth meeting held on July 20, 1983, pending completion of such studies, the Commission reached *ad hoc* arrangements over the Teesta whereby India would receive 39 percent of the flow and Bangladesh would receive 36 percent while the remaining 25 percent would stay unallocated. Those amounts would be revisited after completion of the scientific studies. This *ad hoc* accord was to remain in force for two years, until 1985.[78] This agreement was not concluded in the form of a signed instrument, but was rather included in the minutes of the Joint Rivers Commission. Moreover, it did not specify the point where the allocation would take place, nor did it establish any mechanism, such as a joint committee, for taking responsibility of the implementation arrangements.

This *ad hoc* agreement did not provide any momentum to the stalled augmentation discussions, and the meetings of the Commission did not bring any changes to the positions of the two countries. The dry season of 1984 ended, and with its end the 1982 MOU expired. India refused to extend the arrangements under the 1982 MOU for three more years as proposed by Bangladesh. No new agreement was reached during the monsoon season of 1984, and the dry season of 1985 started without an agreement in place. As in the dry season of 1976 when no agreement was in place, India was at will to divert up to 40,000 cusecs from the waters of the Ganges to Calcutta.

---

[77] For more details on the Teesta, *see*, Chauhan, *supra* note 11, at 138.

[78] For the details of the *ad hoc* agreement, *see* Chauhan, *supra* note 11, at 102; *see also* Bhasin, *supra* note 2, Joint Press Release on the Conclusion of the Three-day Meeting of the Indo-Bangladesh Joint Rivers Commission Arriving at an Agreement on Sharing of the Teesta Waters, at 682.

G. The 1985 Memorandum of Understanding

The President of Bangladesh, H. M. Ershad, and the Prime Minister of India, Rajiv Gandhi, met at Nassau, in the Bahamas, in November 1985, while attending the Commonwealth Heads of Government/State Summit. They agreed that the two countries would sign a memorandum of understanding, for three years, reiterating the water allocation for each country under the 1982 MOU, and setting out the terms of reference of a joint study to be undertaken by experts from the two sides on the available water resources common to both countries. The objective of the study would be to identify alternatives for the sharing of such water resources, including the long-term scheme/schemes for augmentation of the flows of the Ganges at Farakka. Accordingly, the two Irrigation Ministers met in New Delhi from November 18–22 and agreed on a new memorandum of understanding that was signed on November 22, 1985.[79]

The 1985 MOU specified the objectives of the study as: (i) to work out long-term scheme or schemes for the augmentation of the flows of the Ganges at Farakka, and (ii) to identify alternatives for the sharing of the available river water resources common to both countries for mutual benefit. As such, the scope of the study went beyond the scope of the previous studies that were confined to augmentation, and included identifying alternatives for sharing the common river system. The study would be carried out by a new committee called the "Joint Committee of Experts" consisting of the secretaries concerned of the two governments and the two engineering members of the Joint Rivers Commission from each side. The 1985 MOU specified what each part of the study would cover. The first part of the study, sharing the available river water resources system, would cover: (i) ascertaining the available river water resources common to both countries based on the collection, collation and analysis of available relevant hydro-meteorological data in both countries, (ii) studying alternatives for sharing the available river water resources common to both countries for their mutual benefit, and (iii) identifying locations of the points for sharing the rivers, periods of sharing and schedule of sharing, where appropriate. The second part of the study, augmentation of the dry season flow of the Ganges, would cover identification of scheme/schemes for the augmentation of the flows of the Ganges at Farakka by the optimal utilization of the surface water resources of the region available to the two countries.

The 1985 MOU stated that the study would start immediately and would be completed within 12 months from the date of the MOU, with a review of the progress of the joint study at the Ministerial level at the end of six months from the date of the MOU. At the end of the 12-month period, a summit level meeting between the leaders of the two countries would be held to make a decision on the scheme of aug-

---

[79] India-Bangladesh Memorandum of Understanding, New Delhi November 22, 1985, (hereinafter the 1985 MOU; on file with the authors). Unlike the 1982 MOU, this MOU was signed by the Minister of Irrigation, Water Development and Flood Control of Bangladesh, and the Minister of Water Resources for India. This was in line with the 1977 Agreement signed by the ministers of the same portfolios.

mentation of the flows of the Ganges at Farakka, and the long-term sharing of the rivers.

The amounts of the water of the Ganges allocated to each country during the dry season were included in Annexure A (Schedule) to the 1985 MOU. Those amounts were similar to the allocation under the 1982 MOU. The implementation arrangements, dispute settlement procedures, sharing of the excess and deficit flow, including the arrangements for sharing of exceptionally low flow of the Ganges (burden sharing), were all similar to those in the 1982 MOU.

It is worth noting that the 1985 MOU used the name Ganga/Ganges throughout the paragraphs of the MOU. The 1977 Agreement and the 1982 MOU both used the name "Ganga," which is the name used by India for the river. The Side Letter to the 1977 Agreement, which Bangladesh signed first and was later countersigned by India, used the name Ganges, although the Agreement itself used the name Ganga.

Another observation about the 1985 MOU is that the schemes for augmentation to be identified would be by the optimal utilization "of the surface water resources of the region." Those words were used in the Joint Declaration at the end of the visit of the Prime Minister of India to Bangladesh in March 1972, and were interpreted to favor the Indian proposal of using the waters of the Brahmaputra for augmenting the flows of the Ganges.[80]

The 1985 MOU indicated clearly that the two countries came to a conclusion that, after eight years of trial, the Joint Rivers Commission was no longer the right forum for such a study. The Joint Committee of Experts was authorized to determine its own procedures and to take such other steps as may be necessary to ensure completion within the time frame of 12 months.

The Annexure on the arrangements for sharing of exceptionally low flow of the Ganges was signed separately by the Secretaries to the Ministry of Irrigation, Water Development and Flood Control for Bangladesh, and to the Ministry of Water Resources for India. This Annexure was not referred to in the 1985 MOU, but was signed on the same day the MOU was signed. In the case of the 1982 MOU, it was signed separately because it was concluded nine months after the 1982 MOU was signed. It is not clear why it was neither referred to in the 1985 MOU, nor attached to, and signed as part of the 1985 MOU.

The Joint Committee of Experts held its first meeting on January 18, 1986, and agreed on the procedure and method for its work, and the schedule of activities for the joint study.[81] The second meeting was held in February 1986 and the third meeting in July 1986. The Ministerial level review took place on August 27, 1986, nine months after the 1985 MOU was signed. Bangladesh pressed for the storage reservoirs in the upper reaches of the Ganges and called for the involvement of Nepal. Bangladesh also raised the issue of sharing the Teesta in light of the expiry of the *ad*

---

[80] *See* Joint Declaration issued at the end of the visit of the Prime Minister of India, Mrs. Indira Gandhi, to Bangladesh; Dacca, March 19, 1972; in Bhasin, *supra* note 2, at 33.

[81] *See* the Joint Press Release Issued on the Conclusion of the Meeting of the Joint Committee of Experts. Dhaka, January 18, 1986, in Bhasin, *supra* note 2, at 706.

hoc arrangements reached in 1983. On the other hand, India pressed for using the waters of the Brahmaputra to augment the dry season flow of the Ganges. Although a meeting took place in October 1986 between officials from India and Bangladesh with Nepal to discuss the water resources issue, the meeting was limited "to seeking necessary information and data."[82] Another Ministerial level meeting took place in November 13, 1986, at the end of the 12 months stated in the MOU. It should be recalled that the 1985 MOU indicated that a summit level meeting between the leaders of the two countries would take place to reach a decision on the scheme of augmentation and the long-term sharing of the rivers. However, because after seven meetings the Joint Committee of experts was not able to arrive at a proposal acceptable to both parties, the summit meeting was replaced by a ministerial meeting. The ministerial level meeting decided to report the outcome of their meeting to their respective Heads of Government.

No more meetings of the Joint Committee of Experts took place because the duration of its mandate was only one year, and the year was over. Meanwhile, the Joint Rivers Commission held its twenty-ninth meeting and agreed that pending the undertaking of the scientific studies, the *ad hoc* sharing arrangements for the Teesta river as agreed in the twenty-fifth meeting of the Commission would be extended until the end of 1987. Not only did the Joint Committee of Experts fail to reach agreement on the joint studies, the Joint Rivers Commission also failed to undertake the scientific studies for sharing the Teesta. The two countries were left with interim arrangements that would last for two more years for the Ganges, and one more year for the Teesta. And those are the only two rivers, out of the 54 shared rivers, where the two countries had agreements. With the deadlock over the Ganges, no agreement on any other river was expected.

Each of the two countries continued to pass the blame for the failure of the Joint Committee of Experts on the other. The gap between the two proposals remained the same since the discussions over the Ganges started between the two countries in 1972. Whereas Bangladesh's proposal centered on using the Ganges itself to solve the problems of the Ganges, India's proposal aimed at using the Brahmaputra to solve the problems of the Ganges. Summarized differently: "Bangladesh argued that water is best transferred over time, India that it is best transferred over space."[83] It is also noteworthy that each proposal involved the use of the territory of the other country. Part of the link canal proposed by India would be constructed in Bangladesh, and part of the storage reservoirs proposed by Bangladesh would be constructed in India.

1987 ended and so did the *ad hoc* arrangements over the Teesta. May 31, 1988 arrived and passed and with it the 1985 MOU elapsed. The sharing arrangements of the Ganges between India and Bangladesh during the lean season under the 1975

---

[82] *See* Ben Crow, *supra* note 19, at 205. Ben Crow states that Nepal kept inquiring about the benefits for Nepal under any joint scheme, but did not provide the information requested by India and Bangladesh when it failed to get satisfactory answers. *See id.,* at 206.

[83] *Id.*, at 163.

Partial Accord, the 1977 Agreement, the 1982 MOU and the 1985 MOU were all temporary arrangements while the two parties were trying to reach an agreement over the long-term solution of augmenting the flows of the Ganges. Thirteen years and four agreements later, the two parties were still at square one, each playing the same tone it had played 13 years earlier. The dialogue during those 13 years was clearly the dialogue of the deaf, as Verghese called it.[84] So much for Article 6 of the Treaty of Friendship, Cooperation and Peace, concluded more than 14 years earlier, where the High Contacting Parties agreed to make joint studies and take joint action in the fields of flood control, river basin development, hydroelectric power and irrigation.

In August 1988, Bangladesh was devastated by floods, with almost two-thirds of the country submerged. On August 30, 1988, the Ganges flow in Bangladesh reached 72,300 cumecs,[85] which is equal to more than 2.5 million cusecs. This is the same river that flowed at less than 25,000 cusecs in April 1983 in Bangladesh. The problem was clearly the regulation of flow. The momentum and goodwill between India and Bangladesh created by cooperation over the floods was washed away on accusations and counter-accusations on the causes of the floods. Bangladesh blamed the floods on the failure to reach an agreement over the Himalayan rivers, implying that India's bilateral approach to the issue of cooperation over shared rivers was to blame for the floods.

In addition to the Farakka problem, there were many other issues that caused further deterioration in the relationship between the two countries. India had failed to honor its commitment under the Indo-Bangladesh Boundary Treaty of 1974, and the Exchange of Letters of October 7 regarding "Lease of Tin Bigha," to lease to Bangladesh a corridor about 150 meters long called "Tin Bigha." The lease in perpetuity was for the purpose of connecting two enclaves (Dahagram and Angarpota) with Panbari of Bangladesh. This area was given to Bangladesh in exchange for an area of similar size that was already passed to India. India had until that time failed to ratify the Boundary Treaty, and in 1990, the issue of Tin Bigha was still being considered by the Indian Supreme Court.[86] The failure of India to resolve this dispute had certainly strengthened anti-India feelings in Bangladesh.

Another issue that exacerbated the problems between India and Bangladesh was the dispute over the South Talpatty Island in the Bay of Bengal. The island, also known as New Moore, gradually emerged as the result of the silt deposit carried from the Himalayan Mountains by the Ganges, Brahmaputra and other Himalayan rivers flowing into the Bay of Bengal. The island varied in size according to the season, from two to 12 square kilometers. Both India and Bangladesh claimed the island. The issue raised by the dispute over this island was the boundary line in the

---

[84] *See* Verghese, *supra* note 12, at 391.

[85] *Id.*, at 371.

[86] *See* Letters Exchanged Between the Indian Minister of External Affairs, P. V. Narasimha Rao, and Bangladesh Foreign Minister, A. R. Shams-ud-Doha, Regarding Lease of Tin Bigha, New Delhi, October 7, 1982; *see* also Avtar Singh Bhasin, *India-Bangladesh Relations, 1971-1994 Documents,* Vol. 2 (Delhi: Siba Exim, 1996), at 816; *see* also Verghese, *supra* note 12, at 373.

Bay of Bengal. In May 1981 Bangladesh issued a White Paper on South Talpatty Island explaining its ownership of the island since 1971.[87] The Note Verbale handed over by the Indian Ministry of External Affairs to the Bangladesh High Commission in New Delhi in May 1981, brought to the attention of Bangladesh an agreement reached in 1980 to hold further discussion on the issue after study of the additional information exchanged between the two governments. The issue of the Talpatty Island got more complicated in the late 1980s as more Bangladeshi fishermen kept using the island.

A third issue that further complicated the relationship between the two countries was what India saw as a constant infiltration of Bangladeshis to its Northeastern states, particularly Assam and Tripura, and the failure of the Bangladesh authorities to take action to stem such access. There was also a problem with the non-Moslem Chakma tribals from the Chittagong Hill Tracts of Bangladesh, who crossed into the Indian State of Tripura, estimated by India to number more than 50,000 people. India accused Bangladesh of a failure to take action to improve the conditions in the Chittagong Hill Tracts to enable the refugees to return. In July 1991, a Chakma delegation submitted a memorandum alleging violations of human rights of the Chakma tribes by the Bangladesh authorities to the United Nations Commission on Human Rights, Sub-Committee on Prevention of Discrimination and Protection of Minorities, Working Group on Indigenous Populations. Bangladesh accused India of instigating the complaint.[88] Those and other similar issues contributed to the worsening of the relationship between the two countries, and to the hardening of the positions on the Ganges dispute.

In December 1988, Bangladesh proposed a permanent sharing of the Ganges flow at Farakka exactly in the same quantum of waters agreed upon under the 1985 MOU, together with the burden of sharing provisions in case of exceptionally low flow.[89] This concession from Bangladesh was indeed understandable, with another dry season about to start. However, India was in no mood to cooperate, having seen its proposal for augmentation of the flow of the Ganges constantly rejected by Bangladesh. India kept insisting that any water sharing arrangement should be linked to a study of proposals to augment the flow of the Ganges during the dry season. With no agreement for sharing the dry season flow of the Ganges, India continued its diversions of the waters of the Ganges, and again Bangladesh began to

---

[87] *See* Elhance, *supra* note 9, at 179; *see also*, Bhasin, *supra* note 2, Note Verbale Handed by the Ministry of External Affairs to the Bangladesh High Commission in New Delhi on the New Moore Island, New Delhi, May 20, 1980, Volume 2, at 960, and White Paper on South Talpatty Island, Issued by the Ministry of Foreign Affairs, Government of People's Republic of Bangladesh, Dacca, May 26, 1981, at 963.

[88] *See* Verghese, *supra* note 12, at 374; *see also* Bhasin, *supra* note 85, Vol. 2, Memorandum Submitted by Jumma (Chakma) Delegation To the United Nations Commission on Human Rights Sub-Committee on Prevention of Discrimination and Protection of Minorities – Working Group on Indigenous Populations, Geneva, July 29, 1991.

[89] Letter of Bangladesh Ministry of Irrigation, Water Development and Flood Control addressed to the Ministry of Water Resources, Government of India, Containing Proposal for Permanent Sharing of the Ganga Waters, Dacca December 14, 1988, in Bhasin, *supra* note 86, at 741.

complain about the adverse effects of India's withdrawals. Some meetings at the ministerial level, others at the secretarial, were held to discuss the issue of sharing the common rivers, but no agreement on any river, let alone the Ganges, emerged. The Joint Rivers Commission held its thirty-first meeting in Dacca in June 1990, and the issue for discussion, as in the previous meetings, was the sharing of common rivers, including the Ganges. That meeting turned out to be the last meeting of the Commission for a long time, confirming that without the resolution of the Ganges dispute, the parties would simply not be able to discuss meaningfully the sharing of any other river. The diversions of the Ganges to the full capacity of the feeder canal continued and in March 1993, the flow of the Ganges in Bangladesh was reported to be 9,761 cusecs, the lowest since the feeder canal was commissioned in 1975.[90]

With no sharing agreement in sight, and with direct communications growing poorer, Bangladesh raised the issue again at the United Nations when its Prime Minister addressed the General Assembly in October 1993 and accused India of failing to live up to is pledges on the question of water sharing. India immediately condemned this move and accused Bangladesh of playing politics with important river water issues.

Moreover, there was no attempt to involve the South Asian Association for Regional Cooperation (SAARC), a regional organization established in December 1985, which includes Bangladesh, Bhutan, India, Maldives, Nepal, Pakistan and Sri Lanka.[91] With such inclusive membership, SAARC may seem like a suitable organization to address these kinds of issues. However, the objectives of SAARC, as spelled out in its Charter, are of a general nature and include promotion of the welfare of the peoples of South Asia, acceleration of economic growth, promotion and strengthening of self reliance, and promoting active collaboration and mutual assistance. Moreover, the Charter specifies that cooperation within the SAARC framework is based on respect for the principles of sovereign equality, territorial sovereignty, political independence and non-interference in the internal affairs of other states.[92] Based on this, SAARC "...adopted a functional approach, that is cooperation in non-controversial areas like sports, culture and communications...."[93] Moreover, as India has always insisted on bilateral approaches to its problems with its neighbors, no role was envisioned for SAARC in the Ganges dispute.

---

[90] *See* Ben Crow, *supra* note 19, at 219.

[91] For the Charter of the South Asian Association for Regional Cooperation, *see*, *Indian Journal of International Law* 26 (Jan. - June 1986), at 323-326. The Charter was signed in Dhaka, Bangladesh on December 8, 1985, by the heads of the States or governments of SAARC. It is interesting to note that the Charter of SAARC was signed about two weeks after the 1985 MOU between India and Bangladesh was signed on November 22, 1985.

[92] Preamble, Recital 1, SAARC Charter.

[93] *See,* Nahid Islam, *supra* note 10, at 332.

Under those circumstances, it looked quite clear that unless some major political changes took place in both countries, the deadlock would last for a long time. The situation was, to a large extent, similar to the one that prevailed between the two countries after the Consensus Statement was adopted by the United Nations, and prior to the conclusion of the 1977 Agreement between India and Bangladesh.

II. The Ganges Treaty Regime

1. The New Players and the 1996 Treaty

Major political changes did, indeed, take place in both India and Bangladesh in 1996. In India the United Front Government, which consisted of 13 regional parties took power in Delhi. In Bangladesh, the Awami League, which was established by Sheikh Mujib and had close ties to India, was returned to power for the first time since 1975. The United Front announced that better relations with India's neighbors was one of its foreign relations priorities. Its Foreign Minister, Inder Kumar Gujral, announced that India needed to be more generous with its smaller neighbors in seeking more regional cooperation, and should not always expect a *quid pro quo* in such dealings. This principle, which came to be known as the Gujral Doctrine, was a major factor in shaping the political and economic relations of India with its neighbors during the years the United Front was in power.

The political changes in India and Bangladesh created a new momentum that the two countries were able to capitalize on quickly, but cautiously. The foreign minister of each country visited the capital of the other country and the two Prime Ministers met in Rome during the World Food Summit in November 1996. Meanwhile, work on the broad outline for an agreement on the Ganges was going on quietly. The Chief Minister of the Indian State of West Bengal also visited Bangladesh to discuss the sharing arrangements of the Ganges in November 1996. The visit paved the way for an agreement since West Bengal is the key player in the dispute as the Farakka Barrage is located there and is diverting water to Calcutta, the capital of West Bengal. On December 12, 1996 the two countries finally signed a Treaty on sharing the Ganges, ending more than eight years without an agreement, characterized by an acrimonious relationship. The signing of the Treaty was certainly a major breakthrough in the attempts to resolve the long-standing dispute, which by that time, had persisted for more than a quarter of a century.[94]

This is the first time an agreement on the Ganges between India and Bangladesh was called a Treaty; the previous agreements were called a "Partial Accord," "Agreement" and "Memorandum of Understanding." Although the designation of an international agreement alone, according to international law, does not usually

---

[94] Treaty Between the Government of the Republic of India and the Government of the People's Republic of Bangladesh on Sharing of the Ganga/Ganges waters at Farakka, 36 I.L.M. 523 (1997). The Treaty consists of 12 Articles and two Annexures. For a general discussion of the Treaty, *see*, Salman M. A. Salman and Kishor Uprety, *supra* note 59, at 295–343.

matter,[95] the choice of the term "Treaty" should be seen as implying a stronger political commitment on the part of the signatories. Moreover, whereas the 1977 Agreement and the two MOUs of 1982 and 1985 were signed by ministers, either of irrigation or foreign affairs, the Treaty was signed by the two Prime Ministers at that time, Mr. H. D. Deve Gowda, Prime Minister of India, and Sheikh Hasina Wajed, Prime Minister of the People's Republic of Bangladesh. This certainly sent a clear signal of a stronger political commitment to the Treaty. In addition, the Treaty is to remain in force for a period of 30 years, and "…shall be renewable on the basis of mutual consent."[96] On the other hand, each of the four previous agreements, as we have seen, remained in force for a short period of time. All four agreements together remained in force for a total of about 11 years.

2. Sharing Arrangements

One important distinguishing factor between the Treaty and the previous agreements is that the Treaty deals mainly with the sharing of the waters of the Ganges. The issue of augmentation of its flow is recognized in the preamble and dealt with in one three-line article only. The details on the augmentation proposals in the 1977 Agreement and the two MOUs of 1982 and 1985, on the institutional arrangements, specific schedule and higher level reviews, are no longer there. This, coupled with the length of the period of the Treaty of 30 years, clearly indicates that the era of treating the sharing arrangements as an interim measure while the search for the long-term solution is being conducted, is over. It is also clear that India was no longer insisting on the linkage between the water sharing arrangements and the study of proposals for augmenting the flow of the Ganges. This is, indeed, a Treaty for sharing the waters of the Ganges. Augmentation of the flow of the waters of the Ganges is a secondary matter. The wording of Article VIII that "The two Governments recognize the need to cooperate with each other in finding a solution to the long-term problem of augmenting the flows of the Ganga/Ganges during the dry season"[97] is clearly indicative of the fact that the two parties no longer consider this the main issue to resolve. This is certainly a courageous recognition that the dialogue that went on for a quarter of a century and led nowhere should not be repeated, as there was no point in going through it again. Instead, the two parties concentrated on the sharing arrangements of the waters of the Ganges during the dry season.

Another distinguishing factor between the previous four agreements and the Treaty is that the Treaty prescribes an actual formula for sharing the waters of the Ganges between the two countries, in addition to including an indicative schedule giving the implication of the sharing arrangements under the formula. On the other

---

[95] The Vienna Convention on the Law of Treaties (*supra* note 65) defines, in Article 2.1 (a), the term treaty as "an international agreement concluded between States in written form and governed by international law, whether embodied in a single instrument or in two or more related instruments and whatever its particular designation."

[96] Article XII of the Treaty.

[97] *Id.,* Article VIII.

hand, the previous agreements included only a schedule indicating the share of each country from the waters of the Ganges. The sharing formula (Table 7.5) includes thresholds of the water available at Farakka, and the share of each country is stated either as a percentage, or as an amount, of that threshold, as follows:

Table 7.5
Formula for Sharing the Waters of the Ganges Under the 1996 Treaty

Availability at Farakka	Share of India	Share of Bangladesh
70,000 cusecs or less	50 percent	50 percent
70,000 -75,000 cusecs[98]	Balance of flow	35,000 cusecs
75,000 cusecs or more	40,000 cusecs	Balance of flow

Subject to the condition that India and Bangladesh each shall receive guaranteed 35,000 cusecs of water in alternate three, 10-day periods during the period March 1 to May 10.[99]

Source: Annexure 1 of the Treaty.

In addition to the above formula, the Treaty includes an indicative schedule (Table 7.6) of the share of each country between the period January 1 to May 31 each year.

---

[98] It should be noted that the figure "70,000" has been repeated in both the first and second lines of Annexure 1 above (Table 7.5), and the figure "75,000" is also repeated in both the second and third lines above. As such, if availability at Farakka is exactly 70,000 cusecs, the formula in the first or second line could apply. Similarly, if the availability is exactly 75,000 cusecs, the formula in the second or third line could apply. Perhaps a better way of drafting could have been for the first line to read "less than 70,000 cusecs" and for the third line to read "more than 75,000."

[99] In the authors' view, "March 1" in this statement is an error and should read "March 11" instead. This is because the indicative Schedule (Table 7.6 below) specifies only the six 10-day periods from March 11 to May 10. Those six 10-day periods are divided equally and alternately between India and Bangladesh.

Table 7.6
Share of India and Bangladesh of the Waters of the Ganges at Farakka Under the 1996 Treaty

The opening paragraph of the Schedule states that if actual availability corresponds to average flows of the period 1949 to 1988, the implication of the formula in Annexure I for the share of each side is:

Period	Average of total flow 1949-88 (Cusecs)	India's share (Cusecs)	Bangladesh's share (Cusecs)
January			
1-10	107,516	40,000	67,516
11-20	97,673	40,000	57,673
21-31	90,154	40,000	50,154
February			
1-10	86,323	40,000	46,323
11-20	82,859	40,000	42,859
21-28	79,106	40,000	39,106
March			
1-10	74,419	39,419	35,000
11-20	68,931	33,931	35,000*
21-31	64,688	35,000*	29,688
April			
1-10	63,180	28,180	35,000*
11-20	62,633	35,000*	27,633
21-30	60,992	25,992	35,000*
May			
1-10	67,351	35,000*	32,351
11-20	73,590	38,590	35,000
21-31	81,854	40,000	41,854

* *Three 10-day periods during which 35,000 cusecs shall be provided.*
Source: Annexure II to the Treaty

The Treaty maintained the two parameters established by the 1975 Partial Accord and included in the previous agreements, namely that: (i) the quantum of water to be released by India to Bangladesh would be at Farakka, and that (ii) the share of each country would be in 10-day periods (with 11-day periods in the case of 31-day months) from January 1 to May 31. However, there are some major differences in this regard between the Treaty and the previous agreements. The titles of the third and fourth columns of the Schedule to the 1977 Agreement and the two MOUs were "Withdrawal by India at Farakka" and "Release to Bangladesh" respectively. Although Article I indicates that the waters agreed to be released by India to Bangladesh would be at Farakka, the titles of the third and fourth columns of the Annexure 1 to the Treaty are simply, "India's share" and "Bangladesh's share" respectively. This implies an acceptance by India that what Bangladesh is getting is its share and not just a release by India. Indeed, the Treaty embraces the principle of equitable utilization in the allocation of the Ganges waters between the two countries, and includes the term "equity," as we shall see, in three of its articles. Moreover, in line with the 1985 MOU, the name of the river is the "Ganga/Ganges," and not just the "Ganga" as it is called by India and the 1977 and 1982 MOUs.

Another major difference between the previous agreements and the Treaty is the manner in which the flows reaching Farakka is calculated. The 1977 Agreement and each of the 1982 and 1985 MOUs established the flows at Farakka based on 75 percent availability of the average flow of the Ganges from observed data for 25 years covering the period 1948–1973. On the other hand, the Treaty established the flow at Farakka based on 100 percent availability of the average flow of the Ganges for 40 years, covering the period 1949–1988. This is a major departure from the previous agreements and from the established practice in this area when usually less than 100 percent availability of the average flow is shared, to avoid negative surprises. The Treaty has certainly assumed and based the sharing arrangements on higher availability than the previous agreements. Perhaps the year 1988 was chosen, and not a later year, because it was the last year in which joint teams from India and Bangladesh recorded the daily flows of the Ganges at Farakka under the 1985 MOU.

Under the indicative schedule (Table 7.6), India's total share during the lean season amounts to about 48 percent of the total available water during that season, whereas Bangladesh's share represents about 52 percent. For Bangladesh this is a decrease of about 7 percent of its share, from 59 percent to 52 percent under the 1977 Agreement and the two MOUs of 1982 and 1985, and a corresponding increase of India's share from 41 percent to 48 percent.

The Schedule also specifies the three 10-day periods during which 35,000 cusecs shall be provided, alternately, to each of the two countries. For Bangladesh those dates are March 11–20, April 1–10, and April 21–30, whereas for India they are March 21–31, April 11–20, and May 1–10. The period March 11–May 10 is considered the critical period of the lean season because the flow of the Ganges during this period is usually the lowest of the lean season.

Reading Annexure 1 and Annexure II (Tables 7.5 and 7.6) together, the following is noted:

(i) Out of the fifteen 10-day periods of the dry season, there are six 10-day periods that would be governed by the first part of the sharing formula in Annexure 1 (included in the first line of Annexure 1, Table 7.5) which allocates 50 percent of the available water (70,000 cusecs or less) to each of the two countries. However, those six 10-day periods correspond to the period in which each country is guaranteed, according to the indicative schedule, to receive 35,000 cusecs in alternate three 10-day periods. As such, the first part of the formula is not being applied. However, that part of the formula would still apply if the availability of water at Farakka goes down to 70,000 cusecs or less during any of the remaining nine 10-day periods.

(ii) The indicative schedule shows that there are two 10-day periods in which availability of water at Farakka is between 70,000 and 75,000 cusecs. On those two occasions, the second part of the sharing formula (second line of Annexure 1, Table 7.6) has been applied, and Bangladesh's share is 35,000 cusecs, with the balance going to India.

(iii) The third part of the sharing formula (third line of Annexure, Table 7.6) has been applied to the remaining seven 10-day periods, and India's share is 40,000 cusecs, with the remaining balance of the flow going to Bangladesh.

The sharing arrangements under the Treaty followed the principles of equitable and reasonable utilization. There was no longer insistence from Bangladesh on the historical flow, historical rights or natural flow. India, on the other hand, was no longer insisting that the Ganges was an overwhelmingly Indian river, and demanding a proportionate share of its waters. The recognition of the equality of right over the waters of the Ganges led almost to an equal division of such waters.

3. Implementation Arrangements

A Joint Committee similar in structure and responsibilities to the one established under the 1977 Agreement and the two MOUs of 1982 and 1985, has been established under the Treaty. It consists of an equal number of representatives nominated by the two governments, and is responsible for implementing the sharing arrangements under the Treaty. The Joint Committee is authorized to set up suitable teams at Farakka and Hardinge Bridge to observe and record the daily flows of the Ganges at Farakka Barrage, Feeder Canal, the Navigation Lock, as well as the Hardinge Bridge.[100] The Committee has the right to decide its own procedure and method of functioning. It shall submit to the two governments all data collected, in addition to an annual report.

The Treaty also maintained the same provisions as before for dispute settlement, except that the Joint Rivers Commission is given a role, if the Joint Committee cannot resolve the dispute itself. If the difference or dispute cannot be resolved by the Commission, such difference or dispute would be referred to the two governments which shall meet urgently at the appropriate level to resolve it by mutual consent. Again the parties opted for political means for resolving any differences, with no role for a third party.

Excess and deficit flow situations are not dealt with specifically under the Treaty because the thresholds in Annexure I to the Treaty (Table 7.6) deal with such situations. Similarly, there is neither a guarantee clause similar to the one included in the 1977 Agreement, nor burden sharing arrangements like those detailed in the 1982 MOU and 1985 MOU. Instead, Article II (III) states that "in the event flow at Farakka falls below 50,000 cusecs in any 10-day period, the two governments will enter into immediate consultations to make adjustments on an emergency basis, in accordance with the principles of equity, fair play and no harm to either party."

---

[100] The Treaty added the Navigation Lock as an observation point. It was not included in any of the previous agreements.

It should be noted, however, that the sharing arrangements under the Treaty are not binding on the parties for the entire 30-year period of the Treaty. Article X of the Treaty states that "the sharing arrangements under this Treaty shall be reviewed by the two governments at five years' interval, or earlier as required by either party, and needed adjustments, based on the principles of equity, fairness and no harm to either party made thereto. If necessary, it would be open to either party to seek the first review after two years to assess the impact and the working of the sharing arrangements as contained in this Treaty."[101] In addition, Article XI stipulates that for the period of the Treaty "in the absence of mutual agreement on adjustments following reviews as mentioned in Article X, India shall release downstream of Farakka Barrage, water at a rate not less than 90% (90 percent) of Bangladesh's share according to the formula referred to in Article II, until such time as mutually agreed flows are decided upon."

Read together, those two articles guarantee the application of the sharing arrangements referred to above only for the first five years, and if either party requests an earlier review, which could be made after two years from the date of the Treaty, then adjustments may be introduced to the sharing arrangements. If the two parties fail to agree on new arrangements, then India will release to Bangladesh water at a rate not less than 90 percent of Bangladesh's original share under the Treaty. It is worth noting that the 1977 Agreement also included a clause stating that "the Agreement will be reviewed by the two Governments at the expiry of three years from the date of coming into force of this Agreement. Further reviews shall take place six months before the expiry of this Agreement or as may be agreed upon between the two Governments."[102] However, there was no mention of the possibility of a change to the share of either country as a result of such a review under that Article.

Moreover, the Treaty includes a provision that was also included in the 1977 Agreement. Article III of the Treaty states that waters released to Bangladesh at Farakka would not be reduced below Farakka up to the point where the Ganges enter Bangladesh, "except for reasonable uses of waters, not exceeding 200 cusecs, by India between Farakka and the point on the Ganga/Ganges where both its banks are in Bangladesh."[103]

---

[101] The principles "equity, fairness and no harm to either party" are also referred to in Article IX of the Treaty on the conclusion of water sharing agreements with regard to other common rivers. In addition, Article II (iii) of the Treaty on emergency situations (flow at Farakka falling below 50,000 cusecs) provides, *inter alia,* for applications of the principles of "equity, fair play and no harm to either party." It is not clear why this Article used "fair play," whereas Articles IX and X used "fairness." It seems that the principles of "equity, fairness and no harm to either party" are meant to reconcile the principles of "equitable and reasonable utilization" on the one hand, and the "obligation not to cause appreciable harm" on the other hand.

[102] Article XIII of the 1977 Agreement, *supra,* note 59.

[103] Article III of the Treaty. The reason for using the phrase "where both its banks are in Bangladesh" is to exclude the area where the Ganges is a boundary river between India and Bangladesh, which extends for about 112 kilometers.

4. Critique of the Treaty

As indicated above, this is clearly a water sharing Treaty where the augmentation issue has taken a backseat. There are references to other common issues, but such references are cursory. For example, the preamble to the Treaty emphasizes the desire of the parties for sharing by mutual agreement the waters of the international rivers flowing through their territories, and making optimum utilization of the water resources of the region in the fields of flood control, irrigation, river basin management and generation of hydropower. However, only one article of the Treaty, Article IX, deals with one of those issues. That Article states that "Guided by the principles of equity, fairness and no harm to either party, both the Governments agree to conclude water sharing Treaties/Agreements with regard to other common rivers." This is only an "agreement to agree" to conclude agreements on the other shared rivers. The other challenges posed by the Ganges or to the Ganges, such as floods and environmental problems, have not been addressed by the Treaty.

The share of Bangladesh of the waters of the Ganges under the Treaty has decreased, as we have seen, from 59 percent to 52 percent. There is no protection to Bangladesh such as the guarantee clause, or the burden sharing arrangements. In case the flow of the Ganges at Farakka falls below 50,000 cusecs, the only recourse to Bangladesh is entering into immediate consultation to make adjustments on an emergency basis.[104] This Article did not provide help to Bangladesh when the flow fell below 50,000, as we shall see later. The dispute settlement provisions, like the provisions of the previous agreements, are based on political means for resolving disputes and do not provide any room for an intervention by a third party, such as fact finding, mediation or arbitration. India has always insisted on a bilateral approach to matters related to the Ganges, including, as we have noted, the augmentation proposals. Moreover, future reviews of the Treaty could result in a decrease of the share of Bangladesh to 90 percent of the share specified under the Treaty.

Those concessions that Bangladesh agreed to are not without a *quid pro quo*. India was no longer insisting that the sharing of the waters of the Ganges should be an interim measure while the long-term solution is being pursued. "A close look into the main elements of the 1977 Agreement and the MOUs of 1982 and 1985 reveals that the sharing of the Ganges flows under these instruments was always contingent upon Bangladesh's agreement to study the Indian scheme for augmentation of flows at Farakka."[105] It might be recalled that Bangladesh was willing to accept the sharing arrangements under the 1985 MOU for further terms after it expired in 1988. The sharing arrangements under the Treaty are not much different from those under the 1985 MOU. The share of Bangladesh of the waters of the Ganges has, indeed, decreased in proportion to that of India. However, Bangladesh now has a long-term Treaty, in comparison with the previous short-term agreements. It should also be noted that the share of Bangladesh under the Treaty far exceeds the amounts of

---

[104] Article II (iii) of the Treaty.

[105] *See* Khan, *supra* note 11, at 469.

waters that Bangladesh received during the seven years of vacuum, after the 1985 MOU expired and prior to the conclusion of the Treaty, as shown in Table 7.7.

Tables 7.7

Average Flows of the Ganges at Hardinge Bridge in Bangladesh During the Years 1989–1995, and Under the Treaty

Period	Flows During 1989-1995 (Cusecs)	Bangladesh's Share Under the Treaty (Cusecs)
January		
1-10	53,619	67,516
11-20	47,726	57,673
21-31	40,781	50,154
February		
1-10	33,417	46,323
11-20	26,868	42,859
21-28	24,559	39,106
March		
1-10	22,868	35,000
11-20	19,573	35,000
21-31	17,516	29,688
April		
1-10	17,177	35,000
11-20	19,578	27,633
21-30	21,759	35,000
May		
1-10	23,467	32,351
11-20	32,228	35,000
21-31	50,410	41,854

Sources: Ministry of Water Resources, Bangladesh, for the second column and the 1996 Treaty for the third column.

This should not, however, blur the fact that the Treaty includes a number of ambiguous provisions, and provisions that are difficult to implement or are merely agreements to agree. The paragraph in Annexure I, which states that "India and Bangladesh shall each receive guaranteed 35,000 cusecs of water in alternate three 10-day periods during the period March 1 to May 10," is an example of those provisions that are difficult to implement because it is not clear who is the guarantor.

Some of the commitments are no more than obligations of making the best effort. One "best effort" commitment is included in paragraph (ii) of Article II where the reference to the 40 years (1949–1988) 10-day period availability of water at Farakka is included. The Paragraph states that "Every effort would be made by the upper riparian to protect flows of water at Farakka as in the 40-years average availability as mentioned above." It is intriguing that the Article used the term "upper riparian." The terminology of "upper riparian," and "lower riparian" is not included in any other article of the Treaty. Because the Treaty is between India and Bangladesh, it would have to be assumed that the term "upper riparian" refers to India.[106]

It is true that India cannot guarantee that the flow of the Ganges would always remain as specified in the Schedule to the Treaty because natural causes such as drought or slow melting of snow in the Himalayas can affect the flow of the Ganges. However, it should be remembered that the Ganges flows through a number of Indian States including Himachal Pradesh, Uttar Pradesh, Rajasthan, Haryana, Madhya Pradesh, Bihar, West Bengal and the National Capital Territory of Delhi before entering Bangladesh. The expanded use of the waters of the Ganges in those states, particularly the densely populated states of Uttar Pradesh (with a population of 160 million) and Bihar (with a population of 80 million), for irrigation, industrial and domestic purposes, poses a major challenge to maintaining the flow of the Ganges as in the 40 years average availability specified in the Schedule to the Treaty.

Moreover, under the Indian Constitution water is, by and large, a state matter. The definition of water includes "water supplies, irrigation and canals, drainage and embankments, water storage and water power, subject to the provisions of entry 56 of List 1."[107] The Central Government, or the Union as the Constitution calls it, has the authority under entry 56 of List I over "regulation and development of inter-state rivers and river valleys to the extent to which such regulation and development under the control of the Union is declared by Parliament by law to be expedient in the public interest." In addition to these two entries, Article 262 (1) of the Constitution deals with disputes relating to inter-state rivers. It states that Parliament may by law provide for the adjudication of any dispute or complaint with respect to the use, distribution or control of the waters of, or in any inter-state river or river valley. Article 262 (2) states that Parliament may by law provide that neither the Supreme Court nor any other court shall exercise jurisdiction in respect to any such dispute or complaint as is referred to in clause (1), notwithstanding anything in the Constitution. Pursuant to Article 262 of the Constitution, the Parliament adopted "The Inter-State Water Disputes Act, 1956.[108] According to the Act, a water dispute includes any dispute between two or more states regarding the use, distribution or control of the waters of, or in, any inter-state river or river valley, or the interpretation of the terms of any agreement relating to the use, distribution or control of such

---

[106] It should be admitted that the issue of upper riparian/lower riparian may not be that simple when it comes to the Ganges. The river splits into two arms, one flowing towards Bangladesh and the other towards Calcutta, both emptying in the Bay of Bengal. This would technically make both countries lower riparians. It should also be recalled that the river is a boundary river for about 112 kilometers before entering Bangladesh, and that the river originates in China and Nepal, the upper riparians. However, between India and Bangladesh, Bangladesh is considered the lower riparian particularly because India controls the flow of the river.

[107] *See* Constitution of India, Seventh Schedule, List II (State List), Entry 17.

[108] Act 33 of 1956.

waters or the implementation of such agreement. The Act lays down detailed procedures as to how such disputes should be handled. When the central government receives any request from one state regarding a dispute over an inter-state river, and the central government is of the opinion that the dispute cannot be settled through negotiations, it shall constitute a water dispute tribunal. The tribunal, which consists of three judges, has the same powers as those vested in a civil court, including the power for summoning and enforcing attendance of any person and requiring the production of any documents or materials. The decision of the tribunal is final and binding on the parties to the dispute. Thus far, tribunal awards have been issued on the Krishna, the Narmada, the Godavari, the Ravi and Beas and the Cauvery Rivers. None of those rivers is a tributary of the Ganges.[109]

Inter-state water disputes do not necessarily have to be resolved by a Tribunal. The States of Uttar Pradesh, Haryana, Rajasthan, Himachal Pradesh and the National Capital Territory of Delhi signed a memorandum of understanding on May 12, 1994 on the allocation of the utilizable water resources of the Yamuna River, one of the most important tributaries of the Ganges.[110] The five parties agreed under the memorandum of understanding on a final allocation of the surface flow of the Yamuna River, and on an interim seasonal allocation of the annual utilizable flow

---

[109] The Ravi and Beas are two of the three Eastern Rivers of the Indus Basin that were allocated to India, as discussed in Chapter 2 *supra*. As noted in that Chapter, the Indus Waters Treaty allocated the Eastern Rivers, namely the Ravi, the Beas and the Sutlej, to India. It should be noted that the Indian State of Punjab where parts of those rivers flow, was itself divided in 1966 into two states, Punjab and Haryana. As a consequence, an issue arose regarding the mechanism to divide the amount of 7.2 million acre-feet (MAF) of water allocated to Punjab, between the two states. The central Government allocated 3.5 MAF to each of the two states and the remaining .2 MAF to Delhi. Punjab objected to this allocation and filed a case with the Supreme Court. While the suit was still pending, the states of Punjab, Haryana and Rajasthan concluded an agreement on December 31, 1981, on the allocation of the waters of the Ravi and Beas. The Agreement established the total availability of water in the Ravi and Beas as 17.17 MAF, out of which 4.22 MAF was allocated to Punjab, 3.5 MAF to Haryana, and 8.6 MAF to Rajasthan. As a result of the agreement, the suit before the Supreme Court was withdrawn. However, Punjab, concluding that the agreement was unfair, repudiated it in November 1985. An agreement was reached between Punjab and the central Government to refer the dispute to a tribunal. It should be noted that under the Inter-State Water Disputes Act, such a tribunal can only be constituted on receipt of a complaint from one of the parties to the dispute over an inter-state river. Because no specific complaint was received, and because the central Government had no power to establish a tribunal *suo moto*, the Act was amended in 1986 to provide for the establishment of the Ravi and Beas Waters Tribunal. The Tribunal was constituted in April 1986, and it issued its award in January 1987. The award allocated 5 MAF to Punjab and 3.83 MAF to Haryana. The shares of Rajasthan and Delhi of 8.6 MAF and .2 MAF respectively, were left unchanged. Hence, interestingly enough, the Indus dispute that had originated as an inter-state dispute between Punjab and Sind, also ended as an inter-state dispute between Punjab and Haryana. Moreover, similar to the India-Pakistan international dispute, the Punjab-Haryana inter-state dispute could also be resolved peacefully, albeit through judicial mechanism. For more details on the Ravi and Beas award, *see*, Chauhan, *supra* note 11, at 138.

[110] *See* Memorandum of Understanding Between Uttar Pradesh, Haryana, Rajasthan, Himachal Pradesh and National Capital Territory of Delhi Regarding Allocation of Surface Flow of Yamuna" (on file with authors). The Yamuna itself has a number of tributaries and its total length is about 1,376 kilometers. It joins the Ganges near the city of Allahabad in the state of Uttar Pradesh; for further information on the Yamuna, *see*, Chauhan, *supra* note 11, at 133.

of the Yamuna, pending the construction of the storages in the upper reaches of the Yamuna. The allocation was based on 75 percent dependable notional virgin flow. According to paragraph 7 (iii) of the memorandum, surplus flows shall be distributed among the parties in proportion to their allocation. The Union Ministry of Water Resources is not a party to the memorandum of understanding, but the assistance and advice given by the Union Minister of Water Resources in arriving at the settlement is acknowledged in the memorandum. The memorandum, however, did not establish any institutional mechanism for administering and supervising the sharing arrangements. As such, the extent to which the parties are complying with the provisions of the memorandum of understanding is difficult to ascertain.[111]

Two facts are discernible from the above discussion. First, in practice, as in theory, water is a state matter in India, with a very limited role for the central government. Second, the Ganges and its main tributaries run through some densely populated states that have increasing demand for water. It is perhaps because of those considerations that India did not agree to more than making every effort to protect the flow of the Ganges at Farakka as in the 40 years average availability.

It may be argued, however, that every state is required under international law to take all the necessary measures to meet its treaty obligations, and that the treaty obligations supersede domestic laws and agreements. As such, it could be asked whether India was really interested in taking all the necessary measures for guaranteeing the flow of the Ganges at Farakka as in the 40 years average availability. Moreover, if the flow of the Ganges at Farakka is gradually affected by increasing withdrawals upstream, what will the central government in Delhi do to protect the flow under those circumstance, and what will "every effort" entail? Those are certainly difficult issues and only time will show how they are going to be answered.

Although the preamble to the Treaty mentions flood management as one of the areas for cooperation, no provisions for flood control are included in main body of the Treaty itself. The issue continued to be discussed and dealt with on an *ad hoc* basis by the Joint Rivers Commission. Bangladesh blamed India for the floods that devastated it in 1988.[112] Yet, the issue of sharing the lean season flow proved more important and pressing than dealing with the issue of floods. The Treaty, like the previous agreements, operates only during the dry five months of the year. It has no relevance to the remaining wet months. Bangladesh was devastated again by floods in 1998. They were the worst ever. Floods continued from the middle of July through late September, with the Ganges rising to its highest level in 100 years.[113] Three quarters of Bangladesh, including at least 860,000 hectares of agricultural lands, and more than half of Dhaka, were submerged by floodwaters, and more than 40 million people were affected by the floods. The death toll passed 1,000 by late September and diarrhea, "…caused by polluted water or rotten food, led to 208 of

---

[111] It is widely believed that the National Capital Territory of Delhi, with its increasing population, and the corresponding increasing demands for water for domestic, municipal and industrial uses may soon need more than this allocation.

[112] *See* Ben Crow, *supra* note 19, at 212-213.

[113] *See Asia Week*, Vol. 24, Number 37 (September 18, 1998), at 13.

the deaths."[114] By mid-October, "Diarrhea has killed at least 600 people and hundreds of new cases were being reported daily. Almost 500,000 people have been afflicted by the disease since the start of the summer flooding."[115] The flood situation was equally disastrous in India. In the state of Uttar Pradesh, the 1998 flood was rated as the worst in this century, affecting about 25,000 villages. "Until September 7, an estimated 1,250 people had died. The Ganga, the Gandak, the Ghagra and the Rapti rose to unprecedented levels."[116] A similar situation was repeated during the monsoon season of 2000 in the Ganges and Brahmaputra Basins. In India, "the annual monsoon floods have been the most destructive in memory, uprooting or marooning more than 20 million people... in the state of West Bengal, the waters have swamped more than 7,000 villages, and killed at least 1,000 (between September 17 and October 7). Another 500 died in floods earlier this season [2000] here and elsewhere in India."[117]

The problem called for cooperation, but perhaps such cooperation needed to be at the regional level, and needed to include Nepal, China and Bhutan, the riparian states of the Ganges, Brahmputra and Meghna Rivers. The problem showed that the Treaty was too limited in its scope to deal with the issue of floods.

Another important issue that the Treaty did not address is the environmental situation of the Ganges. More than 400 million people live around and depend on the waters of Ganges Basin for irrigation, domestic and municipal uses. The river is also a major source for fishery, and an important mode for transportation, particularly in Bangladesh. It is considered the holiest river in India and millions of people practice the holy dip hundreds of times every year,[118] while the ashes of a large number of dead bodies are scattered there. This heavy population concentration, the absence of strict environmental rules for the use of the river, and the failure to enforce whatever rules that exist, have resulted in the Ganges being one of the most polluted rivers in the world today. As noted by some scholars, "114 cities pour untreated sewage into India's most important river, the Ganges. Its Yamuna tributary picks up a daily 200 million liters of sewage and 20 million liters of industrial waste in Delhi alone. In the industrial city of Kanpur, only 3 factories out of 647 have treatment plants."[119] At the holy city of Varanasi, the water of the Ganges "...is filled with raw

---

[114] *See Far Eastern Economic Review*, Vol. 161, No. 40, October 1, 1998, at 17.

[115] *See Far Eastern Economic Review*, Vol. 161, No. 42, October 15, 1998, at 16.

[116] *See* Kalyan Chaudhuri, et al., "Swamped by Floods," *Frontline*, Vol. 15, No. 20 (September 26 through October 9, 1998), at 69.

[117] *See* Rama Lakshmi, "Clinging to What Little Is Left, India's Flood Victims Risk Lives to Salvage Belongings," *The Washington Post* (October 7, 2000), at A16.

[118] During the pilgrimage to the Ganges that lasted from January 14 to February 21, 2001 (known as the *Maha Kumbh Mela*) an estimated 50 million people visited the confluence of the Ganges and the Yamuna Rivers at Allahabad for the holy dip. The *Maha Kumbh Mela* has a special religious significance since it occurs once every 144 years. *See Frontline,* Volume 18, No. 3 (February 3-16, 2001), at 65–69.

[119] *See* Peter Wallensteen and Ashok Swain, "Comprehensive Assessment of the Freshwater Resources of the World," *International Freshwater Resources: Conflict or Cooperation*, (Stockholm Environment Institute, 1997), at 6.

sewage, human and industrial waste, the charred remains of bodies, and animal carcasses...Not surprisingly, waterborne illnesses—hepatitis, amebic dysentery, typhoid, and cholera—are common killers, helping to account for the death of more than two million children each year."[120] Waterborne diseases caused by the flooding of 1988 and 1998 resulted in a large number of casualties too. Yet, like the problem of floods, the Treaty did not address any of the issues related to environmental protection of the Ganges.

The Treaty failed to address a number of pressing problems surrounding the Ganges Basin, particularly flood and environmental degradation. It should also be added that a number of its provisions are ambiguous and that the share of Bangladesh has decreased under the Treaty in comparison with the 1977 Agreement, the 1982 MOU and the 1985 MOU. However, the fact that this is a long-term Treaty with no linkage to an agreement on augmentation proposals should be taken into account in assessing its importance. It should also be remembered that the Treaty has filled a vacuum that lasted for more than seven years during which Bangladesh received far smaller amounts than those stipulated under the Treaty. Additionally, the Treaty has created momentum for discussing the sharing of other shared rivers. The Joint Rivers Commission started working on an agreement for sharing the waters of the Teesta River, and it is widely expected that the next treaty between India and Bangladesh over their shared rivers would be on the Teesta.[121] It might be recalled that the Joint Rivers Commission reached *ad hoc* arrangements on the Teesta River for two years in 1983. Those arrangements were renewed for two more years, and expired in 1987.

5. Actual Working of the Treaty, 1997-2000

One of the most important features that distinguishes the previous agreements and the Treaty is the basis for calculating the flows of the Ganges reaching Farakka during the lean season. Under the previous agreements, the average flow of the Ganges reaching Farakka was based on 75 percent water availability from observed data for the 25-year period between 1948 and 1973. Under the Treaty, the figures under the indicative schedule are based on the average total flow (and not 75 percent availability) of the Ganges during the 40-year period between 1949 and 1988. As a result, the average total flow of the Ganges under the Treaty for each 10-day period exceeds the average flow under the previous agreements for the same period by a margin of almost 10 percent for each such period. That means that the Treaty assumed a higher level of water availability than the previous agreements.

---

[120] Alexander Stille, "The Ganges' Next Life," *The New Yorker* (January 19, 1998), at 58, 60. The article discusses the reasons for the failure of the first phase of the cleanup project called the Ganga Action Plan. For details on pollution of the Yamuna, *see*, also T. K. Rajalakshmi, "The Yamuna and Pollution," in Frontline, Volume 17, No. 4 (February 19–March 3, 2000).

[121] See *Joint Communiqué of the 32nd Session of the Indo-Bangladesh Joint Rivers Commission Dhaka,* (July 18-20, 1997).

A few months after the Treaty was concluded, actual availability of the waters of the Ganges at Farakka turned out to be far less than the average flow of the Ganges for the period 1949–1988, as reiterated in the indicative Schedule under the Treaty. The first reports of a decline in the flow of the Ganges at Farakka started circulating during the last 10 days of February 1997, when the flow was supposed to favor Bangladesh. During that period, Bangladesh stated that it had received only 24,559 cusecs instead of the 39,106 cusecs stipulated in the Treaty.[122] The situation became quite serious in late March, and on March 27, the Ganges flow in Bangladesh recorded only 6,500 cusecs, the lowest ever.[123] By early April, the flow kept fluctuating between 10,000 and 25,000 cusecs,[124] and by early May water availability at Farakka was only about 40,000 cusecs, instead of the 67,351 cusecs specified in the Treaty.[125] Overall, Bangladesh received less water than was stipulated under the Treaty in twelve out of the fifteen 10-day periods of the dry season of 1997, as shown in Table 7.8. It is ironic to note that this substantially low flow occurred during the period in which "India and Bangladesh shall receive guaranteed 35,000 cusecs of water in alternate three 10-day periods"[126] and the indicative schedule under the Treaty shows the average availability of more than 60,000 cusecs.

Because the flow of the Ganges continued to be below 50,000 cusecs, Bangladesh, without a guarantee clause similar to that of the 1977 Agreement or burden sharing arrangements like those of the 1982 and 1985 MOUs, asked India for "immediate consultation to make adjustments on an emergency basis" as stipulated under Article II (iii) of the Treaty. India agreed to hold immediate consultation with Bangladesh, and a series of meetings were held in both Dhaka and New Delhi. During those meetings Bangladesh demanded that India should ensure that Bangladesh receive the 35,000 cusecs guaranteed under Annexure 1 of the Treaty, and also wanted to know what India was doing to protect the flow of water at Farakka, as per Article II (ii) of the Treaty. On the other hand, India confirmed that the flow at Farakka had slowed down but attributed this situation to the normal hydrological cycle that occurs every four to five years,[127] and argued that it is

---

[122] *See* Ibne Mahfuz, "Water Treaty Remains As Elusive as Ever?" *Dialogue*, April 14, 1997, at 5. *See* also, Asadullah Khan, "Implementation of the Ganges Treaty, a View from Dhaka," *People's Review* (Bangladesh), May 8, 1997, Opinion page, where it was stated "In the last ten days of February, 39,106 cusecs of water should have been available at the Hardinge Bridge point. But Bangladesh got 27,906 cusecs on 22nd of February, 23,094 cusecs on the 23rd Feb., 22,295 cusecs on 24 Feb., 25,654 cusecs on the 25th Feb., 23,006 cusecs on 26th Feb., and 24,559 cusecs on 27th Feb., and on March 27, the flow was lowest in recent times, recording 6,457 cusecs."

[123] *See* John F. Burns, "Sharing Ganges Waters: India and Bangladesh Test the Depth of Cooperation," *N.Y. Times* (May 25, 1997), at 6. This figure is lower than the previous record of 9,761 reported in March 1993; *see* Ben Crow, *supra* note 18, at 219.

[124] *See* Reuters report from Dhaka dated April 4, 1997.

[125] *See* Mahfuz, *supra* note 122, at 5.

[126] *See* Annexure I to the Treaty. This paragraph is unusual in that it does not specify who is the guarantor that such amounts will actually be delivered. Once the availability came down to such low level, the inoperativeness of the guarantee became discernible.

[127] *See* Mahfuz, *supra* note 122. The Minister of Water Resources in Bangladesh told Reuters on

fulfilling its obligations under the Treaty by agreeing to immediate consultation. However, aside from reiterating the commitment of the two countries to the Treaty, those meetings did not result in any adjustments to the share of either country, nor in any concrete actions on how to handle the situation.[128]

Meanwhile, by mid-May unseasonal spring rains eased the crisis, "with the river at Hardinge Bridge back to levels that normally develop later in the spring, when rising summer heat on the north Indian Plains melts snow in the Himalayas."[129] In mid-June an expert-level meeting of the Indo-Bangladesh Joint Rivers Commission was held in Dhaka. After three days of discussions that centered on the Treaty, the two sides recommended the formation of a scientific committee to study the causes of the low flow of the Ganges during the critical period of the dry season. The unusual seasonal variations of water that is one of the main characteristics of the Ganges River continued, and by early August 1997, the Flood Information Center in Bangladesh started issuing messages that the Ganges flow was above the danger mark, and that certain areas could soon be flooded. Thus the 1997 dry season ended with mixed results, a reasonable flow of the Ganges during the beginning and the end of the dry season, and an unusually low flow during the critical period of the dry season.[130]

Unlike during the 1997 dry season, the Ganges flow in Bangladesh during 1998 was quite high. The month of January witnessed a flow that was almost three times the one stipulated in the Schedule to the Treaty for that period. That trend continued, and even during the critical period of the dry season of March/April, the actual flow was higher than what was specified under the Schedule to the Treaty, and in May it was more than double the amounts under the Treaty. The trend continued during the monsoon season and resulted in the far-reaching floods discussed in the previous section.

The flow of the Ganges in Bangladesh during the dry season of 1999 was less voluminous than that of 1998, but was still far more than what was prescribed under the Treaty. The only exception was the last 10-day period of April when the flow was slightly less than that stipulated under the Treaty. The flow of the Ganges during the dry season of the year 2000 was, by and large, similar to the flow during the dry season of 1999, during the first three months. Unlike the flow during 1999, even the last 10-day period of April witnessed an increased flow compared with the flow

---

April 1, 1997, that India informed him that "ice in the Himalayas where the Ganges originates is not melting enough to raise the water level."

[128] On April 11, 1997, the 10-month old government of the United Front, headed by Mr. Deve Gowda, was voted out of office, and it was not until April 21 that Mr. Inder Kumar Gujral (who was until then the Minister of Foreign Affairs) was selected as a Prime Minister of India. The political vacuum, and later, the transition, might have hindered Bangladesh's efforts to resolve the problem through political means. This was manifested by the cancellation of the meeting of the Indo-Bangladesh Joint Rivers Commission that was supposed to take place in April 1997.

[129] *See* Burns, *supra* note 123.

[130] The *Daily Star Newspaper* in Bangladesh reported in mid-May that the Minister of Water Resources of Bangladesh admitted in parliament that the country had received less than the agreed

for the same period under the Treaty. This trend continued, and during the three 10-day periods of the month of May, the flow was considerably higher than the flow during the same period under the Treaty and May 1999. Table 7.8 provides a comparison between the flow of the Ganges during the dry season, as specified under the Schedule to the Treaty (Table 7.6), and the actual flow during the dry seasons for the years 1997- 2000. It shows beyond doubt the variations in the flow of the Ganges not only between the beginning, middle and end of the dry seasons, but also within the dry season from one year to another year. Such variations confirm the pressing need for regulation of the flow of the Ganges.

It remains to be seen whether the unusually low flow of the Ganges during the dry season of 1997 was an isolated phenomenon attributed to natural causes, or a fact that will repeat itself every number of years.

Table 7.8
Ganges Flow in Bangladesh During the Dry Seasons of the Years 1997-2000, Compared with the Indicative Figures Under the Treaty

Period	Treaty	1997	1998	1999	2000
January					
01-10	67,516	70,829	182,263	95,934	94,975
11-20	57,673	55,788	154,292	85,728	79,568
21-31	50,154	50,045	118,313	81,480	62,238
February					
01-10	46,323	48,430	88,363	64,873	55,903
11-20	42,859	38,319	73,584	61,760	53,292
21-29	39,106	25,689	54,242	53,185	46,909
March					
01-10	35,000	23,291	46,686	41,600	44,573
11-20	35,000	19,930	40,192	35,683	39,320
21-31	29,688	13,823	38,685	33,892	35,509
April					
01-10	35,000	17,857	43,960	35,376	37,026
11-20	27,633	24,559	53,241	30,725	35,528
21-30	35,000	27,695	53,627	34,738	41,535
May					
01-10	32,351	26,578	74,886	37,672	56,126
11-20	35,000	26,279	92,039	41,818	50,344
21-31	41,854	27,520	84,965	48,716	85,274

Source: Schedule to the Treaty, and the Ministry of Water Resources, Bangladesh, for the Years 1997 to 2000

quantum of the Ganges water in some of the 10-day cycles during the last four months, but quoted him as saying "we got more water than mentioned in the agreement in some cycles, while less in others."

6. The Search for an Internal Solution – The Ganges Barrage

One clear indication that the search for a long-term solution for augmentation of the flow of the Ganges had ended was the Bangladesh's revival of the Ganges Barrage idea. This is one of the long outstanding issues related to the Ganges River between India and Bangladesh that the Treaty seems to have helped resolve. The idea of building the Ganges Barrage on the Ganges River was first raised by Pakistan in 1963, and a study on the location, design and cost of the barrage was carried out that year. India opposed the idea vehemently. Bangladesh revived the idea and carried out studies in 1984 that examined the technical feasibility and preliminary engineering of the barrage. "The primary justification for the project was irrigated agriculture although additional environmental benefits were identified as a result of augmenting dry season flows in the rivers in the region."[131] India continued its opposition to the construction of the Ganges Barrage because India saw it as a retaliatory measure against the Farakka Barrage and claimed that large areas of Indian territory in the State of West Bengal would be submerged as a result of backwater effect. Following conclusion of the Treaty and further discussion on the barrage, especially its location, India agreed to the construction of the barrage by Bangladesh. The Joint Communique of the Joint Rivers Commission on its 32nd meeting held on July 18-20, 1997, indicating India's approval of the barrage, stated:

> The Commission welcomed the proposal of Bangladesh to implement the Ganges Barrage project. India indicated its intention to consider providing technical assistance through Water and Power Consultancy Limited (WAPCOS), a Government of India Undertaking, which has the requisite expertise in this regard.[132]

India's agreement is indicative, in our view, of its belief that the era of the joint search for an augmentation solution for the Ganges lean flow has come to an end. Bangladesh is currently carrying out studies on the design, cost and environmental and social impact of the barrage. The plan is to build this barrage at Pangsha, 90 miles west of Dhaka, and not the Hardinge Bridge area which is closer to the Indian borders than Pangasha, as was originally planned.[133] Bangladesh considers the barrage the best way for guaranteeing the success of the Treaty because the barrage would enable Bangladesh to utilize its share of the waters of the Ganges. According to the feasibility study for the barrage carried out in 1997, the barrage would allow Bangladesh to make optimum use of the water that would be available under the Treaty, and would permit irrigation of most of the areas in the southwest, the south central and the north western regions of Bangladesh. Similarly, the Study also suggests that water supplies through the Gorai River, which will be fed by water from

---

[131] *See*, Ministry of Water Resources, Government of the People's Republic of Bangladesh, International Seminar on Water Resources Management and Development in Bangladesh with Particular Reference to the Ganges River, Dhaka, 8-10 March 1998, Seminar Proceedings, at 160.

[132] Joint Communique of the 32nd Meeting of the Indo-Bangladesh Joint Rivers Commission, Dhaka (July 18-20, 1997).

[133] The current proposed location at Pangsha is about 40 miles downstream from the Hardinge Bridge. Thus it is further downstream than the Hardinge Bridge from the borders with India.

the barrage, would reduce saline intrusion around Khulna, thus helping to solve the socioeconomic and environmental problems in the area. Moreover, the study suggests that the flows in all tributaries and other rivers in the southwest region would be augmented so that the natural environment, like fisheries, groundwater, forestry, human health and navigation can be restored through the supply of upland water flow and a reduction in salinity.[134] Additionally, the barrage is expected "to irrigate an area of about 1.35 million hectares of land, and to protect another 1.44 million from floods."[135]

An "International Seminar on Water Resources Management and Development in Bangladesh with Particular Reference to the Ganges River" organized by the Ministry of Water Resources in Bangladesh was held in Dhaka, March 8-10, 1998. The seminar discussed the idea of the Ganges Barrage, but adopted a more cautious approach toward the barrage than manifested earlier in the feasibility study. The seminar concluded that the Ganges flow entering Bangladesh under the Treaty that is equal to half the flow that Bangladesh used to receive before Farakka:

> ... must be managed effectively so that it provides the benefits previously brought by the whole flow. To achieve this, the flow must be restored to the area of the greatest need. The Padma still benefits from the continued flows of the Brahmaputra, and it is to the Gorai and the other rivers of the Southwest that the remaining flow must be diverted.
>
> Distribution of the Ganges flows into the Ganges Dependable Area appears to be the answer. Although a barrage solution would be expensive, it appears to be one of the few feasible economic alternatives to permanently restore the flow in the quantities needed.
>
> There remain many issues which have to be addressed, and the lessons of the Flood Action Plan should not be lost. Full social and environmental studies should be undertaken as part of the technical feasibility study, but before then the community should be given the opportunity of defining the scope of the studies, not merely to complain about inadequacies after the studies are made.[136]

Bangladesh's final decision on the Ganges Barrage will depend upon the results of the study that is currently being conducted. If the study confirms that the barrage is the best solution, then Bangladesh will have to convince the donor community of providing the necessary funds for constructing the Ganges Barrage.[137]

---

[134] *See* Government of the People's Republic of Bangladesh, Technical Assistance Project Proforma (TAPP) for the Feasibility Study and Detailed Engineering Design of the Ganges Barrage Project 6 (May 1997, Recast, June 1997).

[135] *See* Reuters report from Dhaka, August 24, 1997, quoting the Minister of Water Resources of Bangladesh, following a meeting with the President of the Asian Development Bank in Dhaka. The figure of "1.35 million hectare" is close to the figure of "1.31 million hectare" specified in the TAPP, *id.*

[136] *See* Seminar Proceedings, *supra* note 131, at 204-205.

[137] The cost estimates for the Ganges Barrage and associated works, according to the study

III. Conclusion

The close relationship that flourished between India and Bangladesh following the emergence of the latter as an independent nation was the product of the geopolitical situation in the South Asian Sub-continent in the beginning of the 1970s. However, the problems between the two countries that were either present or were cropping up, gradually started affecting that close relationship. Those problems overshadowed the goodwill manifested in the conclusion of the Treaty of Friendship, Cooperation and Peace on March 19, 1972 and the establishment of the Joint Rivers Commission and the signing of its Statute on November 24, 1972. The two countries kept emphasizing their cooperation and friendship, and downplaying the existing problems, particularly the Farakka Barrage.

The 1975 Partial Accord was an attempt by both parties to buy time. After its expiry by the end of May, 1975, India continued diversion of the Ganges waters and Bangladesh felt outsmarted. The assassination of Sheikh Mujib less than three months after the expiry of the Accord and the political change that followed complicated the search for a solution to the Farakka problem. Bangladesh's decision to take its case to the United Nations General Assembly was, indeed, a clear indication of the end of the era of friendship and cooperation. It is quite interesting to follow the arguments of both countries with regard to the rules and principles of international water law that are applicable, and the interpretation of each party to those principles.

The political change in India, and to some extent the external factors reflected in the Consensus Statement, resulted in a sudden improvement in the relationship between the two countries, evidenced by the conclusion of the 1977 Agreement. But again the relationship started to gradually deteriorate. The 1982 and 1985 MOUs each represented a negative development for Bangladesh. In 1982 Bangladesh lost the guarantee clause of the 1977 Agreement. By 1985 it became clear to Bangladesh that India would only agree to a continued sharing of the waters of the Ganges if Bangladesh agreed to the joint search for a long-term solution to the lean season flow of the Ganges. That search proved futile as each party insisted on its own proposal. The expiry of the 1985 MOU was followed by a vacuum similar to the one that emerged following the expiry of the Partial Accord in 1975, and India continued its diversion of the waters of the Ganges to the maximum capacity of the feeder canal. As such, not much water was left for Bangladesh, and Bangladesh did not have many options either. The Prime Minister of Bangladesh referred to the dispute in her speech at the United Nations in 1993, but did not ask for inclusion of the issue in the agenda, perhaps concerned that the partial success attained in 1976 may not be replicated. India's rejection of Bangladesh's proposal that the parties sign another memorandum of understanding reiterating the allocation of the waters of the Ganges under the 1985 MOU, without an attempt to search for a long-term solution,

---

carried out in 1984, was approximately $1 billion; *see* Ministry of Water Resources, Seminar Proceedings, *supra* note 131; *see also* "Joint Communique of the 32nd Session of the Indo-Bangladesh Joint Rivers Commission," *The Hindu* (New Delhi), July 21, 1997, at 196.

indicated the deadlock at which the parties had arrived. For all practical purposes, the Joint Rivers Commission ceased to exist, as it was no longer holding any meetings, notwithstanding Article 6 (iv) which states that ordinary meetings of the Commission shall be held as often as necessary, generally four times a year. Although the parties continued to talk to each other, it was clear that those talks were leading nowhere, as other problems, such as the failure of India to resolve the Tin Bigha dispute, the conflicting claims over the South Talpatty Island and the issue of the Bangladeshi refugees in India, all contributed to the deadlock.

Again it took a major political change, this time in both capitals, for the parties to reach an accord on how to share the waters of the Ganges. Such change was more elaborate compared with that of 1977, as it affected both capitals. As such it had far more significant consequences to the Farakka problem. The signing of the 30-year Ganges Treaty in December 12, 1996, is certainly a major breakthrough in the deadlock that followed the expiry of the 1985 MOU in 1988. It is also a breakthrough to the futile and hopeless search for an augmentation solution that shackled all the previous agreements. The doubts about the viability of the Treaty that were raised by the exceptionally low flow of the Ganges in 1997 seem to be overtaken by the exceptionally high flow in 1998 and the Treaty-level flows of 1999 and 2000. And despite the vagueness of many of its clauses and its failure to address other pressing problems, the Treaty has certainly created a conducive atmosphere for discussing and reaching agreements on the issues related to the other shared water resources. The first sign of such a positive atmosphere was the convening of the Indo-Bangladesh Joint Rivers Commission in Dhaka, in its 32nd meeting on July 19-20, 1997. This was the first meeting for the Commission in more than seven years, as the last meeting was held in June 1990. The Commission agreed to monitor and observe the implementation of the Treaty, and to work toward an agreement on sharing the waters of the Teesta River.[138] The preamble to the Treaty stresses the desire of the parties for sharing by mutual agreement the waters of the international rivers flowing through the territories of the two countries. The Treaty itself states that "Guided by the principles of equity, fairness and no harm to the other party, both the Governments agree to conclude water sharing Treaties/Agreements with regard to other common rivers."[139]

The positive atmosphere created by the Treaty has already started to assist with resolving the other outstanding issues such as the transit facility through Bangladesh

---

[138] *See* "Joint Communiqué of the 32nd Session of the Indo-Bangladesh Joint Rivers Commission," *The Hindu* (New Delhi), July 21, 1997.

[139] Article IX of the Treaty. However, it should be noted that the preamble to the Treaty, like the preamble to the 1977 Agreement, states that the desire of India and Bangladesh for finding a fair and just solution for the Ganges River should not be considered as "establishing any general principles of law or precedent." It is difficult to imagine the two countries discussing and trying to conclude treaties on any of the other 53 common rivers without one of them citing some of the provisions the Treaty. It seems that India, as the upper riparian to all the common rivers with Bangladesh, is the one who introduced this provision, as a similar provision is included in Article 11, Paragraph 2 of the Indus Waters Treaty with Pakistan, *supra,* Chapter 2. No such provision exists in the agreements between India and Nepal.

of Indian goods going to or coming from its northeastern states,[140] and the free trade between the two countries. It should be added that on March 19, 1997, the Treaty of Friendship, Cooperation and Peace between India and Bangladesh lapsed, 25 years from the date of signature. Although the Treaty included provisions for its renewal, the parties quietly allowed it to lapse. That Treaty was a political statement needed in 1972. It did not assist in resolving any of the disputes that cropped up since that time. The Awami League that signed it in 1972 realized that, with the changing circumstances, the Treaty was a political burden it was better off without. Indeed the renewed good relationship between the two governments that were in power in the two capitals at that time, and the attitudinal shift in the way New Delhi was dealing with its neighbors, were seen as better guarantees for cooperation and friendship than another treaty with no significance.

One of the questions that has often been asked is, how would the relations between India and Bangladesh have been if the issue of Farakka Barrage never existed, and what shape would the cooperation over the more than 50 shared rivers have taken? The answer is certainly quite difficult to predict. The fact remains, however, that the Farakka Barrage has been, for about a quarter of a century, the focal issue that shaped the relationship between India and Bangladesh, and the centrifugal point around which the relationship revolved.

As has been stated earlier, the Ganges Basin is one of the most populated in the world, with a population that exceeds that of North America. The bulk of the population is the poorest of the world. The challenges of the basin are tremendous: floods, drought and environmental degradation, including bank erosion. The challenges of the other shared water resources between India and Bangladesh are equally staggering. Those challenges can only be met through cooperation, and not just between India and Bangladesh. Nepal, China and Bhutan should be included in a wider Ganges-Brahmaputra-Meghna collaborative basin management arrangement. Such arrangement should go beyond the issue of quantitative sharing of the waters of those rivers to include other areas such as lean season augmentation, hydropower generation, flood control and environmental protection of those rivers. Any basin management arrangement will need to address immediately the issue of expansion and modernization of the irrigation system and efficient use of the waters of those rivers so as to pull the more than half a billion inhabitants of this basin from their misery and poverty.

---

[140] India and Bangladesh signed on November 1, 1972 the Protocol between the Government of India and the Government of Bangladesh on Inland Water Transit and Trade, *see supra* note 8. The difficulties have been with rail and road links that were cut off during the 1965 India-Pakistan war, and were not resumed after the emergence of Bangladesh in 1971. Since 1998, there have been gradual movements to resume those links.

PART FIVE

General Conclusion

CHAPTER 8

Conflict, Cooperation and Treaties: Retrospect and Prospects

Because of the differences in typology and characteristics of rivers, the diversity of problems faced by the countries of the South Asian Sub-continent in relation to one or several rivers, the disparate country priorities, different political agendas and ambitions, and the geopolitical realities in each of the countries concerned, concluding this study is a complex task and cannot pretend to be all-encompassing. This conclusion is thus limited to the comparative submission of issues and common traits among the treaties, rivers and the countries reviewed.

At the outset it should be noted that, worldwide, the trend in recent years with respect to international watercourses has been one of managing conflict and enhancing cooperation. Recognition by the international community of the virtues of cooperation at the bilateral, regional and multilateral levels has resulted in the recent conclusion of a number of treaties, protocols and conventions on international watercourses. Such instruments include, at the multilateral level, the 1994 Convention on the Cooperation for the Sustainable Development of the Danube River, the 1995 Agreement on the Cooperation for the Sustainable Development of the Mekong River Basin, and the 1999 Convention on the Protection of the Rhine. At the Regional level, the Helsinki Convention on the Protection and Use of Transboundary Watercourses and International Lakes of 1992 has entered into force and effect in 1996, and in 1995 the Protocol on Shared Watercourse Systems in the Southern African Development Community Region was concluded (which was replaced in 2000 by the Revised Protocol). Those multilateral and regional efforts built up the momentum for the adoption of the United Nations Convention on the Law of the Non-Navigational Uses of International Watercourses by the General Assembly in May 1997. In parallel, at the bilateral level, the conclusion of the Mahakali and Ganges treaties in 1996 places the South Asian Sub-continent in line with the global cooperative trend over international watercourses. Indeed, the preamble of the Mahakali Treaty reaffirms the determination of India and Nepal to cooperate in the development of water resources, while the preamble of the Ganges Treaty underscores the desire of India and Bangladesh to share by mutual agreement the waters of the international rivers flowing through their territories. The birth of the Nile Basin Initiative is a clear indication that the cooperative spirit could, with persistence and determination, prevail even in basins where there are very diverse riparian interests. Even the Indus Treaty, which was based on dividing rather than sharing, emphasized the importance of settlement of disputes in a cooperative spirit.

1. Purposes of the Treaties

Despite the cultural and geographical similarities among the countries of the South Asian Sub-continent, each of its shared rivers faced its own kinds of problems, and has generated a system of rules of management adapted to address such problems. The countries, riparian to the specific rivers, have conceived or initiated their process of problem-solving, their ventures of cooperation, and their development of projects on the international watercourse by addressing their specific needs and requirements to safeguard their interests of what they considered equitable utilization. What constitutes or does not constitute equitable utilization in a specific case of each transboundary river reviewed under this study has been defined by each of the riparians themselves, considering its individual national interests and sentiments.

All the treaties reviewed and analyzed in this study are bilateral treaties despite the fact that the rivers concerned, in most of the cases, are also shared by countries other than those parties to such treaties. Those treaties have dealt with a wide range of issues, such as allocation of waters, whether for general or specific use, specific projects and the issues regarding irrigation, hydropower production or storage for flood control. The Mahakali Treaty even includes a provision for allocating water for preserving the ecosystem. The treaties have all been entered into during the past 50 years, starting in the 1950s and ending in the 1990s. However, despite significant developments in the field of international law with regard to water or the environment, even the recent treaties have not fully incorporated, in a uniform fashion, the more current thinking about equitable and sustainable use of international watercourses. The lack of political will as well as the unpredictability of hydro-politics in the Sub-continent are perhaps responsible for such outcome. Such unpredictability has also significantly influenced the overall negotiating process of these agreements.

Indeed, the negotiations of all the agreements, albeit with considerable variations, were tense. Arguments and counter-arguments, and theses and anti-theses, regarding the principles of international water law dominated them. In this context, one strikingly noticeable observation is that the posture of countries in the interpretation of the principles of international water law, particularly during negotiations, depending on whether the country is an upper riparian or a lower riparian, has fluctuated. Their theses, in bargaining for water allocation, have varied between territorial sovereignty as opposed to riparian rights, or prior-appropriation as opposed to equitable utilization.

This kind of variation can also be noticed in how the treaties have dealt with the principles they have established. The Indus Waters Treaty between India and Pakistan, for instance, expressly provided that nothing contained in the Treaty was to be construed as in any way establishing a general principle of law or any precedent. A similar provision was included in the preamble to the 1977 Ganges Agreement between India and Bangladesh, and was again reiterated in the preamble to the 1996 Ganges Treaty between those countries. Because of this provision, theoretically, the parties to those treaties, as suggested by some scholars, could revert to their fundamental legal postures in any future water disputes that were not governed by the Indus or the Ganges Treaty. While there are also arguments to support the view that the kind of provision the Indus or the Ganges Treaty has included cannot keep other countries from looking to the settlement as a precedent or from deriving whatever general principles they choose from the terms agreed upon, a clear and deliberate attempt to avoid the rights in either Treaty being replicated or claimed by the other country is obvious. Indeed, it can be legitimately argued that the 1982 and 1985 MOUs between India and Bangladesh over the Ganges used the 1977 Agreement between those two countries as a precedent for some of the issues negotiated under the two MOUs, such as water allocation, despite the caveat included in the 1977 Agreement. Similarly, the 1996 Treaty between India and Bangladesh has included provisions from the previous agreements, particularly the 1977 Agreement, which have most likely been negotiated as precedents. Not surprisingly though, the agreements entered into between India and Nepal do not contain any similar provision. It should be noted in this connection that India is the upper riparian in the case of the Indus and the Ganges, but it is the lower riparian vis-à-vis Nepal in the case of most of the rivers shared with Nepal.

2. Bilateralism Versus Multilateralism

Although detailed discussions over multilateralism versus bilateralism in negotiations of the water related treaties have been taking place over time, it is bilateralism that has been the dominant—if not the only—approach of most countries. Particularly for India, it has been a consistent government prerequisite for negotiations ever since independence in 1947.[1] India's emphasis on bilateralism is based, as noted by some scholars, on its consideration that multilateral negotiations are less focused, more complex and thus lengthy.[2] For Bangladesh and Nepal, on the other hand, although the usefulness of internationalizing their problems has been regularly acknowledged, they have more often opted for bilateral negotiations, particularly because of unavailability, or inaccessibility, of credible data about the region as a whole. All Treaty negotiations reviewed in this study have thus been carried out on a bilateral basis, and excepting for the case of the Indus (in which the third party involvement was significant), said bilateralism has constituted a serious obstacle to achieving the potential of South Asian water resources development.

No doubt, bilateralism can be justified because negotiations are simpler, but more often than necessary it has been used as a shield to avoid opposing coalitions and preserving bargaining power. This has led to limiting the mutual benefits of possible agreements on water development and usage, as the bilateral focus of the bargaining tends to neglect positive as well as negative externalities. The matter gets more complicated because of the perception among countries that the gain of one country is necessarily the loss of the other (the zero sum game). This perception gives the negotiators a particular charge. Any compromise of prior national objectives may be portrayed as a victory for the other side and governments are not easily amenable to changing their perceptions. Indeed, these States have nationally

---

[1] *See* generally Ben Crow and Nirvilkar Singh, *Impediments and Innovations in International Rivers: The Waters of the South Asia* (August 1999), at 8.

[2] *Id.*

constituted—not regionally constituted—visions of water resources development, and they are not willing to make accommodation to the concerns of other states, thereby undermining the fact that compromise among all might achieve greater benefit for the region.

If cross-sectoral, regional, and integrated approaches to water resources development were to be agreed, the huge potential for international transactions that exists in the South Asian Sub-continent could be optimally exploited. For instance, Nepal would be able to supply hydroelectric power to India and Bangladesh. India would be able to supply navigation and transit rights, financing for construction as well as engineering expertise to Nepal, and to grant secure expectations of minimum flow as well as water storage benefits to Bangladesh. Similarly, Bangladesh would be able to provide navigation and transit rights to Nepal. For India, Bangladesh would be able to facilitate navigation as well as transit of Indian goods to or from its northeastern States. But optimizing all these exploitable resources for the common good of the region means that all three countries would have to take a multilateral approach in negotiations with a regionally constituted vision of water resources development, an approach that may continue to meet unexplainable resistance.

3. Third-Party Intervention

In complex negotiations, a third party intervention is considered a useful element. Particularly when the third party is a prominent international body, the role it plays can become more meaningful and attractive. Third-party mediations have facilitative aspects. Many longstanding conflicts in the world have either been settled or reduced in magnitude because of skillful third-party mediation. However, in the case of waters of the South Asian Sub-continent, despite efforts from some countries (such as Bangladesh's attempt to internationalize the Ganges dispute through the United Nations, as already discussed in the previous chapters), third-party involvement has been present in only one dispute. With the exception of the Indus Waters Treaty, the most significant event bearing upon a negotiated settlement in more than four decades, to which the World Bank contributed significantly, there has been no role for a third party in the solution of any other disputes, or treaties related thereto, between India and Nepal or India and Bangladesh.

Certainly, in the Indo-Nepal negotiations on the shared rivers, proposals to involve a third party were not brought forward by either party. As a matter of fact, two of the agreements India and Nepal entered into (the Kosi and the Gandak) were negotiated prior to the Indus, and thus the example set by the Indus Treaty (along with the World Bank's role) and the resulting benefits of such third-party role, were yet unknown. On the other hand, in the case of the Ganges dispute when the Bangladesh Government attempted to involve the United Nations, the attempt failed in particular because of India's insistence that there should be no role for a third party in the Ganges dispute and that the matter should be resolved by the parties themselves.

4. Water Rights and Benefits

The political situation that prevailed in the countries of the South Asian Sub-continent has also been a factor that played a significant role, positive as well as negative, in the outcome of the treaties. If political instability was responsible for the largely prevailing ambiguity in some treaties (India-Nepal), the internal political stability was significant in some other (India-Pakistan). For instance the treaties between India and Nepal would have probably taken a less ambiguous form had political instability, characterized by frequent changes in governments, not prevailed in Nepal. Similarly, the Indus Treaty might have been delayed had a strong government not been in power in Pakistan.

Despite the discrepancy in the political situations and choices of the countries of the South Asian Sub-continent, the parties attempt, through the treaties, to develop water resources for common economic growth, to fix and limit rights of use by the parties, and to confirm amounts of water to be used by the parties on the shared rivers. Essentially they intend to address the paucity of water availability in the region, both in qualitative and quantitative terms. The preambles of those agreements provide a general statement of intent that focuses on the importance of cooperation and the mutual benefits for economic and regional development. For instance, the Ganges Treaty is concerned with sharing the lean flow of the Ganges, the Kosi Agreement is concerned with specific issues of flood control, the Gandak Agreement is concerned with irrigation, power and flood control, and the Indus Treaty confronts the broader question of water resources allocation and management.

In all treaties, the most interesting substantive issues are the description of benefits and allocations as reasonable and equitable. One way of measuring the rights equitably is to have an agreement on the quantity of water available and the guaranteed minimum flows to other riparian states. The calculations of the allocation of waters directly affect the uses that may be made of the rivers being regulated. This has been the most challenging of the issues in all the agreements analyzed in the present study. The Indus Treaty is by all means the most comprehensive of the treaties under this study. Its division of the Indus Basin into Eastern and Western Rivers and allocating it accordingly is a remarkable achievement. No other treaty has succeeded to be so clear and complete on such a complex topic. Also the 1996 Ganges Treaty attempts to clarify the issue of allocation of waters, but the practical problems encountered by Bangladesh and India in the implementation of the Treaty in the first year only permit a cautious approximation. On the other hand, the Mahakali Treaty remains still largely theoretical, and the previous treaties between India and Nepal that pertain to the Kosi and Gandaki Rivers are, as discussed in the previous chapters, too disheveled and ambiguous to be noted.

Most agreements have provisions regarding the enforceable benefits to be gained (such as hydropower to be generated or canals to be built for the diversion of water). However, those between India and Nepal in particular, instead of representing "positive benefits" in the agreement, have opted for dealing with "conditional benefits," which has resulted in the existence of abstract rights for parties (navigation rights in the Kosi and Gandak agreements for instance). On the other hand, the Indus Treaty allocates rights and benefits to parties that are positive and enforceable. The Ganges Treaty falls in between as it provides for some benefits and rights that may not always be enforceable.

Another common trait in some of the treaties concerns the procedures for sharing costs of the project. When applicable, cost issues are delegated to established entities to administer but there is often a statement of intent on how costs will be shared: equally or proportionally. The Indus Waters Treaty triggered the establishment of the Indus Basin Development Fund for financial-packaging. All agreements between India and Nepal have provisions related to financing. The Mahakali Treaty, in addition to the 50/50 principle, refers to the eventual possibility of search for additional financial packages.

5. Institutional Arrangements and Dispute Resolution

While one may record paucity in matters of rights and obligations, all the treaties reviewed in this study are rich in institutional arrangements. Each one has introduced various administrative structures to implement the agreements, or to play advisory roles in its implementation. The powers granted to such commissions could be divided into those that are legislative, administrative or judicial in nature. The legislative functions are those concerned with investigation of river basins and formulation of plans for development, such as those granted to the Joint Rivers Commission. The administrative powers include supervision of construction and administration of relative rights under the respective Treaty. The settlement of legal and technical disputes is a more judicial role. The Permanent Indus Commission established by India and Pakistan, the Mahakali and Gandak Commissions, and the Kosi Committee established between India and Nepal, and the Joint Rivers Commission and the Joint Committee related to the Ganges between India and Bangladesh, are the main institutional frameworks provided for under the respective treaties. Regarding the balance in such joint bodies, all the agreements provide for equal representation of parties therein, and powers of such entities vary according to the nature of the Treaty, the ambit, and the strength of the parties in negotiations. It is not a pure coincidence that of the several commissions, the most effective one is the Permanent Indus Commission between India and Pakistan. Indeed, the Indus Treaty includes very elaborate institutional arrangements for the functioning of the Indus Commission, no doubt because of the political strength of the parties involved in the negotiations. The Commission, and indeed the Indus Treaty itself, continued to function smoothly, by and large, even when war erupted between the two countries. The Joint Rivers Commission that has been established for dealing with the more than 50 rivers shared between India and Bangladesh is certainly an ambitious idea. However, the powers of the Commission center on the formulation of proposals and studies. Moreover, the dispute over the Ganges affected negatively the role that the Commission could have played under its Statute. Obviously, the extent of the success of any treaty depends, to a considerable extent, on the effectiveness of the institution entrusted with implementation of the arrangements under such a treaty. Such effectiveness is usually enhanced by the existence of a permanent entity that functions as a secretariat. Unfortunately, such structure is missing in all of the commissions in the South Asian Sub-continent referred to above.

One other feature common to all the treaties reviewed in the present study concerns the procedures for managing disputes. Dispute settlement is present in all agreements for all the rivers, however comprehensive and effective they may or may not be. All the treaties acknowledge the necessity to address and manage disagreements in a graduated manner. The disputes are to be resolved by negotiations between the parties. If the parties fail to resolve the dispute, the matter is presented either for political decision or arbitration. The arbitral tribunal often consists of representatives of each country and an arbitrator (or umpire) appointed jointly by the two. The processes available are substantive (like in the case of the Indus) or remain a loosely handled diplomatic matter (like in the case of Kosi and Gandaki). In between the elaborate provisions of the Indus and the incomplete provisions of the Kosi and the Gandaki, lie the Mahakali and the Ganges treaties, which also provide for detailed dispute resolution mechanisms. In fact, the Ganges Treaty gives a role in the dispute settlement mechanism to the Joint Rivers Commission, but because the Commission functions on equal representation basis, it should be concluded that the ultimate resolution of the dispute is always a political one.

6. Terms of the Treaties

The terms of the treaties reviewed vary significantly, from being open-ended to the specific term of as few as 30 years. For instance the Indus Waters Treaty is to continue in force until terminated by another treaty concluded for that purpose. Similarly, the Gandak agreement does not contain any specified termination date. On the other hand, the Kosi Agreement is fixed at 199 years. The Mahakali Treaty is to remain in force for 75 years, and the provisions of the Treaty are to be reviewed at 10-year intervals or earlier if requested by either party. The Ganges Treaty is to remain in force for 30 years and is renewable on the basis of mutual consent. It is to be reviewed by the two parties at five-year intervals or earlier as required by either party.

Although the legal principles followed in all the countries reviewed derive from the same system of law, they also contain differing substantive and procedural elements, including those pertaining to rules regarding ratification of treaties. A wide range of constitutional requirements and practices prevail in the South Asian Sub-continent with regard to the ratification of treaties. In India, all treaties that result in financial obligations to the country are required to be presented to the Indian parliament for ratification. In Nepal, while a formal parliamentary ratification was not required until the 1990s, during which time the Kosi and the Gandak Agreements were concluded, the new 1990 constitution requires that treaties with a long-term impact on the country or those dealing with natural resources be formally ratified by the Parliament by two-thirds majority. Thus the Kosi, the Gandaki and the Ganges treaties did not require any formal ratification and they came into force immediately upon signature. The Mahakali Treaty, after a lengthy political debate within

Nepal, was ratified by the parliaments in India and Nepal, upon which it entered into force. The Indus was ratified by both the parties but as discussed earlier, entered into force retroactively.

7. Future Prospects

The historical developments in water resources cooperation in the South Asian Sub-continent in the course of the last 50 years have been complex and varying. The countries of the Sub-continent have had to manage serious water issues in parallel with complex sociopolitical and economic changes. With whatever form of modesty it may be, they have shown willingness to act and have, to some extent, succeeded in managing their problems, favoring more cooperative approaches in tackling such problems and conflicts.

Indeed, any country in conflict owes its vitality to its ability to strike a balance between its aspirations and what it can realistically achieve. From the examples discussed in this study, one can note that each country has, one way or the other, obtained something out of those treaties. This part of the history of the Sub-continent thus teaches us that achievements in bilateral or multilateral water issues do not result from pure empiricism and rhetoric, but the quest of parties for a change and their ability to cooperate in the search for solutions. The South Asian Sub-continent, being one of the most populous and poverty-stricken regions of the world, needs more of those cooperative efforts to address its problems, including those related to allocation and development of water resources, for the benefit of more than one-fifth of the world population who inhabit this Sub-continent. In this context, the prospective role of the South Asian Association for Regional Cooperation can also be noted. Because of the institutional framework it provides, SAARC can facilitate the process of negotiations on several political issues, whether water related or not. Indeed, although the Charter of the SAARC does not include a specific reference to cooperation over shared water resources, it does stress the need for joint action and enhanced cooperation among the respective political and economic systems of its members. Such statements of intent certainly are beneficial for countries in the Sub-continent to generally promote an environment that systematically augurs discussions and decision-making at a higher level.

The realization of the importance of cooperation is obvious in the treaties concluded thus far, and in the ongoing discussions for agreements on other shared rivers as well. And although treaties and other legal instruments over international rivers will not, by themselves, solve all the problems in such rivers, it is equally true that there can be no resolution of water disputes and conflicts without them. Such instruments are indeed the only means for translating cooperative political will into applicable and enforceable action.

Select Bibliography

Abbas, B. M., *The Ganges Water Dispute*. Dhaka: The University Press Limited. (1984).

Ahmed, A. T. S., "Challenges of Governance in Nepal: Politico-Economic and Ethno-Religious Dimensions." *Journal of Contemporary Asia* 24. (1994).

Alam, Undala Z., "Water Rationality: Mediating the Indus Waters Treaty," unpublished Ph.D. Thesis, University of Durham, U. K. (1998).

Ali, Chaudhri Muhammad, *The Emergence of Pakistan*. New York: Columbia University Press. (1967).

Annuaire de l'Institut de Droit International 1911-1997. Reports.

Bandyopadhya, Jayanta and Dipak Gyewali, "Ecological and Political Aspects of Himalayan Water Resources Management." *Water Nepal*. Vol. 4., No. 1. (September 1994).

Bandyopadhya, Jayanta, "Dams for the Third Millennium." Himal South ASIA. (March 11, 1998).

Bastola, Surya Nath, *Water Resources Development of the Mighty Himalayan Rivers*. Kathmandu: Sunil Bastola. (1997).

Baxter, R. R., *The Law of International Waterways*. Cambridge: Harvard University Press. (1964).

Berber, F. J., *Rivers in International Law*. London: Stevens & Sons Limited. (1959).

Bhasin, Avtar Singh (ed.), *India–Bangladesh Relations, 1971–1994. Documents*, Delhi: Siba Exim Pvt. Ltd. (1996).

———, (ed.), *Documents on Nepal's Relations with India and China, 1949-1966*. Delhi: Academic Books, Ltd. (1970).

Bhattachan, Krishna B., "Nepal in 1993: Business as Usual." *Asian Survey* 34. (1994).

Bilder, Richard B., *Managing the Risks of International Agreements*. Madison: University of Wisconsin Press. (1981).

Biswas, Asit K., "Indus Water Treaty: The Negotiating Process." *Water International* 17. (1992).

Blake, Gerald, et al. (eds.), International Boundaries and Environmental Security – Framework for Regional Cooperation. London: Kluwer Law International. (1997).

Bogdanovic, Slavko, *International Law of Water Resources: Contribution of the International Law Association*. London: Kluwer Law International. (2001).

Bourne, Charles, "The International Law Association's Contribution to International Water Resources Law." *Natural Resources Journal* 36. (1996).

Bowman, M. J., and D. J. Harris, *Multilateral Treaties – Index and Current Status.* London: Butterworth. (1984).

Burhenne, W. E., *International Environmental Law – Multilateral Treaties,* Vol. 1. London: Kluwer Law International. (1997).

Chauhan, B. R., *Settlement of International and Inter-State Water Disputes in India.* New Delhi: Indian Law Institute. (1992).

Cosgrove, William, and Frank Rijsberman, *World Water Vision: Making Water Everybody's Business.* London: Earthscan Publications Ltd. (2000).

Crook, John R., and Stephen McCaffrey, "The United Nations Starts Work on a Watercourses Convention." *American Journal of International Law* 91. (1997).

Crow, Ben, et al., *Sharing the Ganges – The Politics and Technology of River Development.* New Delhi: Sage Publications. (1995).

Desai, Bharat, "Sharing of International Water Resources." *Asia Pacific Journal of Environmental Law* 3. (1998).

Dixit, Ajay, "Mahakali Nadi Sajha Ho, Paani Adha Ko Adha Ho." *Mulyankan* Vol. 42. (1997).

Elhance, Arun P., *Hydropolitics in the Third World: Conflict and Cooperation in International River Basins.* Washington, DC: United States Institute of Peace Press. (1999).

Fischer, Georges, "La Banque Internationale pour la Reconstruction et le Developpement et l'Utilisation des eaux du Bassin de l'Indus." AFDI. (1960).

Frederiksen, Harald D., et al., *Water Resources Management in Asia* (Vol. I). World Bank Technical Paper No. 212. Washington, DC: World Bank. (1993).

Friedmann, Wolfgang, et al., *International Law: Cases and Material.* St. Paul, Minnesota: West Publishing. (1969).

Garretson, A. H., et al. (eds.), *The Law of International Drainage Basins.* Dobbs Ferry, New York: Oceana Publications. (1967).

Global Water Partnership, *Towards Water Security: A Framework for Action,* Stockholm: Global Water Partnership. (2000).

Gleick, Peter, *The World's Water 2000-2001, The Biennial Report on Freshwater Resources.* Oxford University Press. (2000).

Godana, Bonaya Adhi, *Africa's Shared Water Resources: Legal, and Institutional Aspects of the Nile, Niger and Senegal River Systems.* London: Frances Printer Publishers. (1985).

Goodland, R., Environmental Assessment of Decreased Ganges Flow in Bangladesh, International Engineering Company and Bangladesh Waters Development Board Special Studies Directorate. (April 1977).

Green Cross International, *National Sovereignty and International Watercourses, Report of the Sovereignty Panel of the World Commission on Water in the 21st Century.* Geneva: Green Cross International. (2000).

Gulhati, Niranjan D., *Indus Waters Treaty: An Exercise in International Mediation.* Bombay: Allied Publishers. (1973).

Gyewali, Dipak and Othmar Schwank, "Interstate Sharing of Water Rights: An Alps-Himalaya Comparison." *Water Nepal.* Vol. 4, No. 1. (1994).

Gyewali, Dipak, "Ke Ke Chan Dosh Mahakali Sandhi Ma." *Mulyankan* Vol. 41. (1997).

Hohmann, Harald, *Basic Documents of International Environmental Law,* Vol. 1. London: Graham & Trotman. (1992).

International Law Association Reports, London, England. 1954-1986.

Khan, M. Y., "Boundary Water Conflict between India and Pakistan." *Water International,* abstracted in Transboundary Resources Report, 5 (1). (Spring 1991).

Khan, Tauhidul Anwar, "Management and Sharing of the Ganges." *Natural Resources Journal* 36. (1996).

Kirmani, Syed, and Guy Le Moigne, *Fostering Riparian Cooperation in International River Basins: The World Bank at its Best in Development Diplomacy.* World Bank Technical Paper No. 335. Washington DC: World Bank. (1997).

Kumar, Santosh, A. K. Sinha, and Nigam Prakash, "Culture and Water Bonds." *Water Nepal* Vol. 4, No. 1. (September 1994).

Le Moigne, Guy, et al. (eds.), *Country Experience with Water Resources Management — Economic, Institutional, Technological and Environmental Issues.* World Bank Technical Paper No. 175. Washington, DC: World Bank. (1992).

Little, I. M. D., and J. M. Clifford, *International Aid: A Discussion of the Flow of Public Resources from Rich to Poor Countries.* Chicago: Aldine Publishing. (1968).

Lyndon Johnson School of Public Affairs, *Water Resources Cooperation in the Ganges-Brahmaputra River Basin,* Policy Research Project Report 101. (1993).

Mason, Edward S., and Robert E. Asher, *The World Bank Since Bretton Woods.* Washington, DC: Brookings Institution. (1973).

McCaffrey, Stephen C., "Water, Politics and International Law." *Water in Crisis: A Guide to the World's Fresh Water Resources,* Peter H. Gleick (ed.), Oxford University Press. (1993).

———, "The Harmon Doctrine One Hundred Years Later: Buried, Not Praised." *Natural Resources Journal* 36. (1996).

———, *The Law of International Watercourses: Non-Navigational Uses.* Oxford University Press. (2001).

McCaffrey, Stephen, and Mpazi Sinjela, "The 1997 United Nations Convention on International Watercourses." *American Journal of International Law* 92. (1998).

Mehta, Jagat S., "The Indus Water Treaty: A Case Study in the Resolution of an International River Basin Conflict." *Natural Resources Forum* 12. (1988).

Merrils, J.G., *International Dispute Settlement.* Cambridge: Grotius Publication, Ltd. (1991).

Michel, Aloys Arthur, *The Indus Rivers. A Study of the Effects of Partition.* New Haven: Yale University Press. (1967).

Nakayama, Mikiyasu, "Successes and Failures of International Organizations in Dealing with International Waters," *International Journal of Water Resources Development* 13. (1997).

Nile Basin Initiative, "Preparatory Phase Working Document," Report No. 01, Entebbe. (June 1999).

Parajulee, Ramjee P., *The Democratic Transition in Nepal.* Lanham, Maryland: Rowman and Littlefield. (2000).

Prasad, Kamala, "Priority and Institutional Development." *Water Nepal* Vol. 4. No. 1. (September 1994).

Rao, A. R., and T. Prasad, "Water Resources Development of the Indo-Nepal Region." *Water Resources Development* 10. (1994).

Rawat, P. C., *Indo Nepal Economic Relations.* New Delhi: National Publishing House. (1974).

Rose, Leo E., *Nepal Strategy for Survival.* Oxford University Press. (1971).

Rousseau, Charles, "Inde et Pakistan: Conclusion du traité du 19 septembre 1960 relatif à l'utilisation des eaux de l'Indus." *Revue générale de droit international public.* 66. (1961).

Salman, Salman M. A., *The Legal Framework for Water Users' Associations: A Comparative Analysis.* World Bank Technical Paper No. 360. Washington, DC: World Bank. (1997).

———, "International Rivers as Boundaries: The Dispute Over Kasikili/Sedudu Island and the Decision of the International Court of Justice." *Water International* 25. (2000).

———, "Legal Regime for Use and Protection of International Watercourses in the Southern Africa Region: Evolution and Context," *Natural Resources Journal* 41. (2001).

Salman, Salman M. A., and Laurence Boisson de Chazournes (eds.), *International Watercourses: Enhancing Cooperation and Managing Conflict.* World Bank Technical Paper No. 414. Washington, DC: World Bank. (1998).

———, (ed.), *Groundwater: Legal and Policy Perspectives.* World Bank Technical Paper No. 456. Washington, D.C.: World Bank. (1999).

Salman, Salman M. A., and Kishor Uprety, "Hydro-Politics in South Asia: A Comparative Analysis of the Mahakali and the Ganges Treaties." *Natural Resources Journal* 39. (1999).

Schwabach, Aaron, "The United Nations Convention on the Law of the Non-Navigational Uses of International Watercourse: Customary, International Law and the Interests of Developing Upper Riparians." *Texas International Law Journal* 33. (1998).

Shah, Rishikesh, "Politics of Water in Nepal." *Water Nepal* Vol. 4, No. 1. (1994).

Sharma, C. K., *A Treatise on Water Resources of Nepal.* Kathmandu: Sangeeta Sharma. (1997).

Sharma, Chandra K., *Geology of Nepal.* Kathmandu: Sangeeta Sharma. (1973).

Shibusawa, A. H., "Cooperation in Water Resources Development In South Asia." *Commerce* Vol. 154, No. 3959. (April 4-10, 1987).

Shrestha, Aditya Man, *Bleeding Mountains of Nepal.* Kathmandu: Ekta Books. (1999).

Shrestha, Govind D., "Himalayan Waters: Need for a Positive Indo-Nepal Cooperation." *Water Nepal* Vol. 4, No. 1. (1994).

Shrestha, K. L., *Mahakali Sandhi Ra Rastriya Hitko Sawal.* Kathmandu: Sumitra Shrestha. (1997).

Smith, Herbert Arthur, *Economic Uses of International Rivers.* London: P.S. King & Sons. (1931).

Tanzi, Attila, "Codifying the Minimum Standards of the Law of International Watercourses: Remarks on Part One and a Half." *Natural Resources Forum* 21. (1997).

Tanzi, Attila, and Maurizio Arcasi, *The United Nations Convention on the Law of International Watercourse.* London: Kluwer Law International. (2001).

Teclaff, Ludwick A., *Water Law in Historical Perspectives.* Buffalo, New York: W. S. Hein. (1985).

Thapa, Bhekh B., and Bharat B. Pradhan, *Water Resources Development, Nepalese Perspective.* Bombay: Konark Publishers. (1995).

Thapa, N. B., *Geography of Nepal: Physical, Economic, Cultural and Regional.* Bombay: Orient Longmans. (1969).

United Nations, *Register of the International Drainage Basins,* Report of the Secretary General of the United Nations, New York: UN DOC. E/C 7/71, 11 March 1977).

United Nations, *Register of International Rivers,* Prepared by the Center of Natural Resources, Energy and Transport, of the Department of Economic and Social Affairs. New York: United Nations. (1978).

Upreti, B. C., *Politics of Himalayan River Waters: An Analysis of the River Water Issues of Nepal, India and Bangladesh.* Delhi: Nirala Publication. (1993).

Uprety, Kishor, "Landlocked States and Access to the Sea. An Evolutionary Study of a Contested Right." *Dickinson Journal of International Law* 12. (1994).

———, "South Asian Regional Cooperation—A Framework for Preferential Trading." *Journal of World Investment* 2. (2001).

Verghese, B. G., *Waters of Hope — From Vision to Reality in the Himalaya-Ganga Development Cooperation.* New Delhi: Oxford & IBH Publishing Co. Pvt. Ltd. (1999).

Verghese, B. G, and Ramaswamy R. Iyer (eds.), *Harnessing the Eastern Himalayan Rivers: Regional Cooperation in South Asia.* Delhi: Konark. (1994).

Verma, U. K., "Socioeconomic Renaissance through Dynamic Indo-Nepal Cooperation in Water Resources Development." *Water Nepal* Vol. 4 No. 1. (1994).

Vitanyi, Bela, *The International Regime of River Navigation.* Alphen aan den Rijn, The Netherlands: Sijthoff and Noordhoff. (1979).

Wallensteen, Peter and Ashok Swain, *Comprehensive Assessment of the Freshwater Resources of the World, International Fresh Water Resources: Conflict or Cooperation.* Stockholm: Environment Institute. (1997).

World Bank, *World Development Report 2000-2001:* Attacking Poverty. Washington, DC: World Bank. (2000).

World Bank, *1999 World Development Indicators.* Washington, DC: World Bank. (1999).

World Commission on Dams, *Dams and Development—A New Framework for Decision-Making. Report of the World Commission on Dams.* London: Earthscan Publications. (2000).

Wouters, Patricia, (ed.), *International Water Law: Selected Writings of Professor Charles B. Bourne.* London: Kluwer Law International. (1997).

Zacklin, Ralph, and Lucius Caflisch (eds.), *The Legal Regime of International Rivers and Lakes.* The Hague: Marinus Nijhoff. (1981).

Appendix
Treaty References

INDIA-BANGLADESH

The Ganges Treaty, 1996
36 International Legal Materials 523 (1997)

Statute of the Indo-Bangladeshi Joint Rivers Commission, 1972
A. S. Bhasin (ed.), *India-Bangladesh Relations, 1971-1994, Documents,* Vol. I (Delhi: Siba Exim Pvt. Ltd., 1996) at 33.

INDIA-NEPAL

The Mahakali Treaty, 1996
36 International Legal Materials 531 (1997), www.south-asia.com/Embassy-India/indneprel.htm

Revised Agreement on the Kosi Project, 1966
A.S. Bhasin (ed.), *Documents on Nepal's Relations With India and China, 1949-1966* (New Delhi Academic Books, 1970) at 156-163.

Agreement on the Gandak Irrigation and Power Project, 1959
A.S. Bhasin (ed.), *Documents on Nepal's Relations with India and China 1949-1966* (Delhi Academic Books, 1970), at 166-170.

INDIA-PAKISTAN

The Indus Waters Treaty, 1960
419 U.N.T.S. 126

Index

Absolute territorial integrity, 14, 32

Absolute territorial sovereignty, 11, 12, 14, 17, 20, 32, 60, 146

Adjudication, 179

Adverse effects, 144, 152, 169

Appreciable harm, *see* No appreciable harm rule

Arbitration, 13, 18, 27, 30, 38, 45, 53, 54, 55, 56

Arbitrations *see* Cases and Arbitrations

Athens Resolution *see* Institut de Droit International

Augmentation of flow, 133, 155-159, 166, 177, 189

Barrage, *see* also Dams, ix, 29, 38, 45, 51, 69, 70, 71, 72, 73, 76, 77, 78, 79, 81, 82, 83, 84, 88, 89, 93, 94, 97, 98, 101, 103, 104, 105, 106, 107, 108, 111, 113, 117, 118, 126, 128, 129, 133, 135, 136, 137, 138, 139, 140, 141, 142, 144, 149, 154, 157, 158, 170, 175, 176, 187, 188, 189, 191

Beneficial Uses, 20

Black, Eugene, 45

Boundary rivers
Ganges, ix, x, 3, 4, 5, 6, 7, 9, 21, 33, 65, 66, 83, 97, 130, 136, 150, 156, 170, 176, 179, 180, 182, 183, 184, 185, 186, 187, 188, 189, 190, 197, 199, 200, 204
Mahakali, ix, 3, 4, 5, 7, 9, 33, 65, 95, 97, 98, 99, 103, 104, 105, 107, 108, 110, 111, 112, 116, 117, 118, 119, 130, 152

Boundary Waters Treaty, *see* Treaties and Conventions

Cases and Arbitrations,
Corfu Channel Case, 13
Gabcikovo/Nagymaros, 29, 31
Gut Dam, 12, 13
Kasikili/Sedudu, 9
Lake Lanoux Arbitration, 12, 111
Nebraska v. Wyoming, 22
Meuse River case, 14, 15
New Jersey v. New York, 3
Oder River Case, 10, 16
Oscar Chinn Case, 10
Trail Smelter Arbitration, 13, 17

Canal
Don Branch, 84, 88, 89
Eastern Nepal, 88
Feeder, 60, 128, 133, 135, 137, 138, 140, 141, 142, 144, 154, 169, 175, 189
Rajasthan, 6, 55
Sarada, 98, 113, 117
Upper Bari Doab, 38, 42, 50, 60
Western Main, 70
Western Nepal, 88

Central Water and Power Commission, 69

Codification and progressive development, international water law, 24

Compensation, 13, 22, 25, 28, 60, 70, 74, 75, 76, 77, 80, 81, 87, 88, 92, 93, 94, 121

Community of interests, 16, 21

Community of co-riparian states, 15, 16

Conciliation, 23, 30

Consent, 16, 17, 18, 157, 171, 175, 201

Conservation, 25, 27, 72, 82, 114

Consultation, 4, 12, 25, 28, 29, 30, 72, 76, 78, 144, 162, 177, 184

Consumptive uses, 108, 111, 112

Conventions *see* Treaties and Conventions

Cooperation, x, 1, 3, 4, 5, 7, 8, 10, 19, 25, 26, 27, 30, 32, 33, 38, 41, 51, 52, 59, 65, 66, 69, 70, 73, 74, 79, 81, 98, 101, 104, 118, 121, 122, 126, 128, 129, 130, 133, 135, 137, 138, 139, 147, 158, 167, 169, 170, 181, 182, 184, 189, 191, 195, 196, 199, 202, 203, 204, 205, 206, 207, 208

Customary International Law, 11, 21, 25, 54

Dams and Barrages,
  Bhakra Dam, 38, 55
  Farakka Barrage, 126, 128, 129, 133, 135, 136, 137, 138, 139, 140, 142, 144, 149, 154, 158, 170, 175, 176, 187, 189, 191
  Gandak, 88
  Ganges Barrage, 137, 187, 188,
  Gut Dam, 12, 13
  Jhelum, 51
  Kosi, 5, 7, 33
  Mangla, 51
  Tarbela, 51

Deuba, Sher B., 103

Detailed Project Report, 105, 107, 108, 109

Dispute settlement, *see* also Adjudication; Arbitration; Conciliation; Mediation, 26, 30, 52, 60, 155, 156, 162, 165, 175, 177, 201, 205

Diversions of waters, x, 12, 15, 29, 58, 199, 111, 133, 135, 139, 142, 144, 145, 146, 152, 189, 199

Downstream benefits, 80, 121

Drainage basin, ix, 3, 13, 18, 21, 22, 23, 24, 26, 27, 146, 157

Drought, 6, 133, 179, 191

Dubrovnik Statement *see* International Law Association

Duty to exchange information *see* Exchange of information

Duty to consult *see* Consultation

Duty to cooperate *see* Cooperation

Duty to negotiate *see* Negotiation

Duty to notify *see* Notification

Eastern Rivers, 41, 43, 46, 47, 49, 50, 54, 55, 57, 58, 137, 138, 180

Environmental law, 10, 19

Environmental protection, 183, 191

Equality of Rights, 21

Equitable apportionment, 22, 59, 146,

Equitable and reasonable utilization, 12, 15, 19, 20, 25, 26, 27, 28, 29, 32, 146, 175, 176

Exchange of information, 52, 118, 122

Existing uses *see* Prior appropriation

Farakka Barrage, 126, 128, 129, 133, 135, 136, 137, 138, 139, 140, 142, 144, 149, 150, 154, 158, 170, 175, 176, 187, 189, 191

Fact-finding Commissions, 30

Fishing, 78, 79, 121, 145

Flood control, x, 4, 23, 24, 69, 70, 71, 80, 83, 109, 110, 112, 113, 116, 121, 126, 127, 129, 134, 135, 138, 140, 152, 162, 164, 165, 167, 168, 177, 181, 191, 196, 199

Gandak Project, 83, 84, 87, 92, 95, 120

Gandak Coordination Committee, 92

Gandhi, Indira, 127

Ganga *see* also Ganges, 129, 133, 138, 139, 140, 145, 152, 154, 156, 157, 159, 165, 168, 170, 171, 174, 176, 182

Ganges Barrage, 137, 187, 188

Geneva Convention *see* Treaties and Conventions

Good faith principle, 13, 19, 29, 30, 115, 122

Good neighborliness principle, 29, 152

Gowda, Deve, 171, 185

Groundwater, 4, 6, 21, 22, 24, 27, 32, 136, 142, 145, 157, 188, 206

Gujral Doctrine, 170

Hardinge Bridge, 137, 154, 175, 178, 184, 185, 187

Hasina, Sheikh, 171

Harm *see* No appreciable harm rule

Harmon Doctrine, *see* also absolute territorial sovereignty, 11, 12, 13, 14, 60, 205

Helsinki Rules *see* International Law Association

ICJ *see* International Court of Justice

IDI *see* Institut de Droit International

IJC *see* International Joint Commission

ILA *see* International Law Association

ILC *see* International Law Commission

Iliff, W. A. B., 37, 41, 48

India's case on Farakka, 144

Indus, vii, ix, 5, 6, 7, 15, 33, 37, 38, 39, 41, 44, 45, 46, 47, 48, 49, 51, 52, 54, 57, 58, 59, 60, 137, 148, 196, 197, 201

Indus (Anderson) Commission, 38

Indus Basin Development Fund, 48, 54, 55, 56

Indus (Rau) Commission, 38

Indus Waters Treaty, ix, 7, 37, 44, 48, 60, 148, 151, 155, 180, 191, 196, 198, 200, 201, 203, 205

Injury, 12, 13, 14, 17, 19, 21, 22, 23, 24, 146

Institut de Droit International, 8, 9, 18, 19, 203
   Athens Resolution (1977), 19, 30
   Madrid Declaration (1911), 9, 10, 16, 17, 18, 19, 22, 23
   Salzburg Resolution (1961), 17, 18, 19
   Salzburg Resolution (1997), 23, 30

Institute of International Law *see* Institut de Droit International

Inter-Dominion Agreement, 43, 44

Inter-States Water Disputes Act 1956, 22

International Bank for Reconstruction and Development, *see* World Bank

International Court of Justice (ICJ), 9, 13, 29, 30, 31, 44, 147, 206

International Development Association *see* also World Bank, 150

International Joint Commission (IJC), 13, 52, 80

International Law Association (ILA), 8, 16, 17, 20, 21, 22, 23, 24, 25, 26, 27, 30, 31, 203, 205
   Dubrovnik Statement, 20
   Helsinki Rules (1966), 11, 18, 21, 22, 23, 24, 25, 26, 27, 28, 30, 32, 146

New York Resolution (1958), 21
Seoul Rules (1986), 24, 27
International Law Commission (ILC), 8, 16, 19, 20, 24, 26, 27, 30
Draft Articles on the Law of the Non-navigational Uses of International Watercourses (1991), see also U.N. Working Group of the Whole, Framework Convention, 8
Resolution on Confined Transboundary Groundwater, 27
Joint Rivers Commission, 104, 134, 135, 137, 138, 139, 141, 156, 157, 158, 159, 160, 161, 163, 164, 165, 166, 169, 175, 181, 183, 185, 187, 189, 190, 200, 201
Joint Committee, 154, 155, 161, 163, 175, 200
Joint Committee of Experts, 164, 165, 166
Judicial decision, *see* cases and arbitrations
Khan, Ayub, 206
Kharif, v, 42, 43, 47, 50
Kosi, *see* rivers, lakes and dams
Kosi Project, 65, 66, 69, 71, 72, 73, 74, 75, 80, 81, 89
Lakes, *see* Rivers and Lakes
Law of the Sea, 31
League of Nations, 10, 11, 25
Limited territorial integrity, 14, 15, 16
Limited territorial sovereignty, *see* Equitable utilization
Lilienthal, D., 44, 45, 46
Madrid Declaration *see* Institut de Droit International
Mahakali Commission, 113
Mahakali River, ix, 3, 4, 5, 7, 9, 33, 65, 95, 97, 98, 99, 103, 104, 105, 107, 108, 110, 111, 112, 116, 117, 118, 119, 130, 152
Mahakali Treaty, ix, 7, 97, 98, 103, 104, 105, 106, 107, 109, 110, 111, 112, 113, 115, 116, 117, 121, 155, 195, 196, 199, 200, 201
Marine environment, protection, 32
McNamara, 150
Mediation, 16, 30, 37, 45, 177, 198, 205
Montreal Rules *see* International Law Association
Navigation, 9, 10, 11, 15, 16, 17, 22, 23, 27, 38, 48, 78, 79, 82, 92, 93, 121, 136, 143, 145, 157, 175, 188, 198, 199, 208
Negotiation, 53, 111
Nehru, 42, 48, 66, 69
New York Resolution *see* International Law Association
Nile Basin Initiative, 4, 195, 206
Non-consumptive uses, 49, 95
Non-navigational uses, 4, 8, 9, 10, 11, 16, 22, 23, 24, 25, 26, 27, 29, 32, 121, 195, 205, 206
Notification, 18, 23, 24, 29, 30, 31, 52, 56, 73
Optimal utilization, 164, 165
Oder River, 10, 15
Pancheshwar Multipurpose Project, 103, 105, 107, 116
PCIJ *see* Permanent Court of International Justice,
Permanent Court of Arbitration, 114
Permanent Court of International Justice, 10, 15, 16, 104
Permanent Indus Commission, 52, 53, 54, 200
Planned measures, 29, 30, 31, 121

Index

Pollution, 18, 19, 21, 23, 30, 183
Prior appropriation, 14, 23, 59, 146
Procedural rules, 30
Protection of international watercourses, 8, 21, 25, 31, 206
Rabi, v, 42, 50
Rahman, Sheikh Mujibur, 126, 139
Rao, Narasimha, 102, 103, 167
Regulation of the flow, 24, 186
Remedies, *see* also Compensation, 12
Riparian rights, 14, 119, 196
Rivers and Lakes
  Bagmati, 88, 129
  Beas, 5, 37, 38, 41, 43, 49, 50, 55, 57, 180
  Brahmaputra, ix, 3, 5, 129, 130, 133, 139, 141, 156, 157, 158, 163, 165, 166, 167, 188
  Chenab, 5, 41, 57
  Colorado, 12
  Columbia, 80
  Danube, 4, 29
  Gandaki, 5, 7, 33, 65, 83, 84, 85, 119, 129, 157, 199, 201
  Ganga/Ganges, ix, x, 3, 4, 5, 6, 7, 9, 22, 33, 65, 66, 83, 97, 129, 130, 133, 136, 138, 139, 140, 145, 150, 152, 154, 156, 157, 159, 165, 168, 170, 171, 174, 176, 182, 170, 176, 179, 180, 182, 183, 184, 185, 186, 187, 188, 189, 190, 197, 199, 200, 204
  Hooghly, 128, 130, 135, 136, 138, 140, 141, 144, 146, 148, 149
  Indus, vii, ix, 6, 7, 16, 33, 37, 38, 39, 41, 44, 45, 46, 47, 48, 49, 51, 52, 54, 57, 58, 59, 60, 137, 148, 196, 197, 201
  Jhelum, 5, 37, 41, 49, 51, 55, 57
  Kabul, 37, 38
  Karnali, 5, 9, 65, 129, 157, 206
  Kosi, 5, 7, 33, 65, 66, 67, 69, 70, 71, 72, 73, 74, 76, 78, 79, 80, 81, 82, 94, 119, 120, 129, 157
  Kurram, 37
  Lanoux, 13, 14, 15, 18
  Mahakali, ix, 3, 4, 5, 7, 9, 33, 65, 95, 97, 98, 99, 103, 104, 105, 107, 108, 110, 111, 112, 116, 117, 118, 119, 130, 152
  Manas, 5, 130
  Mansarovar, 37
  Megha/Barak, 130, 157
  Meghna, 3, 129, 130, 182
  Mekong, 4, 54, 195
  Narmada, 5, 180
  Nile, 4, 12, 195, 204
  Raidak, 5
  Padma, 129, 130, 138, 143, 144, 145, 188
  Ramganga, 5
  Ravi, 5, 37, 38, 41, 43, 49, 51, 57, 180
  Rhine, 4, 15, 195
  Rio Grande, 12, 59, 60
  St. Lawrence, 12
  Sutlej, 5, 37, 38, 41, 42, 43, 45, 49, 50, 51, 55, 57, 180
  Teesta, 3, 5, 163, 165, 166, 183, 190
  Tijuana, 12
  Yamuna, 5
  Yangtze, 133
SAARC, *see* also Treaties and Conventions, 169, 202
SADC, *see* also Treaties and Conventions, 4, 31
Salzburg Resolution *see* Institut de Droit International
Settlement of disputes *see* Dispute Settlement
Seoul Complementary Rules *see* International Law Association
Standstill Agreement, 42, 43

State responsibility, 13
Substantive rules, 48
Sustainable utilization, 25
Territorial integrity, 83
Territorial sovereignty, *see* also Harmon Doctrine, 14, 15, 16, 17, 19, 20, 61, 101, 122, 169, 196
Timber floating, 23
Tokyo Resolution *see* International Law Association
Treaties and Conventions
　Act of the Congress of Vienna (1815), 8, 9, 15
　Agreement between the Government of Namibia and the Government of the Republic of South Africa on the Establishment of a Permanent Water Commission, 22
　Agreement on the Cooperation for the Sustainable Development of the Mekong River (1995), 4, 195
　Barcelona Convention (1921), 10, 11, 136, 137
　Boundary Waters Treaty (1909), 13, 80
　Columbia Rivers Treaty (1961), 80
　Convention on the Cooperation for the Protection and Sustainable Use of the Danube River (1994), 4, 195
　Convention on the Protection of the Rhine (1999), 4, 195
　Ganges
　　Partial Accord (1975), 139, 140, 141, 142, 150, 152, 153, 157, 167, 170, 173, 189
　　Agreement (1977), 151, 153, 154, 157, 159, 160, 161, 162, 164, 165, 167, 170, 171, 173, 174, 175, 176, 177, 183, 184, 189, 190, 197
　　Memorandum of Understanding (1982), 159, 160, 161, 162, 163, 164, 165, 167, 171, 174, 175, 177, 183, 184, 189, 197
　　Memorandum of Understanding (1985), 164, 166, 167, 169, 189, 190, 197
　　Treaty (1996), x, 170, 184, 190, 195, 196, 197, 199, 200, 201
　General Act of the Congress of Berlin (1885), 9
　Geneva Convention (1923), 11, 17, 18, 23, 25
　Helsinki Convention on the Protection and Use of Transboundary Watercourses and International Lakes (1992), 4, 195
　Indus Waters Treaty (1960), xi, 7
　Kosi Treaty (1954) (1966), 70
　Mahakali Treaty (1996), ix, 7, 97, 98, 103, 104, 105, 106, 107, 109, 110, 111, 112, 113, 115, 116, 117, 121, 155, 195, 196, 199, 200, 201
　Protocol on Shared Watercourse Systems in the Southern African Development Community (1995), 4, 21, 31, 195
　Revised Protocol on Shared Watercourses in the Southern African Development Community (2000), 4, 31
　South Asian Association for Regional Cooperation (SAARC) Charter (1985), 169
　Sarada Treaty (1920), 98, 101, 103, 105, 118
　Tanakpur Agreement (1991), 98, 101, 102, 103, 105, 118
　Teesta River (interim agreement 1983),
　Treaty between U.S. and Mexico (1944), 12

Treaty of Friendship, Cooperation and Peace (1972), 127, 128, 129, 134, 137, 138, 167, 189, 191
Treaty of Versailles (1919), 10
United Nations Convention on the Law of the Non-Navigational Uses of International Watercourses (1997), 4, 8, 25, 195, 206
Vienna Convention on Law of Treaties (1969), 102, 157, 171

United Nations
Charter, 30
Charter of Economic Rights and Duties of States, 12, 30
Consensus Statement, 147, 148, 151, 152, 170, 189
Convention on the Law of the Non-Navigational Uses of International Watercourses, 4, 8, 24, 25, 195, 206
Convention on the Law of the Sea, 31
Declaration of the UN Conference on the Human Environment, 146
Declaration on the Right to Development, 30
Integrated River Basin Development, 3
Register of the International Drainage Basins, 207
Register of International Rivers, 3, 207
Working Group of the Whole Framework Convention on the Law of the Non-navigational Uses of International Watercourses (1997), 25

Unity of drainage basin *see* Drainage basin,

Vested rights *see* Prior appropriation

Water quality, 26

Water quantity, 26

Water scarcity,

Western Rivers, 41, 46, 47, 49, 50, 51, 55, 57, 199

White Paper on Farakka, 142, 144

World Bank, 41, 44, 45, 47, 48, 54-56, 59, 148-151, 198
Policy for Projects on International Waterways, 30

World Commission on Dams, 26, 30, 32, 208

World Commission on Water in the 21st Century, 31

World Water Council, 4

www.ingramcontent.com/pod-product-compliance
Lightning Source LLC
Chambersburg PA
CBHW050441240426
43661CB00055B/2471

www.ingramcontent.com/pod-product-compliance
Lightning Source LLC
Chambersburg PA
CBHW050441240426
43661CB00055B/2471